Strategic investment d

Strategic investment decisions is based upon a study of strategic investment decisions in a wide range of UK and international companies. The authors examine these decisions from the perspective of organizational decision-making theory. They find that investments are not made only by the application of formal quantitative procedures but also involve the more qualitative processes of judgement, negotiation and inspiration.

The concept of decision effectiveness is examined and two primary factors identified. These are: the *objectives-attainment* factor and the *learning factor*. A number of case studies are presented to illustrate decisions which achieve different combinations of these effectiveness factors. For example, one case turned out to be ineffective in terms of objectives-attainment but highly effective in terms of the high amount of organizational learning that took place. This learning led to some significant structural and procedural changes in the organization.

Through a combination of case studies and statistical analysis the book develops a general model of decision effectiveness. The essence of this model is that an interaction needs to be achieved between the rational-computational and intuitive-inspirational aspects of decision-making.

There are also implications from this research for capital budgeting theory. The importance of learning as a factor of investment decision-making effectiveness implies the need for greater attention to be given to post decision-evaluation. An important new contribution to corporate strategy, this will also interest those studying human resource management and organizational learning processes.

Richard Butler is Reader in Organizational Analysis at the University of Bradford, Management Centre.

Leslie Davies is Professor at the Bodø Graduate School of Business in Norway.

Richard Pike is Provident Professor of Finance at the University of Bradford, Management Centre.

John Sharp is Professor of Management at the Canterbury Business School, University of Kent.

Strategic investment decisions

Theory, practice and process

Richard Butler, Leslie Davies,
Richard Pike and John Sharp

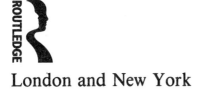

London and New York

First published 1993
by Routledge
11 New Fetter Lane, London EC4P 4EE

Simultaneously published in the USA and Canada
by Routledge
29 West 35th Street, New York, NY 10001

© 1993 Richard Butler, Leslie Davies, Richard Pike and
John Sharp

Typeset in English Times
by Pat and Anne Murphy, Highcliffe-on-Sea, Dorset
Printed and bound in Great Britain by
Biddles Ltd, Guildford and King's Lynn

British Library Cataloguing in Publication Data
A catalogue reference for this book is available from the
British Library

ISBN 0−415−07507−6 Hb
     0−415−07508−4 Pb

Library of Congress Cataloging in Publication Data
has been applied for.

BUSINESS

Contents

List of figures

List of tables

Appendix tables

Preface

The way in which the idea for this book was conceived, eventually resulting in its materialization, by four authors from different scholastic backgrounds, illustrates well some of the decision-making processes it describes.

There was no clear initial agenda. We all had our interests and prejudices. We had the expectation, but not certainty, of financial support for a research project. We had the minimum requirement to bring people together in a co-operative venture in the sense that interests and prejudices overlapped to a sufficient extent to enable us to start talking. The common ground was an interest in investigating the processes of investment decision-making.

Richard Pike, as a member of the Accounting and Finance Group at Bradford Management Centre, had a long-standing interest in studying the capital budgeting processes in firms and had already published widely in this area. John Sharp, as a member of the Management Information Group, had interests in the way in which information is used in complex decisions. Richard Butler, as a member of the Organizational Analysis Research Unit, had already spent a number of years carrying out a major research project on decision-making culminating in the book *Top Decisions* and a number of preceding papers.

Our early talking led to the formation of a new research unit, the Accounting, Information and Decision-Making Unit. The unit has the aim of shedding an interdisciplinary light upon the complexities of investment decision-making within business and other types of organization. We were fortunate in obtaining funding for the project from the Chartered Institute of Management Accountants (CIMA) and from the Economic and Social Research Council of the United Kingdom (ESRC). These funds enabled us to offer a research post to Leslie Davies who, after a period working in the financial services sector in London, had completed a doctorate in International Business at the Management Centre. The interdisciplinary team was now complete.

As the garbage can theory of decision-making (outlined in Chapter 2) tells us, decisions are, in part, the outcome of a merging of problems, people and solutions. We started with our own solutions, but as we worked together a more coherent view of where we were going emerged.

The organizational-behaviour-based literature provides strong descriptions and some explanations of how people behave during complex decision processes but generally lacks a conception of performance. On the other hand, theories of managerial behaviour based on the disciplines of economics, finance and management science have a strong orientation towards performance but tend to lack an understanding of the processes involved in making complex investment decisions.

As the problems of gaining access to organizations to collect data were overcome we increasingly became interested in the notion of decision-making effectiveness. It is due to the need for process theories of decision-making to consider performance, and for performance theories to consider process, that more interdisciplinary research in management is essential. This book presents our contribution towards this end.

Any project of this type can only achieve results through the assistance of a large number of other people whose contribution should be acknowledged. Financial support from CIMA and ESRC (award no. F00232348) for two years is gratefully acknowledged. The empirical field-work involved relied greatly upon the goodwill and kindness of the managers we met and interviewed, and upon general co-operation from their organizations. We can never promise them any direct return for their efforts but we do find that people who are closely involved in the decisions we describe usually like to talk about and reflect upon what it is they are doing. Perhaps, in the long run, the greatest contribution to management that research of this type can offer is to cause managers to reflect upon the activity in which they are involved.

We must also thank our colleagues, in Bradford Management Centre and elsewhere, who are too numerous to name but who, through discussion and in other serendipitous ways, provide invaluable assistance for projects of this type.

Richard Butler   The Management Centre
Leslie Davies   The University of Bradford
Richard Pike
John Sharp

1 The importance of making effective investment decisions

INTRODUCTION

Investment decision-making is the process whereby resources are allocated in organizations in anticipation of future gain. These decisions must, therefore, rank as one of the most critical types of decision made in modern industrial society. It is therefore important that we understand the process by which such decisions are made and the means by which this process can be made more effective. This is the major focus of this book.

The book reports a study of seventeen actual investment decisions made in twelve organizations. We consider investment decision-making as both a formal rational process of trying to optimize financial returns to the organization and as an organizational behavioural process in which local interests, informal interactions, hunches and other aspects of human behaviour that may, to an outside observer, appear as non-rational, play a vital part.

The organizations studied cover a wide range of types, from manufacturing to service sectors, from private to public sectors, and from British-owned to foreign-owned. The size of investments range from under one hundred thousand to several million pounds in value, and the type of investment ranges from investment in large-scale machinery to the purchase of computer software. All the decisions could be regarded as strategic in the sense that they had long-term implications for the organization and helped to set its future course of action.

Some of the study has been reported before (Butler *et al.* 1987, 1991 and 1992) but this book reports on the full set of decisions studied. The data collected during the study gives us insights into the antics of managements as they get embroiled in often complicated organizational processes. Some decisions, however, are relatively easily made;

the data gives a picture of some decisions proceeding smoothly and efficiently. In this respect the decisions reflect those reported by other empirical studies. For example Hickson *et al.* (1986) found some decisions, the sporadic ones, can follow a tortuous organizational path while others, the fluid ones, reach a conclusion under control and with few problems or disruptions.

Underlying our research is a long-standing, but often latent, debate over the way in which organizations operate. On the one hand is an image of organization as an entity that runs as a well-oiled machine whereby decisions are governed by routines and planning; Mintzberg (1983) has described this as 'machine bureaucracy'. This model of organization emphasizes the need for the use of strict evaluation, computations and a congruence of views amongst decision-makers.

The alternative image of organization is a fuzzier (Butler 1991) entity emphasizing the informal and implicit; decision-making according to this model is much more of an inspirational affair (Thompson and Tuden 1956) in which authority counts for less than flair and argument.

Anyone who has experienced organizational life only briefly will know that there is truth in both images; decision-making in organizations is both computational and inspirational, both routine and argumentative. The vital question for us is more to do with unravelling the nature of the interaction between the two images and types of associated decision processes than in insisting that an organization has to choose between one or the other image.

OUTLINE OF THE BOOK

In the next chapter, Chapter 2, this theme is examined in more detail using a now-established body of organizational decision-making theory; the chapter outlines basic theories and models and provides a background against which we can more specifically consider the problem of investment decision-making.

Our data shows processs that will not be unfamiliar to many managers who know the reality of organizational decision-making. What our study does provide, that we find neglected by other reports on the subject, is consideration of the concept of decision effectiveness.

Chapter 3 explores the meaning of decision effectiveness and the factors that can lead to improvement. In doing this we develop a decision effectiveness model (DEM) which provides the guiding framework for the book. The DEM sees decision-making as governed by a number of phases of decision-making, specifically, problem real-ization and definition, strategies for solution and support-building, influencing and timing. The chapter introduces the data pertaining to the study and presents a number of factor analyses from which the key dimensions of each of the variable groupings are extracted. Of particular note in this chapter is the derivation of the two factors of decision effectiveness, objectives-attainment and learning.

Chapter 4 gives an outline of the approach to investment decision-making provided by the theory of capital budgeting, some of the tech-niques used in this process and their apparent effectiveness.

Chapter 5 describes an experiment which investigates the use of some capital budgeting techniques by managers in different organiza-tions and in different positions in those organizations. It is here that the question of evaluation incongruence is explored. Incongruence occurs when decision-makers give different interpretations of the same objective conditions of risk and expected performance, and tend to emphasize different criteria for the acceptance of capital projects. Conventional wisdom suggests that incongruence should be minim-ized. However, our model of decision effectiveness pin-points organ-izational learning as a key aspect of effectiveness in decision-making. Our data raises the spectre of incongruence, under certain conditions, enhancing learning.

Chapter 6 presents an in-depth case study of a decision which turned out to be ineffective from the viewpoint of objectives-attainment but which led to considerable organizational learning. Chapter 7 takes a comparative view of some of the decisions studied in a fair amount of detail and the subsequent Chapters 8 to 10 present further in-depth cases.

Chapter 11 presents some overall findings of the decisions studied with the aim of discovering general patterns in our data that will enable us to draw rather more generalizable conclusions than is possible from case study discussions.

Chapter 12 gives in detail the results of regression and other statisti-cal analyses. These analyses enables the extraction of the key variables that can lead to decision effectiveness. This, and the previous chapters, concentrate upon discovering the interaction between variables; it is here, in particular, that the nature of the complex inter-play between different facets of organizational decision-making emerges.

Our overall conclusions in Chapter 13 emphasizes the importance of finding the right pattern in the different decision strategies and other variables for effectiveness. Here we see that inspirational decision-making needs to be intermingled with the more computational approach.

Many studies of organizational decision-making have emphasized the use of case studies, often studying one case in great depth (Pettigrew 1973). Bower's (1971) study of capital budgeting used a comparative case method as has the more recent study by Marsh *et al.* (1988) where they analysed in depth three major strategic investment decisions. Our approach is to combine both the case study and a quantitative analysis of a larger number of cases.

In developing the decision effectiveness model and reporting the study we see decision-making as both an objective and a subjective process. It is objective in the sense that there are certain minimum standards of performance that decision-makers have to achieve within their organizations. On the other hand, organizational decision-making involves the appreciation of complex situations on the part of a number of actors. This is essentially a subjective process in which the beliefs and values of individual decision-makers will play an important part.

As investigators we have to take both into account. In unravelling the objective constraints of a decision process we take to what is commonly seen as a scientific or nomothetic method of research. This involves the use of a survey, structured interview schedules and of an experiment. With this method, it is necessary to code the data to get comparability across actors and to use statistical procedures for analysis. The aim is to produce generalizable conclusions.

But, in order to appreciate complex decisions, we also use a qualitative or ideographic method. In this method the case study dominates; the aim is to investigate a particular decision in order to try and get behind the intentions and interpretations of the actors. Our study has, therefore, proceeded in the belief that it is necessary to combine both the nomothetic and the ideographic methods (Burrell and Morgan 1979) in order to understand organizational decision-making.

2 Approaches to appreciating organizational decision-making

INTRODUCTION

Interest in studying the processes of organizational decision-making can be seen to have originated from the path-breaking book by Chester Barnard, *The Functions of the Executive* (1938). Barnard's argument was that organizations function through the communication of a common purpose between a number of people. Executive work is a matter of deciding and doing, an idea that was taken up by Simon (1947) in his book *Administrative Bahavior* when he more explicitly outlined a theory of organizational decision-making.

In Simon's theory, decision-making about complex issues is seen to be far removed from economic theories of utility maximization because decision-makers do not possess sufficient information about preferences and the means to reach them. The reality for decision-makers is scarcity of information and lack of ability to determine all possible outcomes; in this condition decision-makers tend to 'satisfice' by using simple rules of thumb or other heuristic devices. Satisficing is a process in which decision-makers select the first satisfactory solution to a problem; what is satisfactory is determined by setting certain minimum performance criteria rather than by trying to maximize.

Simon, therefore, opened up the idea that the highly-rational image of business decision-makers presented by economic theory is limited to a quite restricted set of conditions. As conditions get more complex a different type of decision process begins to take over.

Capital investment decision-making is one obvious area in which the possible tension between the optimal and the satisficing models may become prominent. Since money is involved, and since the surface objective must always emphasize maximizing returns, it is in this situation that settling for anything less may become problematic. As some of the more recent research in the general area of what has become known as behavioural accounting has shown, it is under these conditions that decision-makers may be tempted to indulge in various forms of ritualistic and symbolic behaviour to make it seem as if the ethos of rational accounting is being adhered to but for decisions to be made in some other mode.

THE PROBLEM OF UNCERTAINTY

A decision may be defined as the selection of a proposed course of action. This definition implies a number of aspects of organizational decision-making. First is the notion that there is some choice as to the actions to be taken and that there is uncertainty about which choice to take. There may be uncertainty about preferences as to the ends to be reached or there may be uncertainties about the means of reaching those desired ends. Second, there is the intention to act, although that intention may not be realized during the decision's implementation. Third, decision-making in an organization involves a number of actors; it is seldom that important decisions are taken by one individual.

According to this view, uncertainty is a pre-condition of decision-making. If there was no uncertainty as to the course of action to take there would be no decision to make. It is possible to consider two dimensions of uncertainty (Thompson and Tuden 1956; Thompson 1967). First is uncertainty as to the preferred outcomes; this is ends-uncertainty. Ends-uncertainty may come about as a result of different interests becoming involved in a decision; this is what Hickson *et al.* (1986) call politicality.

The second dimension of uncertainty is uncertainty about the solutions used to achieve the desired ends, this we call means-uncertainty. In an organization means-uncertainty can be seen as a technical problem of how to achieve the ends which in themselves can be uncertain.

In this chapter we examine some of the principal approaches that have developed for the study of decision-making. These approaches are gathered under the headings of four models of decision-making, namely: (1) the rational model, (2) the bounded rational model, (3) the political model, and (4) the garbage can model. As we shall see these models are not mutually exclusive but for the moment it is convenient to proceed as if they were. Each model contains different assumptions as to the processes involved in making decisions.

THE RATIONAL MODEL OF DECISION-MAKING

The rational model requires decision-makers to search for all possible options, to compare and evaluate them and choose the optimal. This model probably represents the predominant view of how decisions *ought* to be made. The theory of capital investment appraisal can be seen to belong substantially to this model.

A number of unifying ideas common to the different presentations of this approach have been well summarized by Mintzberg *et al.* (1976) in terms of a number of distinct routines or stages of decision-making as follows:

- **Recognition** The environment is constantly surveyed for new opportunities using many different kinds of information: financial, industry reports and the like, or informal information. The essential idea is of decision-makers who are constantly alert to opportunities.

- **Diagnosis** The problem is defined in terms of the decision-maker's objectives.

- **Search** Information is sought concerning possible solutions.

- **Design** Possible solutions are created to solve the problem.

- **Evaluation** Each solution is thoroughly assessed.

- **Choice** The optimal solution is selected according to objectives.

- **Authorization** In an organization the choice usually needs to be authorized at a higher level to ensure co-ordination with the overall organizational objectives.

- **Implementation** Since the optimal choice has been selected, implementation will follow.

The overall picture presented by the rational model is of active, highly-alert decision-makers, clear of their objectives, who search until they are in command of a great deal of information and who are knowledgeable about possible solutions, who are then in a position to choose the best course of action which then proceeds to be authorized and implemented. Decision-making becomes a sequence of steps which, if followed, should lead to the best solution, that is, to action which optimizes the decision-makers' utilities.

Some investment decisions undoubtedly do conform to this rational model of decision-making. Whether the vehicle fleet in a company should be renewed or not is a matter of collecting relevant information about new vehicles and their running costs, taking into account the net present value of the money to be spent, and comparing these costs to the cost of increasing repair bills to keep the old fleet going. It is likely that the answer will more or less fall out of the figures, so to speak, with some residual area remaining for judgement to be made concerning, say, likely movements in interest rates or the mileage to be covered by the vehicles. In this kind of decision these areas of judgement are usually fairly limited, although as uncertainties increase the more the process needs to move away from the pure rational model.

This kind of decision can be delegated to a fairly low level in the organization providing the boundaries set by the decision parameters are clearly defined and adhered to. These are programmed (March and Simon 1958) or routine decisions which recur frequently and for which procedures have been worked out by experience. They can also be described as computational decisions (Thompson and Tuden 1956) in the sense that it is assumed that formulae, or algorithms, exist for the solution of problems. They have also been called synoptic decisions (Lindblom 1959) indicating that it is possible for decision-makers to map out accurately the entire tree or hierarchy of all possible cause-effect relations.

THE BOUNDED-RATIONAL MODEL OF DECISION-MAKING

A number of writers on organizations and decision-making (Simon 1947, 1957, 1960; March and Simon 1956; Cyert and March 1963) pointed to the limitations of the rational approach when compared to the way in which actual decisions are made leading them to propose the alternative bounded-rational model.

The essential point about the bounded-rational model is that it emphasizes the need for managers to make decisions with incomplete information, under time pressures, when there may be disagreements over goals, and to accept that an optimal solution cannot always be achieved within these constraints. Rationality, therefore, is bounded.

The bounded-rational approach to decision-making accepts a number of features which are opposite to those of the rational model, as follows:

- **Problemistic search**   rather than complete alertness occurs. This means that managers respond to problems rather than going out of their way to find them. A firm may revamp its products because it finds sales and profits falling rather than as a result of a systematic-continuous searching for opportunities. The spur to decision-making may be outer- rather than inner-directed. Decisions often lie around a long time before becoming active within the decision arena. This gestation time can run to years while decision-makers ponder whether to make the issue more public and perhaps give the game away to others (Hickson *et al.* 1986).

- **Cognitive limits** exist in this search process, meaning that the human mind is limited in its comprehension of problems, thereby making it impossible to achieve the synoptic ideal of mapping out the complete decision tree showing the paths to all possible solutions. Part of the synoptic ideal (Lindblom 1959) is setting objectives and finding paths to achieve them. A complex decision's objectives may not be known beforehand. It is simply felt that there is a problem and something must be done, but what is to be done evolves out of the process of decision-making.

- **Time pressures** frequently apply which may cut short complete search. A decision has to be made even with incomplete information. For example, an investment decision may have to be made quickly to take the opportunity of a special price reduction offered by a supplier.

- **Disjointedness and incrementalism** often occurs (Lindblom 1959) meaning that problems get attended to sporadically and solutions are implemented only partially, rather than decisions occurring through the smooth continuous process of the rational model. Disjointedness might come about because complex problems cannot always be solved, so to speak, in one sitting. Managers may let an issue rest before taking it further and so the decision process appears as discontinuous with stops and starts. An incremental approach may be used in some cases by breaking the problem down into small steps and taking these one at a time. Projects may be implemented in steps, perhaps as a way of testing the ground rather than overcommitting to a course of action early on.

- **Intuition and judgement** may have to be the basis for making a decision rather than computation. Computations may be made to inform a decision but managers realize that the answer cannot fall out of the figures. The decision to launch a new product may, even after all the costings have been carried out, rely upon the judgement of one manager according to a 'feel' for the direction of movement in the market. By drawing upon a reservoir of previous successful and unsuccessful practice a manager can judge the correct action to take although it may not be possible to explicate fully the reasons. Bits and pieces of information gleaned from a variety of sources, especially informal sources, can be used to let the pattern of a solution evolve (Issack 1978; Eisenberg 1984; Simon 1987).

- **Satisficing**   rather than optimal solutions are arrived at. The word 'satisficing' was invented to describe the idea that managers will suffice with satisfactory solutions rather than continuously searching for the ideal one (Simon 1957). Thus minimum performance standards are set and once achieved the problem is considered solved. Satisficing involves setting some key targets and proceeding upon the assumption that complete search is impossible and pointless; the rule of thumb becomes to accept that which first comes to hand which fulfils the minimum performance level (March and Simon 1958: 142). Thus, the decision process to purchase a new computer may be stopped after seeing a particular computer in operation at another company and deciding that this installation fulfilled the minimal parameters.

Conditions for rational and bounded rational decision processes

As descriptions of two possible types of decision processes, the rational and bounded rational approaches provide useful insights but do not, as yet, explain the conditions under which one might be more appropriate for managers to use or give any indication of the possible organizational consequences of each.

Generally we can say that the rational model is more appropriate for routine decisions and the bounded rational for non-routine. Routine decisions are likely to be recurring. For instance, an equipment replacement investment might be routine if it is a matter of replacing an old machine with a new machine of essentially the same technology.

An important aspect of this routineness is that the decisions tend to be programmed into an organization's systems so that particular events stimulate particular actions. Some decisions approach this condition when reordering of a component may be triggered by inventory falling below a minimum reorder level. Conversely, the bounded rational approach is appropriate for non-programmed and more disparate issues. Here problems are unfamiliar and non-routine but also more likely to be contentious.

Mintzberg *et al.*'s investigations of the phases and circularity of decision-making

Mintzberg *et al.* (1976) examined the processes of decision-making used in a range of decisions by comparing twenty-five decision cases in a variety of organizations. They used a model which attempted to describe the decision-making processes in terms of three phases which in turn consists of six routines as already outlined above.

First, there is the identification phase which contains the problem recognition diagnosis routines. The development phase contains the information search and solution design routines. Finally, the selection phase contains the choice evaluation and authorization routines, authorization being required when the individual making the decision does not have the authority to commit the organization to a course of action.

To this point the model appears as another version of the rational approach where decision-making is supposed to proceed in logical sequential steps. As Figure 2.1 shows, the model allows for the possibility of feedback loops between the beginning and end of the routines. Problem recognition may occur first but thereafter routines can be brought in at any time, or completely missed out, or revisited during the decision.

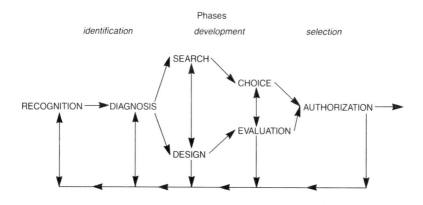

Figure 2.1   Phases and circularity of decision-making
Source: Adapted from Mintzberg, H. *et al.* (1976)

From this basic model Mintzberg *et al.* (1976) collected data concerning the extent to which the various routines were used, and concerning other factors such as the duration of each decision, the extent to which interruptions (interrupts) occurred in the process and the number of branches and recycles that occurred in the sequence suggested by the model.

The organizations investigated covered manufacturing, service and governmental organizations. The duration reported varied from less than one to more than four years. From their analysis of the data collected they attempted to generalize as to possible patterns of decision-making. In order to do this they classified decisions according to:

- **The stimulus giving rise to a decision**   The stimulus was categorized as to whether it was interpreted as providing an opportunity, was seen as a crisis or a problem that was essential to solve. Sometimes solutions were given at the beginning of the decision, conformed to a ready-made organizational solution, were modifications of existing solutions, or were custom-made for that decision.

Using these types of stimuli and descriptions of other routines they were able to identify six generalized types of decision as follows:

- **Simple interrupt**   Stimulus by problem, solution given, recognition and diagnosis stages used with a lot of interruptions. These were the non-complex decisions with given solutions which got blocked.

- **Political design process**   Given solutions or modifications to ready-made solutions were used in these decisions but interruptions were more extensive due to intensive political activity.

- **Basic search**   This type of decision would appear to come nearest to the rational type in that there were few interruptions and the emphasis was upon rational search processes and finding solutions in accordance with organizational precedence.

- **Modified search**   Represents a rather more complex basic search type in which ready-made solutions are modified to a particular decision.

- **Basic and dynamic designs**   These decision types appear to move towards the bounded rational type in that custom-made solutions are found following considerable design and evaluation effort.

Mintzberg *et al.*'s study represents an attempt to derive patterns of decision-making processes by comparing twenty-five cases. Obviously this is a great improvement upon studies which attempt generalizations from one case but their research does indicate how difficult it is to make sense of such complex processes. Above all, they emphasize the essential circularity of decision-making even over fairly simple issues.

THE POLITICAL MODEL OF DECISION-MAKING

The political model of organizational decision-making is based upon the idea that an organization consists of a number of interests who are potentially competing for resources and attention. In the more extreme cases it may mean that interests are opportunistically pursued in the sense that one person may deliberately set out to ensure that a decision is made in that person's favour (Butler *et al.* 1977).

The political approach sees the processes of organizational decision-making as involving shifting coalitions of interests and temporary alliances of decision-makers who can, for the purpose of a decision, come together and sufficiently submerge their differences to make a decision (Cyert and March 1963). A coalition may be formed just for one decision but it is also likely to involve trade-offs in which, say, *A* supports *B* against *C* for this issue, providing *B* supports *A* in the future over another issue.

Hickson *et al.* (1986: 3) describe how a manager in command of certain information in an organization can reactivate an issue when the time is ripe. In the case they illustrated, the outcome of a proposal for a chemical company to invest in a boiler was affected by the interest the production director had in gaining the position of chief executive. If he was successful in persuading the board that a particular type of boiler should be bought, thereby utilizing the waste steam produced during chemical processing for generating electricity, he had a good chance of becoming chief executive in preference to the purchasing director who was opposed to such a project. The purchasing director argued that it was cheaper to buy in the electricity and that a chemical company had no business producing electricity anyway. In this case the decision was driven by personal interest, although that is not to say that this interest was to the detriment of the company.

Some examples of the kinds of processes related to the political model are:

- **Bargaining** Whereby individuals compete for resources and try to get the best deal for themselves.

- **Guile** Which can range from economizing with the truth (not disclosing all information relevant to an issue) to lying. Information can be selectively disclosed or distorted (Pettigrew 1973; Hickson *et al.* 1986).

• **Coalition building**   In order to get support for an issue people combine with others in trade-offs. Of great help here is the ability to build networks of trusted individuals who can be called upon when appropriate.

• **Biasing**   The ability to make the rules of the game by which decisions are assessed can give particular interests tremendous power. This can be done by gradual accretion over time (Butler 1991: 218). One technique is to become the chairperson of committees or task groups (Pfeffer 1981) and hence gain the ability to set agenda.

These are just illustrations of the type of process involved in the political model of decision-making. Overall, the political model provides a highly-dynamic model of decision-making. One danger is that an overemphasis upon this kind of process may lead us to neglect the rational aspect of decision-making.

THE GARBAGE CAN MODEL OF DECISION-MAKING

A colourful and apt description of the way in which some decisions are made in organizations is given by the Garbage Can Model (Cohen *et al.* 1972; Cohen and March 1974). In this approach, events and decisions in organizations are not necessarily even as systematic as the bounded rationality model suggests, but approach those of an 'organized anarchy' exhibiting three main characteristics:

• **Problematic preferences**   Problems, alternatives, solutions and goals are ill defined. Ambiguity characterizes each aspect of a decision process.

• **Ambiguous technology**   Cause and effect relationships are difficult to identify.

• **Fluid participation**   There is a turnover of participants and they have only limited time to allocate to any one problem or decision. Participation in any given decision will be fluid and limited.

The garbage can characterizes organizations as experiencing rapid change and as collegial, nonbureaucratic and fuzzy (Butler 1991). No organization fits these circumstances of organized anarchy all the time, but most organizations will occasionally find themselves in positions of making decisions under problematic and ambiguous circumstances particularly at the strategic level. An important characteristic of the garbage can model is that the decision process is not a sequence of steps beginning with a problem and ending with a solution. It is possible that problem-identification and problem-solution stages may not be connected to each other. Ideas may be proposed as a solution when no problem exists. Problems may exist and never generate a solution.

The reason problems and solutions are not connected is that decisions are the outcome of often independent streams of events within the organization. Four streams of garbage can decision-making can be seen:

- **Problems** Derive from a gap between current and desired performance. They represent points of dissatisfaction but are distinct from choices and solutions since a problem may or may not lead to a solution, and adopted solutions may not solve the problem.

- **Solutions** Participants have ready-made solutions which represent a flow of ideas and alternatives through the organization, with people bringing in new ideas. Participants may be attracted to certain ideas and push them as logical choices and attraction to an idea may cause an employee to look for a problem to which it can be attached. Solutions can exist independently of problems although, over time, there may be a merging of the two.

- **Participants** Participants vary widely in their ideas, perception of problems, experience, values and training. They can come and go and solutions recognized by one participant may not be those recognized by others. Time pressures lead participants to allocate different amounts of participation to a given problem or solution.

- **Choice opportunities** These are occasions when an organization makes a decision and an alternative is authorized and implemented. Choice opportunities arise when any specific stimulus occurs such as the signing of a new contract or a new product is authorized. These opportunities may be precipitated by specific events such as a crisis, an idea, or perhaps a supplier who is pressing for an order to be placed.

From these independent streams of activity emerge patterns in organizational decision-making. Problems, solutions, participants and choices flow through the organization, with the organization acting as a garbage can in which these streams are stirred, and problems, solutions, participants and choices drop in with the possibility of connecting. In this way problems may get solved, or not solved, dependent on whether connections are made.

Any problem and solution may be connected when a choice is made but the problem does not always relate to the solution and the solution may not solve the problem. Organizational decisions are not simply the result of the logical step-by-step sequence of events that other descriptions of decision-making imply. Participants are intendedly rational but events are so ill defined and complex that decisions, problems and solutions are often initially seen as independent of one another.

By using computer simulations Cohen *et al.* (1972) and Cohen (1989) have been able to demonstrate some consequences of this approach to decision-making:

- **Solutions are proposed even when problems do not exist**   A participant may support an idea and may try to sell it to the rest of the organization. An example of this would be if, as we shall see in one of our cases (see Medical Supplier), an engineer is strongly in favour of a particular new production process involving investment in a new machine. Championing this project may now become almost the *raison d'être* of that engineer within the organization as he tries to drive the project through the organization. In some cases ideas like this may fall into disuse, in others they get taken up by the organization and implemented.

- **Choices are made without solving problems**   A choice made with the intention of solving a problem may not solve that problem. Conversely, choices sometimes happen without there being a problem.

- **Problems may persist without being solved**   Participants get used to problems and give up trying to solve them. Or participants may not know how to solve a particular problem. For example, a 'rogue' professor in a university persisted in his post in spite of causing considerable problems for his colleagues because nobody knew how to get rid of him (Hickson *et al.* 1986).

- **Some problems are solved**   Summed over many decisions in an organization things somehow work in spite of the chaos; solutions do, on the average, connect with choices and the organization does move in the direction of problem reduction.

One danger with an organization designed as a garbage can is that participants may spend too much time and effort talking, arguing, interacting, pushing favourite solutions, and so forth. These are errors of decision overcapacity (Butler 1991: 57−9) whereby the organizational rules are too elastic. Inefficiency may result from these conditions and decision-makers proceed upon the false belief that their world is more uncertain than it really is and miss the opportunity to apply crisper structures with associated computational decision-making.

The converse is the danger if managers proceed using the assumptions of the rational model. Here the problem can be that of decision undercapacity (Butler 1991) whereby a too stringent and rigid set of rules is used to assess investment decisions. Here, accounting data that is inherently fuzzy may be treated as accurately representing reality.

A CONTINGENCY MODEL OF DECISION-MAKING

Is there something we can say about the type of decision-making process that is best suited to particular situations? A contingency model of decision-making put forward by Thompson and Tuden (1956) allows us to draw some conclusions towards this end. The model is summarized in Figure 2.2. Here we see the two dimensions of uncertainty about ends and uncertainty about means.

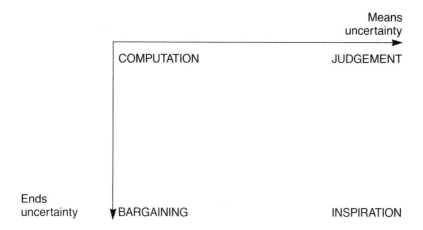

Fig. 2.2 The contingencies of organizational decision-making
Source: Butler, R. J. (1991)

The contingency model gives four conditions corresponding to different values of ends and means uncertainty. Under each of these conditions it is suggested that a different decision strategy is needed. The decision strategies correspond to the features of the four models of decision-making described above.

The computational strategy: suitable for certain ends and certain means

Decision-makers may not know the optimal solution to a problem, indeed if they did there would be no decision, but they may be confident that such an answer is available through the use of particular computational procedures and proceed upon this belief. They are, therefore proceeding with the assumptions of the rational model of decision-making.

The computations may be complex but the expectation is that an answer will come out of the figures. This clarity over ends/means relations will be matched by agreement over ends amongst decision-makers. The overall organizational structure appropriate for computational processes is crisp (Butler 1991); specifically we would expect this organization to feature formalized, demarcated, centralized structures with an appropriate number of experts carrying out analysis and expecting their results to be acted upon. Norms of efficiency will tend to dominate decision-making.

The dilemmas of computation relate to the problems of under- rather than over-decision-making capacity; there is a danger of trying to impose premature closure on issues or trying to force them into the strait-jacket of too tight a control.

The judgemental strategy: suitable for certain ends and uncertain means

This is the process whereby decision-makers cope with the problem of technical ambiguity. These are essentially the processes of the bounded rational model of decision-making, that is, problemistic search, cognitive limits to rationality with limited choice generation and satisficing solutions.

The organization that is suitable for judgement will tend to be fuzzier with specialization professionally based, with more lateral communication than vertical, high participation and expert-based influence.

The bargaining strategy: suitable for uncertain ends and certain means

This is the process of decision-making whereby participants attempt to resolve conflicting objectives. The underlying factor leading to bargaining is disagreement over the desired ends. Two outcomes of bargaining would seem possible: (1) a compromise is reached between involved parties, or (2) one party wins and another loses. Both these suggest that underlying the processes of bargaining is the power that different participants can bring to bear upon a decision issue. This dimension therefore captures the politicality of decision-making (Butler *et al.* 1977).

The inspirational strategy: suitable for uncertain ends and uncertain means

This is the most difficult decision situation and the most demanding in terms of communication and informational requirements. We need, however, to be careful in using the word inspiration since this might imply a decision that is made almost haphazardly or without care. Although as outsiders we may observe some decisions being made as if on the spur of the moment, we should not disregard the feel and intuition for a situation that experience can bring (Issack 1978; Simon 1987).

Overall, we would expect the organization for inspiration to look like that of the garbage can, where solutions, problems, participants and choices are proceeding in parallel waiting for appropriate opportunities to make connections. Interaction will be high and many of the rules implicit rather than formalized. There is likely to be a shifting leadership and the only way in which this kind of organization is likely to get decisions made is through the development of a robust ideology. The likely errors are those of over- rather than under-decision-making capacity.

THE DYNAMICS OF DECISION-MAKING

Decision topics are issues or problems that arise through a combination of an organization's context and structure (Hickson *et al.* 1986; Pettigrew 1990); context sets the scene for decisions in terms of technology, task environment and norms, and structure sets the scene in terms of rules for making decisions. Complex contexts and fuzzy structures give rise to uncertain topics in terms of both ends and means. Outputs follow from the processes, one component of which is the substance of the action taken in the organization, whether it be an investment made, a new product introduced, and the like.

Factors leading to ends-uncertainty

Generally, factors which would increase ends-uncertainty derive from the politicality (Butler *et al.* 1977) of the decision topic. The greater the number and variability of interests involved or the more outside influences exist the greater the propensity for disparity.

Factors leading to means-uncertainty

Some factors which might be seen as leading to means-uncertainty are: (a) incompleteness of knowledge as occurs when new technologies are being developed; (b) the 'object' worked on is dynamic as in the production of a pathbreaking prototype; (c) the unpredictability of the behaviour of outside groups or organizations such as rivals, customers, suppliers or regulators. The combination of high and low scores on these dimensions leads to the possibility of four types of decision process in order to manage these underlying problems of decision-making (Thompson and Tuden 1956; Thompson 1967).

The push towards computation and limitations of time

The model presented would surely suggest that in an organization there would always be a push away from the inspirational towards the computational. In other words, if an issue starts as an inspirational issue the decision processes would proceed until sufficient learning has occurred for algorithms to be developed permitting a decision to be made by computation.

There is, however, a critical limitation, the limitation of time. The above prescription has discounted the value of time but time enters into the equation in two ways (Sharp 1990): (1) through the notion that decision-making takes *managerial time* and therefore imposes a cost upon an organization, and (2) due to the *opportunity cost* of possible benefits forgone while the search for algorithms goes on.

If we say that managerial time comprises the total of the time spent by the various participants in the decision summed over its duration, a time cost, in principle, could be allocated to this. The organization is 'spending' managerial time in anticipation of a future return, not necessarily in the form of a single lump, but over time as the decision proceeds. Managerial time can become a surrogate for money and we can see the impact of the time dimension beginning to emerge; increments of time are 'spent' at Times 1,2,3 and so on in anticipation of a future delayed return; this is a classic investment problem which, given enough information about costs and discount rates, could be solved by means of a discounted cash-flow calculation. Decision-makers, according to this argument, would carry out a kind of intuitive cost-benefit analysis balancing time spent on perfecting decision-making against expected greater return.

This argument becomes more forceful if we extend the notion of opportunity cost. A discounted cash flow assumes an opportunity cost; managerial time (the surrogate for money) 'spent' at Time 1 has a net present value greater than the same amount of time 'spent' at Time 2. But there is a potentially more important aspect of opportunity cost due to opportunities lost in the environment of the organization while a decision is being made. This can be illustrated in the case of market-oriented decisions where time spent perfecting a project proposal whether or not to launch a new product may lose valuable opportunities in the market as other firms take up the challenge. In other words, as a decision is being made the environmental conditions are changing. Assumptions made at the beginning of the process may no longer hold as competitors enter, and prices and costs change.

Conversely, there are occasions when letting a decision lie can improve the quality of the outcomes as new understanding develops or environmental conditions turn favourable.

Kanter (1984) has put the same problem another way by considering the time taken to make decisions and the rate at which events in the context unfold. The basic prescription is to say that the time taken to make decisions needs to be less than the time between arising surprises in order for an organization to maintain adaptability. When time between surprises is short decisions are likely to be made rapidly, thereby approaching the inspirational mode.

Errors of decision undercapacity would be an outcome of premature closure but might be justified on the grounds of opportunity costs; errors of decision overcapacity would be an outcome of late closure but might be justified on the grounds of waiting for favourable conditions to become available. The choice is to err on the side of believing the world more certain than it is by risking acceptance of a false hypothesis, or to err on the side of believing the world less certain than it is by risking rejecting a true hypothesis.

PATTERNS OF DECISION-MAKING: THE BRADFORD STUDIES

It is only recently that a systematic attempt has been made to observe the processes of strategic decision-making across a large number of decision issues in many different types of organization (Hickson *et al.* 1986). Working within the broad contingency framework outlined above, the Bradford Studies investigated the processes of top-level decision-making and noted three principal patterns of decision-making that appeared in the decision studied.

These studies examined 150 strategic decisions in thirty organizations of many different types ranging across a spectrum of manufacturing and service, and public and private organizations. Detailed observations and interviews were carried out concerning the processes used in a range of decisions within each organization and covering a range of topics. Generally, these were high-level or 'top decisions', involving the long-term strategy of the organization covering a range of issues dealing with matters such as the introduction of new products, closing down facilities and factories, reorganizations, mergers or acquisitions, personnel matters or investment in new equipment. Observations were made concerning a number of specific variables (Butler *et al.* 1979) of the processes as follows:

Scrutiny This is the basic process of searching, designing and evaluating solutions and includes the following subprocesses:
- **Sources**:   in an organization participants search for information beyond that which is contained within themselves and an important aspect of this search is the number of different sources and experts that are called upon.
- **Information variability**:   this is the extent to which the information collected is considered to be of doubtful reliability.
- **Information externality**:   this is the extent to which information is sought from outside the organization.
- **Effort**:   some information is more readily available in organizations than other information. Effort is a measure of the work that has to go into collecting, collating and generating that information. Effort may range from information available from personal knowledge or opinions (low effort), through information readily obtained from records, to information synthesized by integrating diverse sources of information (high effort) in order to design optional solutions and to evaluate them.

Interaction   Decision-making within an organization involves social interaction between participants of various kinds. Two types of interaction seemed particularly important:

- **Formal**:   organizations many try to channel a decision formally through committees or any number of formal procedures that may exist.
- **Informal interaction**:   a great deal of interaction in organizations is informal involving discussions over lunch, in corridors or elsewhere.
- **Negotiation**   When decisions involve more than one participant, negotiation is liable to occur in all except the most simple cases. A number of possibilities can be seen ranging from the decision being not open to negotiation, to negotiation occurring only in the final stages, to negotiation resulting in limited consensus.
- **Delays**   Impediments, or 'interrupts' (Mintzberg *et al.* 1976), in the smooth flow of a decision may occur for a number of reasons ranging from problems of sequencing, through awaiting priority in the order of attention, solving and waiting further investigations, to awaiting to overcome resistance to change.
- **Duration**   Some decisions are made more quickly than others as measured by the time between an issue being deliberately considered in the organization to final authorization.
- **Level**   The extent to which a decision is centralized or decentralized is usually considered to be a major variable of decision-making in an organization.

One aim of the research was to discover what happened in organizations as they struggled to make major decisions. The data were subjected to a cluster analysis to establish patterns of decision-making. Three distinct patterns or clusters emerged as shown in Table 2.1. The first, the sporadic cluster, consists of a group of fifty-three decisions with above-average delays, impediments, scrutiny (on all subvariables), informal interaction, duration and were authorized at the highest level in the organization following some negotiation. Overall these decisions may be described as informally spasmodic and protracted.

As a means of making decisions in a very wide range of British organizations, the sporadic method was used in about one-third of the decisions studied. This sporadic cluster may be contrasted to the fluid cluster (consisting of forty-two decisions) where it can be seen that these decisions experienced less delays, impediments, scrutiny (all constituent subvariables) and duration, some negotiation and more formal interaction but were still authorized at the highest level. Overall, these decisions may be described as steadily paced, quick and formally channelled.

Table 2.1   Three ways to make decisions

	Decision process cluster	
CONSTRICTED *(narrowly channelled)*	FLUID *(steadily paced, quick formally channelled)*	SPORADIC *(informally spasmodic and protracted)*
More: Scrutiny, effort Interaction, formal	*Less:* Scrutiny Delays Impediments Duration	*Some:* Negotiation *More:* Delays Impediments Scrutiny
More: Scrutiny, sources	*Some:* Negotiation *More:* Interaction, formal	Interaction, informal Duration
Lower level	*Highest* level	*Highest* level

Source: Butler, R. J. (1991).

The third group, the constricted decision cluster (forty-one decisions), is characterized by less scrutiny effort, negotiation and formal interaction than the other decision types, is authorized below the highest level but, paradoxically, uses more scrutiny sources than does the fluid. Overall these may be seen as narrowly-channelled decisions.

Which method of decision-making?

Is there some guidance we can now give to managers as to the method of decision-making to use when a decision issue arises? To answer this question the Bradford Studies also assessed the associated complexity and politicality of the various decision issues. In general, those decisions displaying the most complexity and politicality were treated in a sporadic way and hence the sporadic issues were found to be those involving many diverse interests, were serious in their potential consequences, contentious and externally influenced (Table 2.2).

Those decisions which were slightly less on complexity but least of all on politicality tended to be treated in a fluid manner. The really distinguishing feature here over the sporadically-treated issues is that the fluid issues were less serious but more rarer. Hence, it appears that top management wanted to hold these decisions in their hands, permitting only that degree of delegation that can be formally managed.

Table 2.2 Decision modes and topic issues

| | *Complexity* | |
	Low	*High*
Low		*rare* *non-contentious* FLUID
Politicality	*familiar* *non-serious* *non-contentious* CONSTRICTED	*unusual* *serious* *interest diversity* *contentious* *external influence*
High		SPORADIC

Source: Butler, R. J. (1991)

Decision issues with the least complexity and politicality were handled by the fluid process. The distinguishing feature is that the issues were familiar (programmed) issues involving internal interests only and were non-contentious.

CONCLUSION

This chapter has surveyed and summarized a range of organizational decision-making theories. It provides a base for developing a model of decision-making effectiveness which is done in Chapter 3.

At the heart of this model are the strategies that decision-makers may pursue in their deliberations over an issue. Following Thompson and Tuden these strategies are computation, judgement, bargaining and inspiration. The important question now is to explore what is meant by effective decision-making and how the decision strategies may impact upon effectiveness.

3 The decision effectiveness model

INTRODUCTION

This chapter outlines a model of decision-making effectiveness. Such a model needs to establish appropriate variables of decision performance and the model to be outlined in this chapter was used to guide our study of investment decision-making. The overall shape of the model is given in Figure 3.1. Decision effectiveness is seen to be the outcome of interactions between four groups of variables:

1 **Definition**, which refers to the shape of the problem as seen by the participants of a decision.
2 **Strategies**, which refers to the approaches used for solution and support building.
3 **Influence**, which refers to the patterns of involvement and authority used during decision-making.
4 **Timing**, which refers to the chronology of a decision.

The discussion of contingency theory in the previous chapter suggests that there should be a relationship between the definition of a decision issue, the strategies used for solution and support-building, and effectiveness. However, the model shown in Figure 3.1 also allows for interaction between all variable groups.

Methodological note

In order to develop and test the ideas contained within this general model of decision effectiveness we carried out a study of seventeen actual organizational decisions.

All these decisions involved major investments for the organizations concerned. Data was collected by means of a structured interview schedule and interviews were conducted with, in all, fifty-five executives who were closely involved in the seventeen decisions. These interviews were tape-recorded and elicited much information about the organizational background and history, the conditions surrounding the decisions and many other aspects of the decision process of a more qualitative nature.

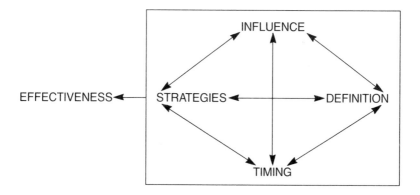

Figure 3.1 The phases of the decision effectiveness model

In identifying decisions for investigation suitable organizations were selected from a range of public, private, service and manufacturing categories. Twelve organizations were selected for the study as shown in Table 3.1.

The difference between the public and private sectors has become increasingly blurred, especially following the privatization programme that has occurred in the United Kingdom, The Electricity and Water Companies were in state ownership at the time of the study, but it was clear that privatization was imminent and that this was having an effect upon the organizations and the way in which they approached investment decisions.

As to be expected with investment decisions, the purchase of equipment, whether computers or manufacturing facilities, dominates the sample. There was also a very wide range of organizational sizes in terms of employment and annual turnover. Although manufacturing predominates, there is one financial services organization and two public utilities. Six of the firms are multinational, Capital Goods and Cloth-Dyer (British-based), Consumer Electrical (Japanese-based), and Household Consumer and Medical Supplier (US-based).

Table 3.1 Sample of organizations and decisions

Organization	Status	Decision		INF	INV (£m)	Size
A Aerospace Company	I,V	AT	New test bed facility	2	35.0	L
B Brewer Company	I,V	BU	Site acquisition UK	1	10.0	L
		BR	Open restaurants in N. America	1	15.0	
C Capital Goods Manufacturer	I,V	CM	Installation of new manufacturing plant	6	4.0	M
D Cloth Dyer	U,V	DK	Totally new plant (kitchen)	5	0.5	S
E Electric Company	I,B	EC	Computer	3	3.1	L
		ES	Computer software	2	0.2	
H Household Consumer Goods Company (US)	U,V	HW	Automated warehouse	1	10.0	L
J Japanese Consumer Goods Company	U,V	JU	Centre opening up in UK	1*	60.0	M
L Electronics Company	I,V	LP	New product introduction	7	0.5	S
M Medical Supplier Company	U,V	MK	Knitting machine	7	0.1	M
		MP	New plant	5	0.2	
O Oil Co (US) Europe subsidiary	U,V	OS	Solvents expansion	1	2.5	M
		OP	Propalyne upgrading	1	5.0	
S Building Society	I,V	SC	Purchase of mainframe computer	2	5.0	M
		SS	Purchase of software	3	0.4	
W Water Company	I,B	WF	Construction of water filtration plant	7	12.0	L
				55		

Notes: Number of organizations = 12. Number of decisions = 17.
Key: INF = number of informants   INV = amount of investment
       EMP = number of employees   TURN = amount of turnover
Status: I = independent, S = subsidiary, B = public, V = private ownership.
* two informants were interviewed simultaneously.

VARIABLES OF EFFECTIVENESS

Butrous (1989) has reviewed the literature concerning the effectiveness of organizational decision-making and concluded that there is little in the way of established concepts and variables for its operationalization. We set out to measure decision-making effectiveness as best we could given the incompleteness of our understanding of the concept at the start of the study. Variables of effectiveness were identified as described.

A dominant theme in the rational model is that decision-making is viewed as a goal attainment process. Hence, variables measuring the extent to which a decision achieves its initial goals (project success) and the extent to which, in retrospect, a 'right' choice was made were used.

The notion of decision-making as a learning process (Vickers 1965) was operationalized by asking whether, and how, the decision led to useful organizational learning. Some side issues here would be captured by the extent to which the decision resulted in unexpected outcomes, either of a positive or negative nature.

Another aspect of effectiveness we considered concerns the extent to which the decision process itself was considered satisfactory.

In all we considered five questions of decision effectiveness as summarized in Table 3.2. These questions on effectiveness were quite exploratory since, at the time, we had no definitive theory of decision-making effectiveness. The approach was to try out the ideas on our sample of executives. The data was collected in the form of responses on five point ordinal scales (a summary of the interview schedule is given in Appendix A) and then subjected to factor analysis.

The factors of decision effectiveness

Factor analysis allows us to see whether there are particular dimensions of the concept of effectiveness in the minds of the executives sampled. Particular variables may be observed as being strongly associated with one another thereby indicating the existence of a dimension of factor. After trying different approaches we found that two principal dimensions could be identified, one dimension is called the objectives-attainment factor of effectiveness and the second the learning factor. These two factors allow us to draw up effectiveness scores for our decisions. This resultant view of decision effectiveness being measured by an objectives dimension and a learning dimension has been supported by parallel work done in the British National Health Service by Butrous (1989)

Table 3.2   The decision-effectiveness model

Phase	Factor (constituent variables)
Dependent variables	
EFFECTIVENESS	*Objectives-attainment*: project success, right choice, $(-)$ unexpected negative outcomes
	Learning: overall learning, $(-)$ satisfactory process
Explanatory variables	
DEFINITION	
Consequentiality	*Failure*: impact of project failure on corporate financial standing, competitive position, performance of company
	Fit: degree of fit with business strategy, $(-)$ project value
Uncertainty	*Rarity*: novelty of project, supplier uncertainties, production and cost uncertainties
	Performance: market uncertainties, internal and external financial uncertainties
Disagreements	*Personal*: personal objectives disagreements, personality clashes
	Objectives: overall organizational disagreements, disagreements about project objectives
STRATEGIES	
Computation	*Rate of return*: payback, internal rate of return (IRR), productivity
	Reported profit: $(-)$ productivity, earnings, overall computation
Judgement	*Personnel*: impact of project on morale, industrial relations
	Image: impact on image, quality
	Judgement: overall judgement
Negotiation	*Negotiation*: overall negotiation, building of alliances
Inspiration	*Inspiration*: overall inspiration
INFLUENCE	*Internality*: internal involvement and direction
	Externality: external involvement and direction
TIMING	*Deliberation*: duration of decision process, decision building up slowly, delays, pace worries

Note: $(-)$ denotes a negative loading on a variable.

High scores on the objectives-attainment factor are achieved where the decision is seen as: (a) leading to a generally highly-successful project, (b) with hindsight making the 'right' choice was made, and

(c) not leading to significant unexpected negative outcomes. The composition of the objectives-attainment factor reinforces a general rational approach to decision-making where a number of variables which are concerned with the achievement of goals are related to one another.

High scores on the learning dimension are achieved where (a) the decision resulted in a great deal of useful organizational learning, and (b) there was considerable dissatisfaction with the process by which the decision was arrived at.

The learning factor, however, contains a noteworthy and not altogether expected result. There is a tendency for decision processes that are viewed as generally satisfactory to result in less learning and for unsatisfactory processes as being seen to foster learning. The implication is that dissatisfaction can be a spur to creativity, whereas satisfaction may breed a complacency that does not encourage a search for better solutions.

This effect is well illustrated by several of our case studies. In particular, decision *MK* which is summarized in Table 3.3, and is the subject of a detailed case study in a later chapter (Medical Supplier: to weave or to knit). The creative potential of certain types of dissatisfaction and disagreement amongst decision-makers is a major thread that runs through much of the remainder of this book; this notion lends weight to the current theories of organizational change which give considerable emphasis to the importance of organizational learning (Kanter 1989). Table 3.3 summarizes the constituent variables of the effectiveness factors along with the other factors to be described later. Appendix B, section 3.10, gives fuller details of this factor analysis.

The effectiveness of the decisions

It is now possible to assess each of the decisions studied as to their degree of effectiveness on the objectives-attainment and learning dimensions.

Each decision is presented in Table 3.3 according to its code. The top part of the table gives the scores on the two effectiveness variables for each decision. The decisions are ordered according to the learning scores and then according to the objectives scores.

It should be noted that there are sixteen, not seventeen decisions, and eleven, not twelve, organizations represented in Table 3.3 and the subsequent analysis since one decision and one organization has been left out of this analysis. Aerospace and decision *AT* have had to be

Table 3.3 The decisions and their variables

								Decision										
Variable	LP	BR	WF	DK	SC	EC	JU	SS	ES	OP	CM	HW	OS	MK	BU	MP	*scale*	*mean*
EFFECTIVENESS																		
Learning	(H)30	30	27	26	(M)25	23	23	23	(L)15	15	18	10	0	(H)34	30	(L)12	0–40	20
Objectives-attainment	(H)35	35	35	31	(H)38	39	30	31	(H)40	30	34	30	30	(L)18	20	(L)20	0–40	31
DEFINITION																		
Interest: career	0	1	10	18	5	13	0	10	15	0	3	0	20	11	0	12	0–40	7
Consequentiality: fit	27	40	40	40	30	37	30	40	25	35	37	30	40	34	40	32	0–40	33
failure	33	30	6	26	20	20	10	30	5	5	16	30	10	7	8	10	0–40	15
Uncertainty	14	15	8	12	9	10	27	18	9	8	16	23	21	18	8	13	0–40	14
rarity	6	40	13	22	20	3	0	33	20	0	10	10	0	23	40	18	0–40	16
market	21	20	3	4	5	7	40	7	0	20	28	30	10	17	10	30	0–40	16
Disagreements (type)	mar	reg	fin	sup	tec	fin	tec	tec	cos	ire	cos	fin	cos	cos	cos	pec		
Disagreements	3	30	18	24	15	10	4	14		8	8	10	0	24	33	12	0–40	13
personality	0	20	8	12	0	0	0	7	0	0	15	0	0	24	0	2	0–40	6
objective	2	20	8	8	0	10	20	7	0	0	7	0	0	9	40	12	0–40	9
objective (type)	obj	obj	obj	per	pro	pro	obj	obj			pro			per	obj	obj		
objective (type)	eth	per	obj	pro		obj	pro	pro			obj			pob		pro		
STRATEGIES																		
Computation	23	28	32	30	20	33	40	27	30	40	35	30	40	21	10	28	0–40	29
payback	27	20	2	26	5	20	10	27	15	10	27	10	20	21	0	30	0–40	17
productivity	27	24	24	24	15	27	20	30	20	0	35	20	20	21	0	30	0–40	21
Judgement	28	26	20	36	25	20	10	30	30	30	35	10	10	23	20	28	0–40	24
information	4	0	7	6	5	0	30	3	2	10	5	0	0	0	10	6	0–40	4
image	32	22	26	18	0	13	0	33	15	20	27	30	20	24	0	18	0–40	20
Negotiation	18	30	11	20	10	10	0	10	5	10	11	0	0	14	30	12	0–40	12
alliances	2	10	5	18	0	7	0	0	10	0	5	0	0	23	30	8	0–40	8
Inspiration	1	10	1	14	0	0	0	1	0	0	1	0	0	26	20	12	0–40	6

INFLUENCE / TIMING data table

	LP	BR	WF	DK	SC	EC	JU	SS	ES	OP	CM	HW	OS	MK	BU	MP		
INFLUENCE																		
Involvement	8	6	8	5	5	6	6	8	4	6	9	9	9	9	5	7	units	6.7
Direction	3	3	5	2	1	5	5	4	3	3	5	5	5	5	5	4	units	3.9
External	0	3	1	1	1	2	4	3	2	1	1	1	0	1	1	1	units	1.3
Authority	T	T	T	T	T	T	T	T	T	P	P	P	P	O	T	O	*	
TIMING																		
Build-up	1	20	6	26	0	0	30	23	5	0	10	0	0	21	0	12	0–40	9
Delays	1	30	22	32	10	20	40	30	20	20	30	20	30	31	20	22	0–40	25
Duration	77	277	900	269	6	150	60	19	162	175	200	129	169	350	−	350	$\text{yrs} \times 10^2$	219
Pace disagreements	1	1	1	1	0	0	1	1	1	0	0	1	0	1	1	1	0–1	no–yes

* *Authority:* T = strong top management guidance, P = well-defined parameters set, O = little control or guidance

Abbreviations: (H) = high, (M) = medium, (L) = low, cos = cost, eth = ethical, fin = finance, ire = industrial relations, mar = market, obj = objectives, per = personality, pob = personal objectives, pro = procedures, reg = regulatory, sup = supplier, tec = technical

Note: rounded-off numbers are given, therefore means need not corresponds to the means of the row numbers.

omitted due to the unavailability of data on project effectiveness since implementation was still in progress.

The ordering of the decisions in this fashion enables us to create five groups of decisions. The first group, consisting of four decisions, is a high learning/high objectives-attainment group; the next group contains four decisions and is a medium learning/high objectives-attainment; the third group contains five decisions and is a low learning/high objectives-attainment group. Two decisions are in a high learning/low objectives-attainment group, and one decision shows up as low on learning/objectives attainment.

Table 3.3 also gives the mean score for each variable and it can be seen that learning has a mean of 20, the mid-point on our rating scale which runs from 0 to 40. The mean for objectives-attainment is 31, indicating that, in general, decision-makers see themselves as attaining their initial goals in decision-making to a quite high extent. Only one out of the sixteen decisions was considered ineffective from the viewpoint of both these dimensions (decision *MP*).

This result is, in itself, significant since it tells us that, going on the evidence of sixteen strategic investment decisions taken in companies operating in the United Kingdom, about 6 per cent of decisions turn out to be overall failures. This presents a picture of industry that is less sensational than that often portrayed in popular reporting on British industry.

Scores of the most significant variables for the whole model are also given in this table which, therefore, represents the core data base for the decisions studied. Each column in Table 3.3 provides a kind of numerical sketch of each decision. It is from these sketches that we will develop, on the one hand, more detailed portraits in case-study-form of some of the decisions, and on the other hand, comparisons between the decisions to draw more generalized conclusions about the processes of effective decision-making.

THE DEFINITION OF DECISION ISSUES

An issue gets defined as a problem in an organization which has to be resolved by building solutions and support for those solutions. Definition of an issue means facing the possibility of making a choice about future actions. Once participants in an organization arrive at the point of perceiving that a choice is available there is no going back. The very fact of perceiving choices that were not previously perceived changes the appreciation of a situation.

We used a number of specific variables to capture the process of definition.

Interest

An issue has to be recognized and given an impetus in the first place. The impetus has to be given through the interest of participants.

Individuals need motivation to become involved in an issue. One measure of this is the extent to which participants see the issue as having career implications for them personally. Table 3.3 shows that this was not generally seen to be of great importance since the average score is only 7 out of a maximum of 40.

Decision *DK* is notable in scoring 18 on this variable. This is described in more detail in the chapter 'A New Kitchen at Cloth-Dyer'. In short, the decision involved buying a new dye-mixing 'kitchen' which was vital to the future survival of the organization. The interest in this decision came about as a result of the quest for commercial survival in a very direct way.

Consequentiality

Another aspect of definition concerns the consequentiality, or importance, of the issue to the organization for its growth and survival and, in particular, what the consequences of failure would be.

A number of variables were used to measure consequentiality and a factor analysis gave two factors (Appendix B, section 3.12):

1 *Fit* The first factor, which we called 'fit', is concerned with the effect of the decision on fit with overall corporate strategy. However, this dimension is also negatively loaded on the size of the investment in money terms; the implication of this is that the important aspect of this dimension is concerned with strategicality in terms of reshaping corporate direction rather than in the sense of the size of the investment.

2 *Failure* The second factor we dubbed 'failure' since it is primarily concerned with the effect of the decision on the possibility of failure and overall performance of the organization. Decisions score high on this dimension if they are perceived as having: a high impact on corporate financial standing if they fail; an important effect on the competitive standing of the organization and an important effect on organization performance.

The mean for failure is 15 (Table 3.3), below the midpoint for the scale but some decisions score very high. Decision *LP* is an example of this (33 out of 40). A new product was introduced into the Electronics Company which relied upon a limited range of products. Failure in this project would have been catastrophic for the company.

The mean for fit is 33 thereby indicating the importance of this variable in the investment decisions investigated. This is easily the most highly-weighted aspect of issue definition as we can see from Table 3.3.

- *Technical note*: The scores presented in Table 3.3 are the scores of the most significant individual variables that make up a particular factor and factors are, in general, named after this variable. Factor loadings have not been given in this chapter but are given in the relevant Appendix section. This has been done in order to assist the clarity of the presentation. In no way does this simplification alter the direction of the argument presented.

Uncertainty

Uncertainty was measured by a number of different variables and computed into an overall uncertainty score as shown in Table 3.3. The mean score is 14 on a 0 to 40 scale. Also shown are the scores for two of the most significant items making up uncertainty, namely, uncertainty about market factors and the rarity of the decision.

Table 3.3 also indicates the most prominent aspects of uncertainty in each decision covering features such as market, regulatory or technical factors. We can see from this analysis the predominance of uncertainties about financial, cost and technical matters.

The highest overall uncertainty is found in decision *JU* (27 out of 40). This decision concerned the opening of a manufacturing plant in Britain by a major Japanese company. The uncertainties particularly concerned technical factors relating to the reliability of British suppliers thereby confirming a common complaint of Japanese companies in connection with the unreliability of foreign industry.

The uncertainty variables were also factor analysed in order to discover the principal dimensions. Two appropriate dimensions were discovered (Appendix B, section 3.13):

1 *Rarity*   The first factor is strongly determined by the novelty of the decision to the participants; hence we called this the rarity factor. Other variables making up this factor concern uncertainty about suppliers, and production and cost uncertainties. The interrelationships between the variables indicate that the greater the rarity of a decision the more likely these aspects are to become sources of uncertainty during the decision. It is interesting to note that technical uncertainties did not appear in the factor. This confirms our impression from the interviews and case studies that, despite the

considerable technical complexity of many of the investments that we studied, our organizations were confident of their technical abilities; it was their ability to cope with outside influences (such as suppliers) and to produce economically that was the major concern.

2 *Performance* The above observation is further reflected in the second uncertainty dimension which involves uncertainties about the market, and external and internal financial considerations.

Disagreements

Disagreements between participants in the decision process were taken as the main measures of the political dimension of decision-making. A number of variables were used to measure disagreements and an overall disagreements score was computed for each decision giving a mean of 33 (on the 2 to 40 scale) with a range of 0 to 24.

The scores for two prominent items in the overall disagreements measure are personality clashes and disagreements over objectives; these scores are provided for each decision in Table 3.3. Also given (as abbreviations) are the two most prominent causes of disagreements. We can see the predominance of disagreements about objectives across all the decisions. Procedural disagreements is the next most common type.

The decision in which disagreements were greatest is *BU* (33 out of 40). This decision involved a Brewery moving into a new market and there was considerable disagreement about the objectives the management was trying to reach.

Factor analysis again gave rise to two disagreement factors (Appendix B, section 3.14):

1 *Personal disagreements* This factor is strongly influenced by disagreements over personal objectives and personality clashes. The factor analysis also shows that these two variables are strongly related to disagreements about the procedures to follow during decision-making.

2 *Objectives disagreements* This factor is the weaker of the two disagreements factors and is about disagreements over the objectives of the decision.

It is possible that participants disguised the extent of disagreements over decisions. Our interviews, however, suggested that was unlikely; the participants were, in the main, sophisticated executives well aware of organizational politics. There seemed no reason to believe that they were incapable of identifying disagreements over objectives where it was a serious issue.

STRATEGIES FOR BUILDING SOLUTIONS AND SUPPORT

The core of the decision effectiveness model consists of the strategies that decision-makers use in building solutions to the problem as they have defined it and in building support for proposed solutions within the organization. In considering more specific variables of solution and support-building we draw upon the insights of Thompson and Tuden (1956) already outlined in Chapter 2. They outline four strategies for making decisions: computation, negotiation, judgement and inspiration.

Computation

Computation was operationalized by an overall question concerning the extent to which numerical calculations were carried out during the development and analysis of options. A number of more specific items were also used, particularly in relation to the kinds of appraisal methods commonly used in organizations.

Table 3.3 shows that the mean overall computation score is 29 (0 to 40 scale) with a minimum of 10 and a maximum of 40. The payback method of assessing investments was the most strongly used, with a mean of 17, while productivity calculations were also prominent (mean 21).

A number of other more specific variables were also used to capture the degree to which various procedures were used for assessing investments quantitatively. The computation variables were then factor analysed. Two factors emerged as a result of this analysis (Appendix B, section 3.15):

1 *Rate of return* A number of variables that measured, in one way or another, the rate of return of an investment formed the first factor. These variables are: importance of payback period, profit and sales target computations, the use of internal rate of return (*IRR*), and impact upon productivity.
2 *Reported profit* This factor contains two positive variables, the impact upon the current year's earning and the overall computation variable (decision evolved out of facts and figures). In addition to these two variables, a third variable, effect on productivity, was found to be negatively related to the other two variables.

The two computation factors touch upon some interesting aspects of the issue of short- versus long-termism in investment decision-making. The rate of return dimension may be seen as representing an economic rationality insisting that investments must give a sufficient return in the long term to compensate for risk. The reported profit dimension may be seen as representing a managerial rationality whereby the economic rationality of productivity, and the like, is de-emphasized and shorter-term earnings, as reported to the stock market, are given priority. Even so, we have to note the greater prominence of the shorter-term payback method rather than longer-term measures of profitability.

Judgement

Judgement is taken to mean the use of more qualitative and intuitive type of data than is provided by computation. Judgement was operationalized by a general question assessing the extent to which qualitative information was used during decision-making.

Other more specific questions covered aspects such as affect on company image (mean 20 on 0 to 40 scale) and also whether the decision was made with inadequate information.

In addition to the general question, a number of other variables were used to measure judgement. Factor analysis gave three factors (Appendix B, section 3.6).

1 *Personnel* This factor consists of variables concerned with the possible effect of the decision upon morale and industrial relations.
2 *Image* Variables concerning the importance of product quality and corporate image are represented in this factor.
3 *Judgement* This factor consists of the overall judgement question and a question concerning the extent to which decision-makers would have liked additional information.

The judgement factors demonstrate that decision-makers are prepared to make a decision on the basis of inadequate information, which is the essence of the concept of satisficing (March and Simon 1958; Simon 1964). The distinction between the personnel and image factors, although both were originally defined as comprising the use of qualitative variables, can be interpreted as one (image) representing qualitative variables concerned with presenting the organization to the outside world, while the personnel factor is a more internally-directed concern.

Negotiation

Negotiation is operationalized, in part, by a general question concerning the extent to which negotiation and give and take were used in arriving at a decision. A number of more specific variables were used, particularly the extent to which alliances were built during decision-making (Appendix B, section 3.17).

The general negotiation variable has a mean of 12 (0 to 40 scale) with a minimum of 0 and a maximum of 30 (Table 3.3). A factor analysis revealed only one factor (Appendix B, section 3.17). This factor shows, perhaps not surprisingly, a high correlation between overall negotiation and the extent to which alliance building was used during the decision process.

Inspiration

Inspiration literally means the breathing of life into something. As far as decision-making is concerned the notion of 'breathing life' into a decision process is an appropriate way to see the concept. We see inspiration as referring to the extent to which someone takes a decision issue into their hands and brings it to a conclusion. Inspiration sees decision-making as a creative process in contrast to computation which sees it as a matter of applying algorithms and procedures for solution and support building.

At six (0 to 40 scale) inspiration shows a mean score across the sixteen decisions that is considerably less than the mean for the other strategy variables. However, there is a large range with a minimum of 0 on a number of decisions and a maximum of 26 for decision *MK*, which is a high learning/low objectives-attainment decision.

The interactive nature of the strategy variables

Although the original framework proposed by Thompson and Tuden presented their types of decision-making strategies as discrete categories, we do not assume that computation ceases with increasing uncertainty. Rather, the model allows for these processes to interact with one another.

Our data support this notion. In none of the decisions is one process completely dominant over another. All decisions appear to need a mix of strategies for solution and support-building. We also note that there is a ranking of the strategy variables with computation being used the most strongly used (mean 29), then judgement (mean 24), then negotiation used the next most strongly (mean 12), and finally inspiration which is used the least strongly (mean 6).

All decisions use computation and judgement, but three decisions do not use any negotiation. Seven decisions do not use any appreciable inspiration. The relative weightings of the different strategy variables suggests that management sees the need to build a base of computation from which to move to other kinds of strategy. The term computation is a catch-all term to capture the total process of collecting hard factual and quantitative data for decision-making. The predominance of computation in decision-making confirms Pike's (1988) finding that companies have increasingly and almost automatically use a number of basic financial evaluation methods.

INFLUENCE

Decisions involve patterns of influence amongst participants (Hickson *et al.* 1986). These influence patterns occur against a background of interests and organizational power and can be seen as related to who gets involved, who has most influence over a decision (direction), the extent of external influence and the way in which authority is used.

Involvement

Different levels of influence can be seen in decisions. Involvement is the extent to which there are interests who have some influence, but with these interests remaining relatively uninfluential, but who, nevertheless, can play an important part in the process (Butler *et al.* 1977, Hickson *et al.* 1986). These may be, for instance, functional individuals or groups who work on some aspect of a decision but who do not see the whole process through.

Data was collected concerning the various 'units' that exerted some influence; these units comprise individuals, groups, departments or external organizations. The degree of influence was assessed on a 0 to 4 scale. Any unit that had an influence greater than or equal to a score of one on this scale was counted as being involved. Table 3.3 shows the number of units thus involved for each decision. The mean is 6.7 with a minimum of 4 and a maximum of 9.

Direction

Direction refers to the number of units that exert a high degree of influence. This was taken to mean any unit that scored at a level of 3 or greater on our 0 to 4 scale. These are the 'heavyweight' interest units (Hickson *et al.* 1986) that really influence the course of events.

The mean number of units directing decisions was found to be 3.9. The highest score, found across eight of the decisions, is five units and the lowest, found in only one decision (*SC*), is one unit.

Externality

Included in those interest units exerting influence can be any external organization or individual. The externality of influence was found by Hickson *et al.* (1986) to be an important aspect of decision-making. This was measured by considering those external units that exerted influence at the level of 1 or more.

Table 3.3 shows that there was a mean of 1.3 external units with a minimum of 0 and a maximum of 3.

Influence factors

The above aspects of influence were subjected to factor analysis to explore the existence of different factors. Two factors were found (Appendix B, section 3.11):

1 *Internal*   This factor consists of those internal units that have both involvement and direction over the decisions.
2 *External*   This factor consists of those external units that have both involvement and direction over the decisions.

A greater degree of variance is explained by the external factor. Thus, although internal influence is clearly always much higher than external influence, the degree of variability of internal influence (both in terms of involvement and direction) is less than for external influence. Organizations take internal influence far more for granted than external influence. It is, after all, the nature of organization that people should be influencing more internally than externally.

Authority

The use of authority is a major feature of how people exert influence in decision-making. The nature of this authority can vary between decisions. The important aspect of authority that was considered in this research was the extent to which top management guided and controlled the decision rather than simply rubber-stamping a decision.

This idea was converted into a nominal scale as follows:

T Strong top management guidance. No evidence of 'rubber-stamping'.

P Well-defined parameters set within which decision-makers have to keep.

O Little management guidance or control evident.

Two decisions were found to have little management guidance or control. It is noteworthy that both these decisions (*MK* and *MP*) are both low in terms of objectives-attainment.

TIMING

One other, but vital, aspect of decision processes concerns timing. Organizations operate in the temporal world; building solutions and support takes time, time is limited and managerial time has a cost. Decisions often have to be made up against deadlines and delays can occur.

Timing refers to any aspect of the temporality of decision-making. Variables cover those already used in the earlier Bradford studies (Butler *et al.* 1977, 1979; Hickson *et al.* 1986), such as duration and delays. The notion of pace (Wilson 1980) is also a significant aspect of decision-making. The pace aspect of decision-makers is distinguished from duration in that decision-makers can feel a pressure to make a decision that may be independent of chronological time.

Case studies of decision-making often stress how critical the timing of events can be in the effecting of decisions, participants can often deliberately time actions to make the greatest effect. In general, our understanding of timing at this stage requires that uncertain and political decisions be required to build up over a longer time period than less ambiguous decisions.

Build-up

Build-up is the extent to which a decision issue gathers momentum without the participants necessarily having a clear idea of where things were going. This variable, therefore, captures aspects of what Lindholm (1959) calls incrementalism.

Delays

The extent to which decisions were disrupted or delayed has been pointed to as an important variable of decision-making by Hickson *et al.* (1986).

Duration

Duration refers to the length of time the decision took from its inception as an active topic for consideration to the final authorization.

Pace

The final variable of timing is disagreements about pace. We found that in many decisions, even though they moved quickly in clock time, the pace at which the decision moved was a cause of dissatisfaction.

The deliberation factor

A factor analysis was applied to the timing data and we found that all the variables of timing loaded positively on one factor. This we called deliberation, indicating that decisions which took a long time by clock time, tended to build up slowly over time and had delays as decision-makers took time to come to a deliberate choice.

The Japanese subsidiary, *JU*, lived up to the reputation of their country's management methods by showing high deliberation. The decision to open up a plant in the UK took a great deal of time to build up. The overall strategy was to open a manufacturing facility in a European Community country in order to overcome the restrictions on importation of finished products. The questions were, in which country, where in that country and when would they set up the subsidiary?

The company had to achieve a certain percentage of components made in the UK thereby putting a great emphasis upon the reliability of local suppliers. Highly-detailed analyses of opportunities offered by each county and by each locality within these countries were conducted and eventually the decision involved agreement amongst 40 people. It was also found that this decision showed high uncertainty about suppliers. Deliberation was part of the process of building solutions and support.

DYNAMICS OF THE DECISION EFFECTIVENESS MODEL

The decision effectiveness model follows the general thrust of the principles of organizational decision-making outlined in Chapter 2, but provides a more specific treatment of the notion of decision effectiveness and provides opportunities for a more sensitive understanding of the interactions between the variables.

Following the contingency theory framework, as issues are defined as more uncertain, political and more consequential, we would expect more solution and support building to be needed in order to achieve effectiveness. More specifically, we can propose that this would require high degrees of computation, judgement and negotiation, with relatively high involvement and direction.

The above discussion has concentrated upon identifying the variables of the model and the key intervariable relationships within each overall variable category. The model provides us with a framework for looking at the processes of decision-making. Of particular importance in the model is its dynamic nature and the allowance for relationships between variables. Hence, although the rational model of decision-making emphasizes the need to define objectives before searching for solutions, we accept that the process of solution and support-building via the decision strategies will affect the definition of the issue as the decision proceeds.

DISPARITY OF VIEWS

In order to allow us to capture the dynamic processes involved, and to make comparative statements about effective decision processes, the adopted methodology combines the theory building aspect of a quantitative-nomothetic method with the in-depth understanding of processes that can be achieved from a case study or ideographic method (Burrell and Morgan 1979).

Multiple informants were used in ten of the decisions to build up a picture of the processes involved. In all, fifty-five executive interviews were carried out for seventeen decisions, an average of over three per decision with some decisions having as many as seven informants. If there is a disparity of views over an aspect of the decision process this is turned to good use in this research. Our technique is to create a parallel set of variables measuring disparity; this is done by the simple device of using a measure of the dispersion of each variable. The simplest of such measures is the range of a variable which is the difference between the lowest and the highest scores. The range was used in calculating dispersion for Figure 3.2 below and for discussions in the case studies. For the more statistically-based regression analysis used later in the book more sophisticated methods were used as will be described.

As an initial exploration of the effect of disparity upon effectiveness we calculated, using the range method, an overall disparity measure for each of the ten decisions for which we had multiple informants.

(a) *Objectives-attainment and overall disparity*

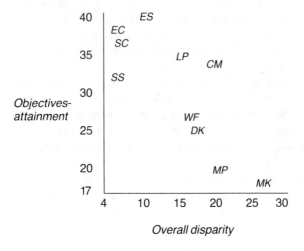

(b) *Learning and overall disparity*

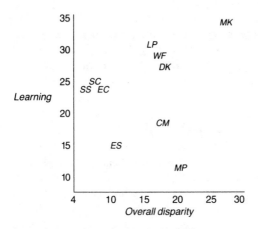

The Decisions
   CM Capital Goods – install manufacturing plant
   DK Cloth-Dyer – new 'kitchen'
   EC Electric Co. – new computer
   ES Electric Co. – computer software
   LP Electronics Co. – new product introduction
   MK Medical Supplier Co. – new knitting-machine
   MP Medical Supplier Co. – new plant
   SC Building Society – purchase of mainframe computer
   SS Building Society – purchase of software
   WF Water Co. – construction of water filtration plant

Figure 3.2   **Disparity and decision effectiveness**

This disparity score was then plotted against each of the two effectiveness dimensions with the results as shown in Figure 3.2. These plots reveal two potentially significant aspects of the impact of disparity upon effectiveness. First is the apparent negative association between disparity and the objectives-attainment effectiveness factor. Second is the weaker but still apparent positive association between disparity and the learning factor of effectiveness.

This finding suggests an inherent tension in decision-making that has already been referred to in the discussion of Chapter 2. This tension derives from the need for organizations to strive for efficiency in the short-term goal attainment meaning of the term while, at the same time, striving for learning. The results of the factor analysis of the effectiveness data has also pointed to the notion that dissatisfaction with the process of decision-making can enhance learning.

A methodological note

Our aim was not so much to attempt to reach the 'true' story but to build upon the fundamental idea that there is not necessarily a single truth in complex decision-making. Rather, there are interests, viewpoints and perspectives which, in some way, develop an 'appreciation' of what a decision is about.

The truth in investment decision-making, as in any other type of organizational decision, comes in the reality testing (Vickers 1965) to which such actions must eventually be put. The basis of such testing is whether an organization can gather sufficient support from its environment (Butler 1991) in order to survive. For business organizations operating in a competitive environment this reality testing comes through action in a market-place. For other kinds of organization the reality testing may come from, for instance, persuading government to provide funds.

The problem for the decision-makers, in all but the very simplest of decisions, is that the connection between their appreciation of a decision and the eventual reality testing is often unclear and incomplete, hence it is not immediately obvious who, if anyone, is in possession of the 'truth'.

SUMMARY

The decision effectiveness model gives us a way of appreciating decision-making processes in organizations. Effectiveness, it is suggested, can be viewed as consisting of two dimensions or factors, the objectives-attainment factor and the learning factor.

The explanatory variables for this model are given by the broad variable categories of definition, strategies, timing and influence. Each of these categories is comprised of a number of variables.

The original variable categories have been grouped into factors as suggested by the factor analyses. Factor analysis is often used as an inductive approach to data whereby patterns emerge out of the data itself. However, underlying the factors is a model of decision-making which has at its core the classical decision strategies as outlined by Thompson and Tuden (1956). Our factor analyses were, therefore, essentially confirmatory in nature.

Contained within this model is the fundamental tension between the computational and the inspirational approaches to decision-making. Different authors have given different names to what are often seen as opposite ends of the spectrum describing decision-making. This tension has already been pointed out in the data presented for this project. A disparity of views between decision-makers is seen to reduce the likelihood of objectives-attainment, a view belonging essentially to the computational model of decision-making; a disparity of views, however, is seen as leading to the possibility of increased learning during a decision process, a view belonging to the inspirational model. These are all aspects to be explored in subsequent chapters.

4 Capital investment decisions

INTRODUCTION

Capital investment decisions must rank as one of the most important forms of decisions made in our economic society: in aggregate across different sectors of the economy they account for a large proportion of the national resources and set the course of activities for the next generation. To the individual enterprise, whether public or private, the success of these decisions will affect its very survival and future prosperity.

The investment decision is the decision to commit the firm's resources (capital, people, know-how, and so on) to particular projects with the intention of achieving greater financial and other benefits in future years. These assets may be *tangible*, such as land and buildings, plant and equipment and inventories, or *intangible*, such as investment in patents, brands, know-how and people. Increasing recognition has been given in recent years to the significance of intangible assets, sometimes accounting for more than one half of a firm's market capitalization value.

Capital budgeting is the term given to the process by which organizations reach capital investment decisions. In larger organizations it is simply not possible for senior management to handle all capital projects from start to finish. The formal capital budgeting process, together with other structures and controls, provide the mechanism by which investment decision-making can be delegated whilst still retaining control.

A FINANCIAL PERSPECTIVE

John Maynard Keynes once described the theory of finance as 'a technique of thinking which helps its possessor to draw correct conclusions'. However, the 'correctness' of such conclusions rests, in part, on the reality of the assumptions underlying the theory. All too often we find that the assumptions underlying capital budgeting theory do not accord with the practical realities of business life.

Modern finance theory prescribes selection rules consistent with the assumed goal of the firm of wealth maximization. One such selection rule concerns net present value (NPV). Given certainty and perfect capital markets, the wealth of the firm's shareholders is maximized when projects with after-tax positive net present values are selected. Long-term investment decisions give rise to changes in corporate cash flows in different future periods. It is necessary to incorporate into the decision analysis a means of taking account of the differences in timing between cash flows, and the NPV approach achieves this by discounting all cash flows at a rate commensurate with the time-value of money reflecting the opportunity cost of funds. A related selection rule employs the internal rate of return (IRR) approach. Projects should be accepted where the IRR – that rate of return which equates the initial cash outlay with future cash flows – exceeds the cost of capital.

Once we recognize that decision outcomes cannot be forecast with perfect accuracy (that is, we introduce the reality of uncertainty), the cost of capital, representing the opportunity cost of funds, is no longer constant. Firms should accept projects where the expected net present value is positive when discounted at the appropriate risk-adjusted opportunity cost of funds for the projects, risk being viewed in terms of how the project's expected return co-varies with the stock market's expected return. (Readers unfamiliar with the finance theory approach are referred to Brealey and Myers 1991.)

Selecting capital projects with positive net present values is very much like picking undervalued shares on the stock market using the fundamental analysis approach of assessing the share's underlying cash flows. Such an approach is really only appropriate for shares if there are financial market imperfections that do not allow asset prices to reflect their equilibrium values. Such imperfections are more commonly found in the markets in which businesses operate. Organizations may have a degree of monopolistic control over product or factor supplies giving rise to economic rents or excess returns; such above-normal returns, when applied to new capital projects, create positive net present values. Within the context of major, strategic projects, it is the creation and exploitation of such market imperfections that characterizes much of corporate strategic decision-making.

It is clear from the foregoing that the focus of attention in the finance literature has been directed towards the formal appraisal of investment options, the assumption being that application of theoretically correct methods leads directly to optimal investment selection and, hence, maximizes shareholders' wealth. The decision-maker is viewed more as a technician than an entrepreneur, making decisions according to a neat algorithm. Inherent in this view are the assumptions that investment ideas simply emerge; information is available and costless; projects are viewed in isolation and have no interactions; risk can be measured in a precise manner; non-quantifiable investment considerations are unimportant; and cash flow estimates are unbiased.

Managers, however, frequently operate in a somewhat different environment. Most large capital investment projects may be defined as ill-structured problems, calling for decision processes that have not been previously encountered in quite the same form and for which no explicit set of ordered responses exist. Novelty, complexity, ambiguity and irreversibility are the hallmarks of many capital investment projects. While financial theory fulfils an important role in saying how capital investment decisions should be made under specified conditions and given a wealth-maximizing goal, it gives the mistaken impression that sound capital budgeting is all about selecting the right technique and criteria. Increasingly it has become apparent that the emphasis on formal investment appraisal techniques rather than on the whole process is misplaced (Haynes and Solomon 1962; Adelson 1970; Cooper 1975; King 1975).

CAPITAL INVESTMENT – THE DECISION PROCESS

One way of viewing capital budgeting is to see it as a process with a number of distinct stages. According to this view, decision-making is an incremental activity, involving many people throughout the organization hierarchy, over an extended period of time. While senior management may retain final approval, actual decisions are effectively taken much earlier at a lower level, by a process that is still not entirely clear. We tend to regard investment decision-making as a rational process of resource allocation, although, in reality, decision-making may be somewhat less ordered and rational than supposed.

Within a capital budgeting context, various authors have attempted to describe this process (for example, Bower 1971; King 1975). For the purposes of this chapter we will employ the four-stage process suggested by Mintzberg *et al.* (1976), applied to capital budgeting by Pinches (1982). These are:

1 Identification of investment opportunities.
2 Development of an initial idea into a firm proposal.
3 Selection of projects.
4 Control of projects, including post audits.

Figure 4.1 illustrates this process.

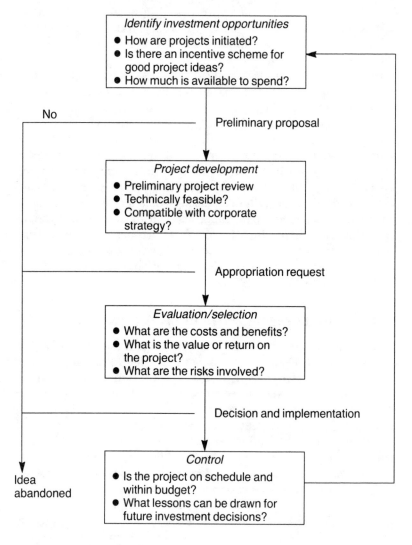

Figure 4.1   The capital investment decision

STAGE ONE: IDENTIFICATION

Economic theory views investment as the interaction of the supply of capital and the flow of investment opportunities. It would be quite wrong, however, to assume that there is a continuous flow of investment ideas. Possibly the most important role which top management can play in the capital investment process is to cultivate a corporate culture which encourages managers to search for, identify and sponsor investment ideas. Questions to be asked at the identification stage include:

1 How are project proposals initiated?
2 At what level are projects typically generated?
3 Is there a formal process for submitting ideas?
4 Is there an incentive scheme for identifying good project ideas?

Generating investment ideas involves considerable effort, time and personal risk on the part of the proposer. Any manager who has experienced the hurt and frustrations of having an investment proposal dismissed or an accepted proposal fail is likely to develop an in-built resistance to creating further proposals unless the organization culture and rewards are conducive to such activity. There is some evidence that firms employing long-term incentive plans encourage the initiation and implementation of capital investment projects (for example, Larcker 1983).

For the identification phase of non-routine, strategic capital budgeting decisions to be productive, managers need to conduct environmental scanning, gathering information which is largely externally oriented, much of which is non-financial and *ex ante* (Gordon and Pinches 1984). We should not expect the formal information system within most organizations to be particularly helpful in identifying non-routine investment ideas. Informal channels of communication are frequently more important in identifying investment ideas.

STAGE TWO: DEVELOPMENT

The second stage in the capital investment decision-making process is the screening of all investment ideas and development of those showing sufficient promise. This is sometimes termed the preliminary project review.

It is neither feasible nor desirable to conduct a full-scale evaluation of each investment idea. The screening process is an important means of filtering out projects not thought worthy of further investigation.

Ideas may not fit with strategic thinking, or fall outside business units designated for growth or maintenance.

The investment process usually forms part of a wider strategic process. Capital projects are not normally viewed in isolation, but within the context of the business, its goals and strategic direction. In a recent UK study of strategic investment decisions, Marsh *et al.* (1988) found that explicit strategic planning, even at a divisional level, seemed to have only limited impact on the generation and approval of investment projects; it was more 'emergent' than 'deliberate' (see Mintzberg and Waters 1985). Screening proposals therefore address such questions as:

Is the proposal compatible with corporate strategy?
Is the idea technically feasible?
Do we have access to the required resources (for example, finance, technology, skills, and so on)?
Does the project need further development?

Another element of the development phase involves defining projects, the detailed specification of the proposal, together with its technical and economic characteristics. Projects must be created:

capital projects do not begin life in a filing cabinet awaiting only the tedious collection of the information necessary for their evaluation. They must be created. The choice of the form of a project occurs at the screening and definition stages where information is limited, search required and analysis sequential.

(King 1975: 78)

In one study this stage was rated by executives as the most critical and the most difficult of the whole capital investment process (see Gitman and Forrester 1977).

The very act of gathering information necessitates communicating with other managers and seeking support for the project. Commitments are made and alliances formed early on in the process, usually well before any financial analysis has been conducted:

In order to collect information, it is necessary to communicate with people, to make certain decisions, and often to give tacit promises. In this process commitments are accumulated until a situation is created which leads inevitably to investment.

(Aharoni 1966)

The amount of information gathered is largely determined by the data perceived as necessary to gain a favourable decision, and the extent to which the proposer will be held responsible for later performance related to the data (Carter 1971).

STAGE THREE: SELECTION

The selection phase involves evaluation of the project and the decision outcome (for example, accept, reject, request further information, and so on). Project evaluation, in turn, involves the assembly of information (usually in terms of cash flows) and the application of specified investment criteria. Each firm must decide whether to apply rigorous, sophisticated evaluation models or simpler models which are easier to grasp yet capture many of the important elements in the decision.

In order to provide a suitable context for the investment case studies and analyses reported in subsequent chapters, we summarize the survey findings on capital investment practices from a recent study by Pike (1988) into 100 large UK firms.

Investment appraisal techniques

Table 4.1 shows that while all firms sampled conduct a financial evaluation on capital projects, the particular methods of analysis employed differ widely. Discounted cash flow (DCF) techniques, of which the internal rate of return (IRR) and net present value (NPV) methods are the best known, have greatly increased in usage from 58 per cent in 1975 to 84 per cent in 1986, making it a fairly standard technique for the larger firm.

The capital budgeting literature (for example, Klammer 1972; Pike 1983; Haka *et al.* 1985) distinguishes between 'naïve' or simple and sophisticated methods of investment analysis. Simple methods include payback period and accounting rate of return techniques, while 'sophisticated' techniques include most, if not all, of the other methods listed in Table 4.1. While sophisticated methods have clearly increased in popularity over the years, the observed increase has not come at the expense of simpler methods. The payback method continues to gain support and is now almost universally employed (92 per cent), approximately one half of the sample using it on every occasion. Prior studies (for example, McIntyre and Coulthurst 1986) have also shown it to be highly popular for smaller firms. The obvious conclusion to be drawn is that managers prefer to employ a combination of appraisal methods, sophisticated and naïve.

Table 4.1   Capital investment evaluation methods: trend analysis of usage in
100 large UK firms

	1975 (%)	1981 (%)	1986 (%)
Firms using:			
Financial appraisal techniques			
Payback	73	81	92
Average accounting rate of return	51	49	56 −
DCF methods (IRR or NPV)	58	68	84
Internal rate of return	44	57	75 +
Net present value	32	39	68 +
Risk analysis techniques			
Sensitivity analysis	28	42	71 +
Analysis under different assumptions (best/worst)	n.a.	n.a.	93 +
Reduced payback periods	25	30	61
Increased hurdle rates	37	41	61 +
Probability analysis	9	10	40
Beta analysis	0	0	16 +
Management science techniques			
Mathematical programming	11	17	21 +
Computer simulation	12	21	40 +
Decision theory	3	3	34 +
Critical path analysis	23	31	49

Note:
+ indicates significant association (at 5 per cent level).
− indicates a significant negative association with the frequency of use of computer
   applications in capital budgeting using the Spearman Rank correlation and *t*-tests
   conducted on 1986 data only.

Risk analysis

An assessment of the risks involved in making investment decisions is
a crucial element of the evaluation process. Although the techniques
employed in analysing risk in capital projects vary considerably across
firms, all techniques have witnessed considerable increases in usage
(Table 4.1). The most popular approach involves testing the sensitivity
of critical investment inputs and underlying economic assumptions.
The high usage of sensitivity analysis (71 per cent) and specifying
investment outcomes based on 'best' and 'worst' case scenarios (93
per cent) suggests a strong movement towards applying multipoint
estimates. In the following chapter we will be assessing the importance
managers give to 'best' and 'worst' case analysis in reaching investment decisions.

   A strong movement towards the application of probability analysis is also witnessed, most notably by the larger firms surveyed. However, of the 40 per cent applying probability analysis and the 16 per cent using beta analysis (a measure of the impact of cash flows on non-diversifiable risk), very few operate them on a regular basis.

There now seems to be a greater awareness of the value of risk analysis and management science techniques, which may largely be attributed to the availability of relatively inexpensive computer software. With the exception of probability analysis, a significant and positive association was found between the use of all sophisticated risk analysis methods and the application of investment computing software (see Table 4.1).

Approval

Following evaluation, larger projects may require consideration at a number of levels in the organization hierarchy until finally approved or rejected. The decision outcome is rarely based wholly on the computed signal derived from financial analysis. Considerable judgement is applied in assessing the reliability of data underlying the appraisal, fit with corporate strategy, and track record of the project sponsor. The selection phase is essentially a political process. Projects put forward at lower levels in the organization need the 'impetus' of sponsorship by a higher level manager with a good track record to secure a rapid and safe passage to final approval level (Bower 1971). In many organizations relatively few projects are rejected at the final approval stage since to do so would indicate a lack of confidence in the decision-making judgement of those involved at earlier stages (King 1975). However, Marsh *et al.* (1988) found that top management was more involved in the decision process than the earlier literature suggests.

STAGE FOUR: CONTROL

The capital budgeting literature frequently assumes that control occurs after the selection phase. In fact, for most projects, relatively little real project control is possible then, the process being more that of monitoring implementation and performance through post-audit and other procedures. These 'controls' do, however, provide useful feedback on how well the capital budgeting process is operating, for example, the realism of assumptions.

The capital budgeting control process may be divided into pre-decision and post-decision controls (see Scapens, Sale and Tikkas

1982). Pre-decision controls are mechanisms designed to influence managerial behaviour. Examples of such controls include the selection and training of subordinates to possess goals and risk attitudes consistent with senior management (selection controls), setting authorization levels and procedures to be followed (intervention controls) and influencing the proposals submitted by setting goals, hurdle rates, cash limits and identifying strategic areas for growth (influencing controls).

Table 4.2. provides a summary of the capital budgeting control procedures found in large UK firms. Almost two-thirds of the firms sampled prepare a capital budget which looks beyond two years. The trend towards adoption of longer-term capital budgets has halted since 1981, indicating that a level of stability has been reached among large UK firms. One way of influencing managerial investment behaviour is by formalizing control procedures in the form of an up-to-date capital budgeting manual, or equivalent. Table 4.2 reveals that 84 per cent of responding firms operate such a manual; non-users are primarily the smaller organizations within the sample.

Table 4.2 Capital budgeting control procedures within 100 large UK firms

	1975 (%)	1981 (%)	1986 (%)
Pre-decision controls			
Firms with:			
Capital budget looking beyond two years	57*	64*	64*
An up-to-date capital budgeting manual	65*	76*	84
A formal screening and reviewing body	78	84	83
At least one person fully engaged in capital budgeting	31*	33*	26*
A specific search and screening of alternatives	76	84	98
A regular review of hurdle rates	43	61	71
A formal financial evaluation	93	95	100
A formal analysis of risk	26*	38*	86*
Post-decision controls			
Firms which:			
Monitor project performance	69	76	84
Reconsider major projects after approval if cost over runs are likely	72	82	85
Require post-completion audits on most major projects	33	46	64

Note:
*Size significant at 5 per cent level using chi-square test.

Increasing attention is devoted to setting and reviewing investment hurdle rates: 71 per cent of firms review these levels on a regular basis compared with 43 per cent in 1975. One effect of a regular review of the required rates of return on investment projects is that it keeps the financial considerations high on the decision-making agenda. There is, however, evidence from the survey that unduly high hurdle rates adversely affect the number of proposals put forward for consideration.

Post-decision controls are introduced to help managers implement the project on schedule and to achieve the planned levels of performance. The most notable increase is the requirement to conduct post-completion audits. Such audits seek to compare the actual performance of a project after, say, a year's operation with the forecast made at the time of approval. Although a common feature in North America, post-audits have hitherto been little used in the UK. Table 4.2 reveals that since 1975 there has been a marked increase in adoption with 64 per cent now regularly conducting audits on larger capital investment projects. The main justifications given by respondents for their use are:

1 learning from the investment experience to improve the quality of future decisions, and
2 ensuring accountability of managers in an attempt to deter over-optimistic forecasts.

Pike and Neale (1992) identify a number of problems with post-auditing which may explain the initial reluctance within firms to introduce such a practice:

- **Biased selection** By definition, only accepted projects can be post-audited, and among these only underperforming ones are singled out by many firms for detailed examination.
- **The disentanglement problem** It may be difficult to separate out the relevant costs and benefits specific to a new project from other company activities, especially where facilities are shared and the new project requires an increase in shared overheads.
- **Prohibitive cost** To introduce post-audits may involve interference with present management information systems in order to generate flows of suitable data. Since post-auditing every project may be very resource-intensive, firms tend to be selective in their post-audits.
- **Projects may be unique** If there is no prospect of repeating a project in the future, there may seem little point in post-auditing,

since the lessons learned may not be applicable to any future activity.

- **Lack of co-operation**   If the post-audit is conducted in too inquisitorial a fashion, project sponsors are likely to offer grudging co-operation to the review team and be reluctant to accept and act upon their findings. There is thus a need to assemble a balanced team of investigators.
- **Environmental changes**   Some projects can be devastated by largely unpredictable swings in market conditions. This can make the post-audit a complex affair as the review team is obliged to adjust analysts' forecasts to allow for the 'moving of the goal-posts'.
- **Encourages risk aversion**   If analysts' predictive and analytical abilities are to be thoroughly scrutinized, then they may be inclined to advance only 'safe' projects where little can go wrong and where there is less chance of being 'caught out' by events.

INVESTMENT DECISION ANALYSIS AND DECISION EFFECTIVENESS

While the Pike survey reveals that in almost all aspects, larger firms have become more sophisticated in their approach to capital budgeting, it does not necessarily imply that they have become more effective.

An obvious question which can be raised at this stage is: does the adoption of sophisticated and theoretically-sound investment techniques actually improve investment decision effectiveness? Such a question is not easy to answer. So many factors influence the performance of companies that it is virtually impossible to detect the effects of one variable, such as the investment techniques employed. Empirical studies on the association between use of investment techniques and corporate performance are generally inconclusive or questionable (for example, Christy 1966; Klammer 1973; Kim 1982; Scholl *et al.* 1978; Pike 1984; Haka *et al.* 1985).

To address this important issue, changes in each of the investment methods between 1981 and 1986 were computed as independent variables, together with the company size variable which has been shown to be an important factor in capital investment studies. These variables were incorporated into a regression model to estimate the change in investment effectiveness, measured in terms of respondents' perceptions of the change in capital budgeting effectiveness over the 1981–6 period. If sophisticated methods, such as DCF and management science techniques, give rise to greater effectiveness they should yield positive associations with effectiveness, while naïve methods should yield negative signs.

Table 4.3 summarizes the step-wise linear multiple regression output giving significant variables at the 5 per cent level. The equation explains nearly half of the variation in the dependent variable; all regression coefficients have signs consistent with *a priori* predictions. Five sophisticated methods (including net present value and internal rate of return) are positively associated with effectiveness. The simple risk analysis technique of reducing payback period has, as predicted, a negative sign, although the payback method itself is not significant (possibly because it is used by virtually all firms). It is interesting to note that, while all management science techniques surveyed have increased considerably in uptake, none enters the regression equation, suggesting that respondents are not yet convinced of their decision-making utility.

Table 4.3 Project perceived effectiveness and methods of analysis

Explanatory variables	Predicted sign	Coefficient	Standard error	T-significance
Intercept		2.789	0.274	0.000
Coefficients of independent variables (changes 1981–86)				
Investment specialist		−0.787	0.287	0.009
Internal rate of return	+	0.753	0.292	0.014
Formal financial analysis	+	1.328	0.595	0.031
Monitor cost overruns	+	0.617	0.229	0.010
Post-completion audits	+	0.416	0.177	0.024
Inflation considered through sensitivity analysis		−0.587	0.240	0.019
Net present value	+	0.625	0.227	0.009
Shorten payback for risk	−	−0.573	0.212	0.010
Size	+	0.271	0.088	0.004
Adjusted R^2		0.483		
Overall F-test significance		0.001		

To summarize, significant positive associations were obtained between the change in use of investment methods (actual and perceived) and perceived change in the effectiveness of project evaluation and control. The regression analysis found that more sophisticated techniques such as DCF methods and post-completion audits were significantly associated with higher levels of capital investment effectiveness while less sophisticated techniques were negatively associated. Whilst most previous studies have been unable to detect a significant positive association between capital budgeting sophistication and firm performance, this study found that adoption of such methods is associated with greater perceived effectiveness in selecting and controlling capital projects. Senior finance executives, dealing with investment decisions on a regular basis, believe that it pays to employ discounted cash flow selection techniques, post-completion audit reviews and other control mechanisms.

SUMMARY

In this chapter we have summarized the four main stages in the capital investment process: identification, development, selection and control. The literature on capital budgeting processes shows that it is a complex, lengthy process of a series of stages through time, in which the earlier activities and choices are crucial. The traditional financial emphasis on the investment selection as the main element is misplaced. Second, the whole capital investment activity should be viewed within a wider political context, embracing potential differences between various groups and personal stakes for managers. The reliability and accuracy of information underlying projects should be viewed within this context. Third, all activities within the process are interrelated and are, to some extent, influenced by structural context, including the formal organization, control procedures, information systems and performance.

While the survey findings outlined in this chapter provide a useful overview of UK capital budgeting practices, large-scale cross-sectional studies do not attempt to view capital budgeting within the contexts in which organizations operate, nor do they really help us understand how investment decisions are made. These issues are addressed in the remainder of the book.

5 Congruence in capital investment evaluation

In the previous chapter we considered the investment decision-making process, paying particular attention to the more financial aspects. From this discussion we make certain observations: investment decision-making is a complex, often lengthy process involving a number of stages. The traditional emphasis in the finance literature on financial appraisal, while important, is given undue prominence and is often far removed from the emphasis in the actual decision-making process within organizations. There is little hard evidence to support the view that increased attention to the computational aspects of investment decision-making leads to improved performance, although managers seem to believe that they lead to softer measures of effectiveness such as improved evaluation and control of capital projects.

The plethora of capital budgeting surveys (for example, Scapens and Sale 1981; Pike 1983 and 1988) has only partially enriched our understanding of the role of financial measures, such as discounted cash flow and risk analysis techniques, in reaching investment decisions. Two limitations of such surveys are: the emphasis on formal – to the exclusion of informal – methods of assessing investment worth, and the tendency to survey only one individual per organization – typically a finance executive. The result is that we probably know more about what the finance function prescribes, in terms of investment techniques to be performed prior to approval, than we do about how such decisions are actually made.

Capital investment decision-making is not just an economic activity, it is also a political activity taking place within a wider political context where groups and individuals have vested interests. One example of this is seen in the investment choice. In theory at least, all capital projects (either individually or collectively as programmes) could be offered to the capital market for funding. Investment choice then becomes essentially an economic event, the availability of funds for each capital project or programme and the rate of interest required being a function of the market's perception of each project's prospective returns and associated risks.

In practice, multidivisional organizations operate an internal capital market (Williamson 1970), with fund-raising being the task of the treasurer and fund allocation the task of senior management. The logic for this separation of sources from uses of capital is part practical, but primarily based on the assumption that top management is better informed than the capital market and therefore better able to assess the attractiveness of capital projects. Given the risks associated with investment and the possibility that managers are seeking to promote their own interests at the corporate expense, the operation of an internal capital market is often essential. However, it is also a political activity, frequently giving rise to choices which could never be justified on purely economic grounds.

In this chapter we seek to improve our understanding of how managers evaluate capital projects and the extent to which evaluation congruence, at least in terms of how managers perceive 'acceptable' and 'unacceptable' projects, is attained.

EVALUATION CONGRUENCE

Activities within the investment decision process are interrelated and influenced by such organizational contextual factors as the control procedures, accounting information system, performance measurement and reward mechanisms in operation. The organizational context within which investments are generated, developed, selected and controlled should, wherever possible, be conducive to sound decision-making compatible with corporate goals. Top management seeks to create and manage an investment environment where lower-level managers are encouraged to put forward the very kind of projects that senior-level managers desire. Such goal congruence is less likely when the organizational context encourages managers to promote their own interests at the expense of the longer-term organizational interests. Capital budgeting becomes a 'game' with the control procedures, accounting systems, performance measurement and reward mechanisms 'rules' of the game to be exploited and, where possible, manipulated.

Dysfunctional behaviour in the area of capital investment may well occur when divisional managers are encouraged to pursue short-term divisional accounting targets such as Return on Investment (see Dearden 1960, 1969). Such behaviour is even more likely when organizations, intentionally or otherwise, create or operate in a climate within which dysfunctional investment decision-making can flourish (Kaplan 1984). These climatic conditions include high managerial mobility, large organizational size, strong market pressure for short-term financial performance and the operation of bonus plans linked to accounting performance measures.

The influence of accounting performance measurement on managerial behaviour can be considerable and far reaching. It has been related to the nature of tasks being controlled (Hofstede 1978; Perrow 1977), the organization strategy (Govindarajan and Gupta 1985; Simons 1990), leadership styles (Hopwood 1973; Otley 1978), and structure (Bruns and Waterhouse 1975). Each of the above has important implications for investment decision-making.

Investment goals may not be attained because lower-level managers have different interests and biases to senior-level managers (for example, Carter 1971; Ackerman 1968). In decentralized organizations senior management possesses far from complete knowledge of how lower-level managers generate and appraise capital projects. Such uncertainty, or incomplete knowledge is, perhaps, the primary justification for introducing management control.

Senior management can adopt various control strategies for bringing lower-level management thinking more in line with corporate investment goals. It can influence the investment process through appropriate training and instituting investment criteria to be met and procedures to be followed. Further encouragement can be given through appropriate reward and incentive schemes. Senior managers can impose intervention controls, becoming personally involved under certain conditions (for example, based on authorization levels, risk, and so on). A third control strategy involves screening lower-level managers, through recruitment and promotion policies, to ensure that those involved in the investment process have similar decision-making preferences to senior managers.

Strategic planning is a further means by which congruence can be achieved and dysfunctional behaviour minimized. By focusing on longer-term objectives it provides a context which transcends divisional activity based on short-term accounting performance measures. Where managerial mobility is low, managers have greater opportunity to absorb corporate goals and values and adopt them as their own. Incongruent, dysfunctional behaviour is thereby reduced. One approach to assessing the effectiveness of the control system in achieving decision-making congruence is found in the area of experimental research on human judgements (see Libby and Lewis 1982; Snowball

1986). Carter (1987), in a laboratory experiment on capital investment selection for over one hundred managers in a single firm, found significant differences in the importance attached to the financial variables employed, these differences being explained partly in terms of training and background. More recently, in a study of the capital budgeting preferences of seventy-eight managers within a major Canadian organization, Zanibbi and Pike (1989) found a relationship between managerial investment preferences and both organizational level and background training.

We seek in this chapter to examine how managers in ten organizations make trade-offs in selecting capital investment proposals through an analysis of an investment decision-making experiment. To set this experiment within the context of the whole study, it is appropriate at this point to describe the sample and approach adopted.

INVESTMENT EXPERIMENT

The case studies and findings reported in this book are based upon structured interviews and experiments conducted in a variety of organizations as explained in Chapter 3 and summarized in Table 3.1.

A capital investment experiment was designed to discover how managers evaluate capital projects and whether there exists a high degree of evaluation congruence within organizations. All organizations identified in Table 3.1, except *A* and *J*, participated in this exercise, giving forty-four respondents in total.

The basic approach adopted was to ask managers who were heavily involved in capital investment decision-making to rate various case profiles of capital investment proposals in terms of their attractiveness. Each investment profile was described using attributes, or cues, typically present in the capital budgeting procedures within larger firms. Managers were presented with eight synthetic investment proposals, each proposal containing five pieces of information covering the project's strategic fit, internal rate of return, payback period, best-case return and worst-case return. These information variables are generally viewed as important in capital investment analysis and commonly found on capital expenditure request summary forms. Participants were familiar with these information variables.

To ensure that the experiment should appear as realistic as possible, the individual proposals were presented in a way similar to the summary sheet that many organizations use as a frontispiece to capital investment proposals. It seemed unlikely that realism could be maintained if a large number of proposals were presented. No attempt was made to prescribe how the investment decisions should be examined; our aim was to tap the actual decision-making style of the individual manager. The exercise was conducted following an interview with subjects so that it was possible to verify the results of the exercise with interview findings.

Each information variable had two or more possible levels, as shown in Table 5.1. The general design, including the number of investment proposals and levels for each variable, were consistent with Addelman's (1961) suggested fractional factorial experimental design. It is generally accepted that experiments of this type should be based on orthogonal experimental designs. These designs have useful statistical properties. However, their assumption that the different determinants are uncorrelated was, we felt, incompatible with our wish for realism. Specifically, payback period and internal rate of return (IRR) are negatively correlated in practice. Our investment scenarios were accordingly developed to exhibit a realistic degree of negative correlation between payback period and IRR (in fact -0.59). The remaining three determinants were taken as orthogonal to themselves and to payback period and IRR.

Managers were asked to rate investment proposals on a scale $(0-100)$ and to indicate whether they would accept or reject the proposal. Regression analysis was then employed to estimate the importance of each attribute.

Table 5.1 Investment attributes and associated levels

| Investment attribute | Experimental level | | | |
	Level 1	Level 2	Level 3	Level 4
Fit with corporate plan	Poor	Excellent		
Internal rate of return (expected)	9%	17%	25%	33%
Payback period (months)	84	60	40	24
Best-case internal rate of return (over expected IRR)	+ 5%	+ 20%		
Worst-case internal rate of return	− 20%	− 5%		

As a first stage of analysis the data was analysed on an individual basis. The scores for each synthetic investment were used as the dependent variable for regression purposes, explaining 70–90 per cent of the variance. There were considerable similarities in the weights computed for different individuals as measured by the betas for those weights; in particular, few managers appeared to pay much attention to the Best-Case Rate of Return as a cue in rating capital projects.

The results are given in Table 5.2 which displays the number of respondents per organization and the importance ranking for the five information variables. Concentrating on the total picture, the table shows that the forty-four managers placed greatest importance on the strategic fit of the particular investment proposals. Unless a capital investment proposal made sense at the strategic level, contributing to strategic goals or falling within strategic business units targeted for development, managers were generally unwilling to support it. A close second to strategic fit was the project's economic performance as measured by its internal rate of return. Of somewhat less importance in the appraisal process was Payback Period and the 'worst case' economic return. There was no evidence of any statistical significance being attached to 'best case' rate of return. Investment decision analysis, at least for larger projects, would therefore seem to be dominated by strategic and expected performance considerations, with investment risk being a less important factor.

Dummy variables and interaction terms were introduced as independent variables to enable significant deviations of individual weights from the average to be detected (see Barry and Feldman 1985).

Separate regressions were conducted for each individual and organization, given the importance weightings (beta values) for each attribute. Where an individual's beta weights exhibited a statistically significant deviation from the organizational mean for certain attributes, these were deemed to be idiosyncratic or incongruent. The greater the idiosyncrasies, the lower the evaluation congruence.

Idiosyncracy is clearly related to the notion of disparity as outlined in Chapter 3. Both refer to the situation where decision-makers are not in agreement over their views about a decision-process. We keep the two terms, however, because idiosyncrasy is here referring to the extent to which members of an organization would use different evaluation techniques in assessing synthetic decisions. Disparity refers to a more general phenomenon concerning the extent to which there are disparate views over many different facets of a particular decision.

The final column in Table 5.2 lists the incongruent individuals in each firm as assessed by the number of idiosyncratic weights. For example, all four managers from the Building Society (*S*) exhibited remarkably similar importance weightings for investment attributes, with corporate fit and IRR predominating the exercise. This would appear to be an organization exhibiting relatively high investment

Table 5.2 Average importance of investment attributes

Organization	No. of respondents	Investment attribute importance					Adjusted R^2	Idiosyncratic betas
		CORP	IRR	PBK	WCASE	BCASE		
S	4	1	2	4	3	5	0.70	0
W	6	3	1	3	2	5	0.75	2
E	4	1	3	4	2	5	0.77	1
L	6	2	3	1	4	5	0.87	3
C	6	1	2	3	4	5	0.80	1
M	8	1	2	3	4	5	0.83	2
D	5	1	2	4	3	5	0.59	1
O	2	1	2	3	4	4	0.83	0
B	2	2	1	4	2	4	0.87	1
H	1	1	2	3	4	5	0.73	0
TOTAL	44	1	2	3	4	5	0.70	11
Beta		0.46	0.40	−0.32	0.26	0		

Notes: 1 Importance scale: 1 – most important, 5 – least important.
2 Areospace (A) and Japanese Consumer goods (J) are not represented here due to missing data.
3 CORP = corporate fit
   IRR   = internal rate of return
   PBK   = payback
   WCASE = worst case
   BCASE = best case
4 'Idiosyncratic betas' refer to number of respondents in each organization for whom their regression equations gave statistically significant deviations from organizational mean for attributes.

evaluation congruence. A rather different picture emerged from the Electronics Company (*L*) where three of the six managers exhibited disparate views in appraising synthetic projects. While most organizations had at least one respondent taking a significantly different view on the attractiveness of the proposal examined, the overall impression gained is that a consensus exists within firms as to the important cues in appraising investments. These findings indicate that the operation of various investment control strategies (screening, invervention, influencing, and so on) and the development of corporate values ensure that differences between managers as to what constitutes an acceptable investment proposal are minimized.

An interesting finding from Table 5.2 is the remarkably consistent ranking of investment attributes. For example, corporate fit was the most important attribute in seven of the ten organizations, while best case considerations received a zero weighting in all regression equations. This again suggests a fair degree of consensus of views across all organizations studied.

Table 5.3   Comparison of survey and experiment rankings

	Average response	*Ranking for the experiment*
Degree of corporate fit	3.32	1
Effect on product quality	3.08	
Level of agreement/opposition	2.42	
Effect on productivity	2.42	
Growth rate of related market	2.42	
Contribution to corporate image	2.15	
Internal rate of return	2.07	2
Payback period	1.98	3
Impact of project failure	1.60	4 (worst case)

Note: Average responses have been calculated on basis of original 0–4 scale across all informants. Averages cannot be directly compared to averages in Table 3.2.

The structured interviews, based on sixteen key investment decisions in eleven organizations, revealed broadly similar findings (see Table 5.3). Managers were asked how important they regarded various factors in reaching a decision on specific investment decisions (scale of 0 to 4).

What is interesting is that certain other variables not included in our experimental exercise ranked extremely high. For example, effect on quality and productivity were viewed more highly than any of the financial factors. No doubt there is a link between these factors and ultimate performance, but it seems that managers prefer to dwell on disaggregated data (data on the market, quality, productivity and corporate image, and so on) than on the financial aggregate in the form of IRR or Payback. Arguably, all the variables rated more highly than economic performance are strategic in nature: the strategic imperatives of quality, corporate image and developing key markets dominate all else.

It is also interesting that managers were extremely concerned with the level of agreement or opposition between interested parties, scoring a mean of 2.78, third in importance to corporate fit and quality. This is an indication of just how important investment evaluation congruence is viewed. On the other hand, two questions asked on short-termist, dysfunctional behaviour regarding the impact on the current year's earnings and impact on personal career/earnings were viewed as relatively unimportant. Although we should see such a finding with a degree of caution, it does suggest that the managers were able to transcend any tendency towards dysfunctional short-termist behaviour, and to seek congruency based on strategic and economic goals.

SUMMARY

To summarize, we have sought to improve our understanding of what managers involved in assessing capital investment proposals regard as important and the extent to which there is agreement within and across firms.

There was a generally high degree of agreement about the relative weights to be attached to the five variables under consideration. As expected, the greatest consensus was found within firms, indicating that the investment control process was going some way towards achieving investment evaluation congruence.

Further analysis revealed that across organizations by organizational level, by organization role or by sector, no particularly strong systematic differences between respondents emerged. The lack of attention paid to the Best Case Rate of Return – though not unexpected (see Mao and Helliwell 1969) does give cause for concern. If managers systematically ignore best case assumptions, it suggests either that, from experience, they very rarely occur and that 'expected' or 'most likely' performance levels are, in reality, somewhat optimistic, or (b) that managers are so obsessed with 'downside risk' (possibly due to their perception of the managerial appraisal and reward processes) that they adopt a highly cautious capital budgeting approach. Such an approach would inevitably lead to some higher-risk projects with exceptional performance prospects being passed over.

It is arguable that firms should not seek total agreement in what are the important investment variables. The capital budgeting process should encourage an element of ambiguity; a degree of 'idiosyncratic' behaviour and diversity in decision-making can sometimes improve the analysis and final outcome. Indeed, the minor differences identified by this study lends support for this view. Perhaps a degree of incongruency in investment appreciation and support-building enhances the learning aspects of investment effectiveness.

This tension between congruence and disparity in decision-making has already been referred to in Chapter 3. There we presented an overall finding that disparity reduces the ability to improve objectives-attainment, one measure of effectiveness, but enhances the ability to learn from decisions, our other measure of effectiveness.

Such a finding is obviously of great import. However, we will need to look beneath the surface of this generalized observation as to whether, for instance, there are certain variables more likely than others to give rise to this phenomenon. This is an important purpose of the subsequent case study and overall sample analysis which follows.

6 Medical Supplier: to weave or to knit

Our investigation of investment decision-making has, to this point. developed a conceptual framework for thinking about the processes and given some broad results from our analysis of the survey of seventeen investment decisions. The theoretical development and survey results give some idea about the kinds of features we might expect to find in effective decisions.

We now move to an analysis based upon case studies which have the advantage of allowing greater insights into the processes involved. In order not to lose sight of the comparative aspect of what we are seeking to understand, however, we also compare and contrast what we see in these cases.

Our concern with case studies starts with Medical Supplier. The story is built up, in part, by using the perceptions of the various actors involved in the decision and, in part, using the factual information about the case gathered from interviews and a variety of documentary sources. The actors, their fictitious names and location in the organization, are indicated in Figure 6.1.

What we will see is a very cloudy process but what we must not assume is that all complex decision-making has to be this way. Neither must we assume that, if a decision exhibits processes of this type, that disaster must ensue for the organization; as we shall see, even cloudy decisions can have silver linings.

THE BUSINESS OF MEDICAL SUPPLIER

Medical Supplier is the British subsidiary of a US-based multinational company manufacturing and selling products that may be broadly classified as medical or medically related. By far the largest single customer is the British National Health Service.

There are three divisions. The Hospital Division manufactures a

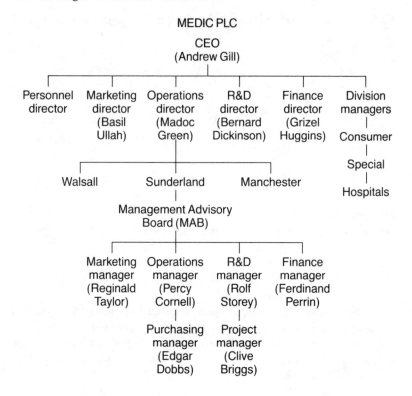

MEDIC PLC

CEO
(Andrew Gill)

| Personnel director | Marketing director (Basil Ullah) | Operations director (Madoc Green) | R&D director (Bernard Dickinson) | Finance director (Grizel Huggins) | Division managers |

Walsall   Sunderland   Manchester

Consumer

Special

Hospitals

Management Advisory Board (MAB)

| Marketing manager (Reginald Taylor) | Operations manager (Percy Cornell) | R&D manager (Rolf Storey) | Finance manager (Ferdinand Perrin) |

Purchasing manager (Edgar Dobbs)

Project manager (Clive Briggs)

	HOSPITAL	Division SPECIAL	CONSUMER
Turnover 1988	20	14	8
Growth 1985–8 average %	2	10	25
Gross profit margin %	25	40	12

Figure 6.1   Organization of Medical Supplier

wide range of surgical dressings and related items with 80 per cent of its production being sold to National Health Authorities throughout the UK; at the conclusion of this decision it had a turnover of £20m with an average growth rate of 2 per cent, and a long-standing gross profit margin of 25 per cent, but declining and expected to reduce to about 22 per cent within three years. The Special Division manufactures and markets a range of special aids for disabled people and many surgical appliances; again the largest proportion of output is sold to the National Health Service; turnover is approximately £14m with a growth rate of 10 per cent and gross profit margins of 40 per cent. The

Consumer Division represents the fastest growing market with a growth rate of 25 per cent on a turnover of £8m but gross profit margins are comparatively low at 12 per cent; the products include a wide range of medical dressings, cosmetics and related products sold to retail outlets such as pharmacies but also increasingly to supermarkets.

The surgical dressing business, the subject of this case, is worth about £4m with a gross profit margin of 20–25 per cent.

THE KNITTING SOLUTION

It had been realized for some time that knitting could be used to produce the wide range of dressings that Medical Supplier sold. The company had filed a patent for a knitting process thirteen years previously, but the present story really begins with Clive Briggs, an MBA-qualified project engineer in his early thirties working in the Consumer Division's R&D department:

> The idea came from me. I convinced the guy in marketing that it was a good idea and that there was potentially quite a large cost saving and some unique features that we could build-in using this knitting technique and provide real user benefits in terms of performance and cost, and make a distinctive product, branded possibly, using 'high-tech' to stop the competitive action that we were beginning to see at that time. It meant using different machinery but such a machine was available on the market. It is very modular and will cover three sizes simultaneously. You could easily get a Portakabin or a building, bolt on filter and systems; it's not an expensive exercise to get off the ground and it's only the sterile product that requires clean room conditions. The bulk product can be made anywhere. It was very good value for money.

Rolf Storey, research and development manager and Clive's boss, saw the issue in terms of using a new manufacturing concept for surgical dressings:

> to protect a substantial profitable business that was under permanent attack; this process offered protection through a distinctive product that appeared to offer some cost saving. The company has a culture that is all about weaving. There is a massive weaving facility only a mile down the road; in the textile industry you're either a weaver or a knitter.

The knitted SuperDress product would not comply with some existing specifications for the British Pharmacopia (BPC) which describes the construction of some products sold to hospitals. The specification describes so many threads in the warp and so many threads in the weft but these concepts do not apply to a knitting process. However, the product can still be sold alongside the more conventional woven product which can be used when compliance with BPC is needed. Nevertheless, Rolf Storey accepted that this did add 'a degree of difficulty'.

Edgar Dobbs, purchasing manager of many years standing in the company, cast a different light on the idea: 'It's not the first time that an idea perceived as a good idea by R&D has been pushed along without approval'. The operations manager, Percy Cornell, also noted that:

> we knew R&D were looking at a knitted dressing but it was a project which came to operations fairly late in the day. We weren't involved, for example, in what type of equipment was to be used. We assisted with setting the machine up, e.g., services, electrics, basic installation, and that type of thing.

DECISION TO HIRE A KNITTING-MACHINE FROM AVANTI

A knitting-machine was hired for an initial period of six months from a French company, Avanti, who build specialized one-off knitting machines and worked with Medical Supplier Company to make recommendations as to the design of the machine. At this stage £80,000 spending was committed. During this period a number of trials were conducted at Avanti. As Clive Briggs said:

> We did a number of proving trials and we actually ran that machine ourselves. I took myself over to France, found out how to make the stuff, came back and started producing. There was very high level of commitment by R&D to make this thing work.

After three months the machine was brought over to Sunderland for trials. Ferdinand Perrin, the finance manager, noted that:

> it was very much R&D driven and when the machine came in on trial the manufacturer's fitter came over and basically showed Clive and one other employee how to work a fairly complicated machine. Because of its height we had to site it in a warehouse which wasn't totally adequate. At that stage, without knowing the capital investment, I had to say it looked like a good runner given the information we had. The optimistic view was the one that was spread around and therefore generated the enthusiasm for the product. But that spreading was done at the development stage by R&D.

Momentum on the project was maintained particularly by Clive Briggs:

> it was perceived as being the major product at the time. Nothing was more important than this. Certainly from my point of view. I was interested in it technically but there was a whole lot of kudos, it was a very high profile project and Rolf Storey made no bones about it when we entered into this. He said; 'imagine yourself as being a fly on the wall and there's lots of people shining torches, that's exactly how it's going to be. Because we don't enter into this type of project lightly it is high profile stuff. If it works when you launch your product there could be a lot of kudos in it for you. If you bomb out you go out in a big way, sort of thing'. It was quite clear.

Clive also noted that:

> it was, incredibly quick. We needed this momentum. We did a fair amount of messing around; we had any number of problems in trying to run that machine on site and that was partly the reason why everybody here sort of cooled to the idea of doing it themselves. They could see me struggling with it, what they didn't take into account was the fact that I'm a chemist by trade, I'm not a machine operator. I managed to get the raw feedstock, the cotton yarn into the machine, thread it up, run the machine, make a reasonably acceptable product. We built any number of dressings for trial purposes and got very good results in the marketplace.

Ferdinand Perrin emphasized that the Consumer Division has been a drain on total cash flow because of the continual launching of new products with an investment level in the region of £1m; in comparison a £100,000 on SuperDress 'didn't rate perhaps as much enthusiasm'.

Marketing was keen to find a 'super' product. In the view of Reginald Taylor, marketing manager, the knitted SuperDress was more absorbent, 'had a cleaner look about it, a tidier finish to the product and the plus point to us was we were looking originally at 25 per cent reduction in cost. Quite a big saving on a £2.5m brand'.

Once the machine was in the warehouse to produce samples the decision gathered pace. Madoc Green, operations director, described the project as a 'Rolls-Royce compared with a Ford' with initial costings indicating that it was going to be cost effective.

> That is when I first became involved and got called up to meeting with one of my colleagues, and Bernard Dickinson (R&D director)

and Rolf Storey. Probably from the first meeting I had to pour cold water on it because it was such a bitty project.

Designs were registered and patents taken out within the first few months. Rolf Storey, R&D manager, emphasized that 'Clive had enough energy and perspective to drive this through, although I think we were optimistic on the costs that were quoted in the early days and that wasn't really helpful'.

The machine was taken to another site on hire to demonstrate the samples. Edgar Dobbs became involved 'when it sounded as if the enthusiasm for it was going to grow because we were unable to house the machine ourselves. It was the height that wouldn't fit our existing buildings'.

The competing 'Hyper' line

It was during this period of machine trials that other changes were taking place in the organization. The overall strategy was changing from an emphasis on the high volume/low margin medical market to a higher margin but more ephemeral consumer market.

This change in strategy was exemplified by the 'Hyper' line. A new range of consumer products were introduced that required considerable investment in a new production line. At this time the 'Hyper' line was occupying a considerable amount of attention from production.

APPOINTMENT OF EDGAR DOBBS AS PROJECT LEADER

About three months after the hire of the machine a meeting of the Management Advisory Board (MAB) was held to discuss a number of aspects of productivity in the company. The MAB had a membership including Clive Briggs, Rolf Storey, Percy Cornell (operations manager) and Edgar Dobbs. Part of this discussion included the SuperDress project which was presented by Clive as having long-term significance for productivity.

At the same time Edgar Dobbs was appointed as project leader for the SuperDress project. Clive Briggs described the process by which this happened:

> In R&D we believed that the way to maintain momentum was to get support from MAB. One of Rolf Storey's ploys was, in effect, to say; 'let's appoint Edgar Dobbs to be a project champion. He would take a particular interest in this important project and would make sure that arses were kicked and time scales kept'. Edgar is a

bit volatile, he's psychotic, and we could see that this guy would either make this project go like a train or he'd kill it stone dead. We thought that Edgar Dobbs might be a stumbling block so by putting him on the team it was thought that he might do some good. It was Rolf Storey's decision, under the table if you like, none of this was overt. Rolf is a political animal and tends to manipulate; seems quite good at it and gets away with it.

Rolf considered that:

Edgar Dobbs manages by conflict to achieve his version of what should happen in any particular situation. When we get a similar bully or a strong individual with that kind of style, then that's the time for conciliation. But he's got strong views. He is specifically responsible for outworker relationships and supply of materials. He was nominated to lead the project. It was a bit of skulduggery in the Divisional Board, especially by the Board Chairman to try to bring him round to be more positive; 'it's your baby, adopt it, kind of thing'. It was a mistake actually.

AUTHORIZATION OF PURCHASE OF THE KNITTING-MACHINE

Consideration was now being given to purchasing the machine. Costings were produced and as Clive Briggs noted:

we were hopeful the cost saving would be in the order of 30 per cent. Even if we'd spent a quarter of a million it wouldn't be a bad return. So we submitted our normal PAR (project appropriation request) form to finance. They crunched the numbers, came back and said, 'with these outputs and these yarn costs and these efficiencies we should be getting cost savings between 20–30 per cent.

Edgar Dobbs, who generally handled relationships with suppliers, was concerned about relations with the machine's makers, Avanti, who, he said:

were getting edgy about the length of time the machine was on hire. We would have been much happier to take the thing further on an experimental basis in order to test whether this investment should be made. I felt we were always trying to prove a negative against Marketing and R&D. Marketing liked the numbers they got from R&D because they showed cost savings; we were always having to try and justify the numbers that we were producing rather than the

other way round. You see, Clive Briggs has not much of an investment track record. The accountants can only produce costs based
on the information they are given. At one stage we did convince
Ferdinand Perrin that he should stop using Clive Briggs's figures
and start using ours. By the time we'd finished the installation, constructed walls, installed the bleaching equipment we had spent
£130,000. The bleaching equipment that we then found to be needed
was an extra £20,000. There was a failure to recognize that there are
things like wastage in the process, that theory and practice are not
the same thing.

Ferdinand Perrin was also expressing doubts since there was

difficulty in defining the process. I was costing the thoughts of R&D
if you like. It took another two years before we actually defined the
process. This is the amount of yarn used, time taken, wastage and
so forth. Costs indicated at best, 25 per cent cost reduction, at worst
equivalent cost, with three years of Clive Briggs, a year of a purchasing officer and two years of an accountant. There were significant revenue costs that weren't identified in the PAR; we
identified a further £15,000 as product work-up costs. Trial
quantities of yarn, very high wastages during commissioning of the
machine, those kinds of costs. We put £15,000 into the original
project. Our total commitment to that project up to launch date was
somewhere in the region of £300,000, including labour. Purchasing
quoted us the wrong price for sewing the product; it was mis-read as
being per-thousand rather than per-200 dressings and we used the
per-thousand figure in the costing when they had meant 200. We
managed to have conflict within the whole project between Purchasing and R&D, R&D and operations, and operations and
purchasing. And probably finance and purchasing as well.

Uncertainty over costs was reinforced by Percy Cornell, operations
manager: 'Finance have to take the base data that's supplied by R&D
and that's the element under dispute, especially concerning waste.
There are well trusted formulae for allocating overheads; capital spent
is known and depreciation easily calculated'.

Similarly, the operations director, Madoc Green, noted that there
had been costings:

it's just that I don't believe them. Marketing strongly supported the
PAR due to the advantages of having a better product at a better
price to take a bigger share in that market; for them it was a survival
issue as much as anything; if you can undercut by a few pence that

might be all that's needed to take the business. The threat's been there for a number of years and Basil Ullah (marketing director) pushed very, very hard to have this approved. I was under the impression that this was something that was quite unique and so by buying into it we would preclude competitors from coming in, providing the costs were going to be the same or less. Should we spend that £150,000 in a business like ours? I've been spending millions, not hundreds of thousands on consumer product machinery, so to put it into proportion, to spend £120,000 at that time to safeguard a 3.5m market which was profitable, seemed like a pretty good investment.

From the R&D perspective Rolf Storey noted what he called 'poor information and dog-in-the-manger attitudes. The complexity of the knitting process was eons away from what we were familiar with. We had to make such big steps in our work philosophy'.

The decision to authorize the purchase of the machine was put on the board meeting minutes for discussion and the purchase was authorized; by now three years had elapsed since the preliminary discussions on the project. In the opinion of Percy Cornell 'there was a very large degree of rubber stamping. They hadn't scoured the market for other equipment, for example.'

EMPLOYMENT OF AN OUTWORKER

After another month or so, due to the problems of trying to produce SuperDress and the shortage of skilled labour, thoughts were turning to the idea of using an outworker. As Clive Briggs said: 'Let's get into bed with a warp knitter and find someone who is used to running this type of machine'. It had become increasingly apparent that SuperDress was a different type of product to what was normally processed, not only in terms of the differences between knitting and weaving but also in terms of its subsequent processes of bleaching and scouring.

As purchasing manager, Edgar Dobbs became more closely involved since the nogotiation of contracts was usually his remit. The selection of an outworker was taken after obtaining quotations from a short list of three companies taken from forty-seven member companies of the Warp Knitters Association. As Edgar Dobbs said:

We took the view that, of the three, Lion was the best company. Clive Briggs was enthusiastic about their technical expertise and we put our quality assurance people in to look at the premises. They are very good. So we went ahead and installed the machine on their premises.

This investigation of outworkers, however, brought to light the fact that, in the eyes of the companies approached, there had been no need to purchase the machine because a far cheaper alternative was available; they all had machines which for a relatively small investment of about £6,000, could have been modified to do the work. Edgar Dobbs:

> This is one of the difficulties. We're talking about a technology that none of us had knowledge about; to some extent we were swept along by the 'expert' (Clive Briggs) and accepted statements that were not subjected to the normal line of checks; we weren't even invited to look outside.

Production at Lion started after about four years from the beginning of the decision process. There were problems in obtaining accurate costings as Ferdinand Perrin relates:

> We didn't have a firm commitment on yarn price or on Lion's make-up charge. Because their works weren't as clean as they should be we built a wall within their factory to take this process which cost us £15,000. They were beaming other materials and fly (fluff from other weaving processes) was getting into our yarn. After building the wall they couldn't use the area for anything else and charged us £30,000 a year for under-utilization of that area.

As Edgar Dobbs put it,

> We didn't actually say to them, 'you mustn't put anything adjacent, you mustn't do this or the other'; if you put a machine like this into a factory that's producing net curtains and alongside conventional yarns ladened with optical brighteners there will be contamination.

Other problems also arose, in particular the need to install bleaching equipment and the charging by Lion at £170 per week for any time the machine stood idle.

Now that the outworker was involved, interdepartmental relations became more important. Edgar Dobbs continued:

> We do have some demarcation disputes. I've no problem with R&D. I don't take the view that purchasing has a monopoly of knowledge; we certainly were going to have to start learning about facilities but I do take exception to the meeting that I convened because we had cost problems and Clive Briggs arriving with, 'well

here's a new costing since I just happened to call in at Lion, I just happen to have some material, they just happened to have been able to bleach it for me and what do you think of that? And it's only going to cost this'. And suddenly the cost problems disappear, so we get on our bikes and go to see Lion again. By this time Lion was getting a bit fed up with us. We also had to spend £150,000 if we wanted to do our own drying. So, the numbers game changed again.

Clive Briggs cast a different light upon relationships between functions. 'Edgar took the project over and he interpreted that as "I'm going to be project champion". He came down very heavily on you if you didn't keep him informed. He wasn't the true project champion of the type that nurtures and makes things happen.'

LAUNCH OF 'SUPERDRESS' ON THE MARKET

A date, approximately four years after the beginning of the decision process, to launch SuperDress was set but this was delayed for six months due to the problem of the outworker and due to the more competitive conditions in the Health Service with buyers becoming more professional, picking and choosing between suppliers.

Ferdinand Perrin summed up the general attitude: 'As we had put £300,000 into this product, we couldn't not spend an extra £50,000 to test the market and see whether it "flies" or not'. Madoc Green reinforced this view: 'If we didn't take this on board then almost certainly a competitor would'.

A lot of effort was now put in to bring the project to completion. A further few months saw most production problems at Lion resolved and some SuperDress was in stock. SuperDress was then launched on the market. The first order from the National Health Service was for four months forecast output.

Clive Briggs:

Suddenly we find ourselves with a forecast that is eight times too small. So we do all the costings again because the volumes have grown. We want two machines and that totally changes the cost structure. Once we start to get the volume, we don't have one man running one machine, we have one man running two or three machines. That's the potential.

Some views on the project success

Various participants in the decision gave their overall assessment of the decision process.

Edgar Dobbs:

> I tried to influence the decision the other way. There was over optimism about the market response to the product. The first samples that went out to the marketplace were received favourably and people were enthusiastic about them. That is not the case now and in fact I can't hear that anybody's got a good word for the product. The market simply doesn't seem to want to know, regardless of price. I'm hearing that it's too harsh, that surgeons don't like it. . . . The impact on Clive Briggs seems to have been he's got promotion.

Ferdinand Perrin said that he was:

> strongly supportive of this in November last year; if it does fly, maybe we've got a good product here. In retrospect, I wouldn't invest; the market has changed to being very price conscious, we always assumed that we could charge a premium for this product in the marketplace. Now the marketing argument is that we have lost contracts for our existing Dress product in areas where we launched SuperDress. Therefore, we're trying to buy the business back with a superior product at a similar price and that's not what we intended. It's not what I intended as the accountant associated with the project.

Percy Cornell:

> The cost reduction element of it was bulldozed through by R&D but did not come to fruition. Operations is not always very popular but has a lot of experience because at the end of the day we are the people who are responsible for manufacturing goods at a price.

Madoc Green:

> I didn't pour cold water on it for any reason other than I was edgy. Of all the projects I've been involved with, it's the one that's given me the most cause for concern. We can produce a very fine dressing, we are probably first in the market-place here in this country with this type of product. I think it's an 'iffy' situation still.

Rolf Storey:

> I actually feel that this was a model of how not to conduct any project. I think this was a catalogue of hidden agendas and politics in a situation where the prize was so important to the business that we should have been acting in concert and we just weren't.

THE CHRONOLOGY OF EVENTS AND SUBDECISIONS

As a long, complicated decision process, the timing and intercon-
nections between different events played an important part. In this
respect it is possible to think in terms of a hierarchy of decisions in the
way that Simon (1956) describes with high-level decisions setting the
values for lower-level factual decisions. A subdecision is a choice that
is made as part of the process of a larger decision. The decision, itself,
fits in a hierarchy of meta-decisions.

If we are not careful we could impose upon ourselves a procedure of
infinite regression in which decisions get broken down into ever
smaller components. Our purpose in identifying the concept of a
subdecision is to point to the notion that decisions are built up by
means of a series of subdecisions. To some extent it is arbitrary where
we say that a decision starts and where a decision finishes. As has been
stressed in the description of the decision effectiveness model,
the effect that a decision has upon the wider organization leads to
further decisions. The overall effect that a decision has, then, is
ultimately determined by how it fits into an overall pattern of
decisions.

Decisions are subjected to the impact of key outside events that may
conspire to change the norms of performance for a particular decision
or to in some other way affect the processes involved.

It is instructive to look at this involved decision at Medical, and we
will do likewise to other decisions, in terms of the subdecisions and
key outside events. The key subdecisions are identified in Table 6.1.

Subdecision one: hire of the machine from Avanti

The hire of the knitting machine was a step that began to commit the
organization to the introduction of the knitting process. As Staw and
Ross (1978) point out, the commitment of resources to a course of
action tends to make a withdrawal from that course more difficult.

Event: introduction of 'Hyper' as a competing line

Investments are always competing with one another in an organization. The development of the competing consumer line, 'Hyper', put
knitting at a disadvantage in terms of the managerial attention that
could be devoted to it. It also highlights the uncertainties that had
developed in the organization as regards the strategy to follow.

Table 6.1 SuperDress decision chronology

Date	Event	Subdecision
c 1977	Patent filed for knitting process	
c 81/82	Discussions with Basil Ullah, Rolf Storey and Clive Briggs about knitting dressings and 'getting thoughts together'	
mid 82	Preliminary costings from Ferdinand Perrin	
3/83	*The decision to hire the machine from Avanti of France*	SD 1
9–10/83	Trials at Avanti	
10/83	Clive Briggs visits Avanti	
83/84	Consumer 'Hyper' investment occupies minds of production	
11/83	*The decision to appoint Edgar Dobbs as project leader*	SD 2
1/84	Machine arrives at Sunderland and installed in warehouse for 6 months	
early 84	Trials at Sunderland, machine still on hire from Avanti, Avanti getting 'edgy'	
6/84	*The decision to authorize purchase of the knitting-machine*	SD 3
84	Machine idle at Sunderland	
end 84	Clive Briggs asks Edgar Dobbs to find outworker	
early 85	Outworkers visited. Realized there could have been a low cost alternative to knitting	
mid 85	*The decision to employ Lion as an outworker*	SD 4
85	Trials at Lion. Contamination problem. Wall built. Lion losing interest. Bleacher bought for Sunderland	
85	Andrew Gill becomes CEO. Change in policy with shift away from 'hyper'. Reorganization on product lines	
4/85	Production first planned. Did not happen	
86	Machine idle in Lion, Edgar Dobbs objects to paying rent for space in Lion	
8/86	Finishing problems	
12/86	Started producing 3 months expected sales at Lion	
1/87	*The decision to launch SuperDress on the market*	SD 5
4/87	Wastage and reliability still unsure	

Notes: SD denotes a subdecision.

Subdecision two: appointment of Edgar Dobbs as project leader

This was a key subdecision since there was manipulation on the part of the research and development manager to co-opt the person who he saw as offering the most resistance to the knitting solution. As an attempt to co-opt it backfired since Edgar Dobbs was now given a more prominent platform from which to voice his opposition. When guile gains the upper hand in an organization then the scene has been set for a great deal of managerial effort to be wasted with undesirable effects for the whole organization.

Subdecision three: machine purchase authorized

The purchase of the machine seems almost to have been an inevitable decision since the organization had gone so far down the road towards incorporating the knitting solution.

Subdecision four: outworker selected

The outworker decision was one that was forced on the organization due to the lack of internal expertise with knitting as a manufacturing process, an aspect of the decision that was given very little attention by the organization, and due to the lack of manufacturing capacity.

Event: shift in strategy away from 'Hyper'

An important reason for the selection of an outworker was to give manufacturing capacity for knitting SuperDress. The shortage of capacity came about as a result of the attention being given to the consumer products, but there was a down-grading of this policy that would have given the capacity to manufacture the SuperDress product in-house.

However, the use of an outworker had one very useful advantage from the viewpoint of learning; it had shown that a mistake had been made in the first place through buying such an expensive machine when it was discovered that a much cheaper home-grown solution was available.

The change in company strategy was also associated with the incoming of a new chief executive and led to subsequent structural changes.

Subdecision five: SuperDress product launch

The product was launched although demand was still uncertain.

ORGANIZATIONAL LEARNING

Shortly after the purchase of the machine Andrew Gill was appointed as the new chief executive of Medical Supplier Company. He commented:

> We have learned some lessons about how to handle capital expenditure. In addition to SuperDress a series of bad projects have focused our minds; we are less likely to make the same kind of decision again. The main problem is the inappropriateness of the decision in terms of what we are trying to do overall.

Following Andrew Gill's appointment, considerable changes were made to the organization. As he said:

> I think we handled it badly; authority for capital decisions had been delegated too far down the organization. It seems to me that the driving force (of SuperDress) was Bernard Dickinson; he believed in knitting technology. The man who handled it was Clive Briggs but he was too junior to have swung it on his own; the reports on his ability were favourable and one dud project is not sufficient reason to abandon the man. Now we don't have a research director, only a manager; Bernard went abroad.

Andrew Gill continued:

> The organization climate has changed a great deal. Today we have a small nucleus executive management group consisting of myself, finance, marketing and production directors who will consider capital investments. R&D will not be there, in the short term at any rate.

In these comments we see here a considerable change in the performance norms of investment decisions, not only as a result of the SuperDress project, but due to the change in top management. The particular point of note is how a series of bad projects have caused a rethinking of the treatment of investments. This is aimed at clarifying the premises for future capital projects. The question of organizational learning will be taken up in a later chapter.

7   The appreciation of effectiveness

INTRODUCTION

Our appreciation of effective decision-making now concentrates upon the ten decisions, out of the overall sample of seventeen, for which we gathered the views of multiple participants. These are developed, either in the form of larger cases, as for the preceding Medical Supplier case, or in the form of 'mini-cases' which present outline cases and analysis. Our aim is to develop further understanding of the processes of decision-making which cannot be achieved through a broader but shallower survey.

Our approach is to analyse contrasting pairs of decisions to try and understand the dynamics of how the achievement of objectives and learning, our two principal dimensions of decision effectiveness, takes place. The development of such cases relies as much upon qualitative as quantitative data.

Figure 7.1 plots each decision on the two effectiveness dimensions, objectives-attainment and learning. From this we select pairs of cases for deeper examination and comparison.

A HIGHLY-EFFECTIVE AND THE LEAST EFFECTIVE DECISIONS COMPARED: ELECTRONICS COMPANY (LP) AND MEDICAL SUPPLIER (MP)

We start the development of the mini-cases by comparing and contrasting two very different decisions. The decision to introduce a new product at Electronics Company (decision *LP*) is considered to be the most effective all-round decision of our sample because it rates highly both on attainment of objectives and on learning.

Conversely, the decision to invest in a new surgical dressing manufacturing and packing plant at Medical Supplier (decision *MP*), must

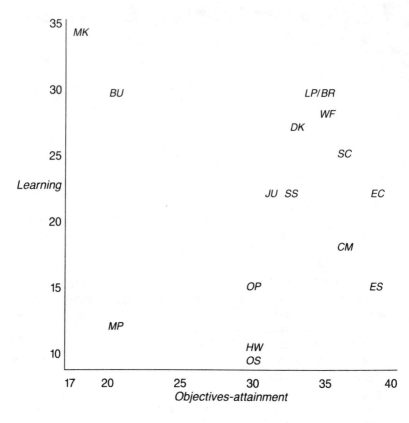

The Decisions
BU   Brewer Co. – UK site acquisition
BR   Brewer Co. – opening restaurants in N America
CM   Capital Goods – install manufacturing plant
DK   Cloth-Dyer – new 'kitchen'
EC   Electric Co. – new computer
ES   Electric Co. – computer software
HW   Household Goods – warehouse
JU   Japanese Consumer Goods Co. – opening up in the UK
LP   Electronics Co. – new product introduction
MK   Medical Supplier Co. – new knitting-machine
MP   Medical Supplier Co. – new plant
OS   Oil Co. – solvents expansion
OP   Oil Co. – propylene upgrading
SC   Building Society – purchase of mainframe computer
SS   Building Society – purchase of software
WF   Water Co. – construction of water filtration plant

Figure 7.1   Two dimensions of decision effectiveness

undoubtedly be seen as the least effective decision. This decision scores lowest on both learning and objectives-attainment.

Settings and definitions

LP Electronics is a medium-sized company of about £25m turnover (late 1980s figures) specializing in the manufacturing, selling and servicing of one central product line and related products. The decision concerns the introduction of a new product line, a form of 'intercom' for use in homes for the elderly to allow the occupants to communicate with the outside world in the event of an emergency or other occasion. The investment involved was approximately £450,000.

The technology of this product is almost irrelevant to our understanding of the decision other than to say that it is fairly advanced but not exactly breaking radically new ground by the standards of the electronics industry. Interest in this issue arose out of a realization that the existing product line was becoming outdated relative to the competition. As the company was dependent upon a limited product range change was considered important.

The chief executive of the company was new and determined to keep the company at the forefront of developments within its market and industry. Hence, we see that this was appreciated as a highly consequential decision, especially in terms of the consequences of failure for the company. The chief executive was instrumental in arousing and maintaining interest in the issue. This interest had a high degree of support from others in the organization.

In spite of its consequentiality, the participants could readily agree upon the main parameters of the issue as regards the main uncertainties. The major uncertainties involved uncertainties about market response and some technical problems, reflecting the technical nature of the product. Disagreements over the objectives of the decision were low.

MP The organizational setting of Medical Supplier is that it is the British subsidiary of an American multinational company, but is given a fair degree of autonomy over its investment policy, although investments do have to be approved by headquarters. This is sometimes seen as a rather laborious and restrictive process by local management. Traditionally, the company has operated in what is sometimes called the 'ethical' field, so called because they manufacture and supply a wide range of medical products which have to be made to precise standards of hygiene.

In the United Kingdom the main customer is the National Health

Service but competition has been increasing in recent years with the Health Service adopting a policy of buying from the cheapest source even if it means importing. One strategic response to this situation has been to develop the consumer product side of the business with lines such as cosmetics.

This particular decision involves the investment in a new manufacturing facility with the intention of increasing capacity; an important factor here was the desire on the part of the UK subsidiary management for their company to become the principal European manufacturing facility and to pioneer use of new technology. Again, the precise details of the technology are not important to the understanding of the decision processes other than certain critical aspects which will be explained as we proceed.

Interest in the decision was prompted very much by the market, and research and development departments who pressed for the new plant. Although consequential in terms of strategic fit and competitive factors, the decision was not, overall, as consequential in terms of the consequences of failure to the organization as the Electronics decision *LP* was within its own organization. Interest in the decision also involved some external influence.

Possible implications for career were seen to be high by the participants in this decision. Overall uncertainties were also fairly high and the decision was seen as quite rare. The noteworthy feature is the lack of agreement amongst participants as to what the major uncertainties are; this is particularly noticeable as regards the objectives of the decision. Disparities over objectives are particularly high compared with the Electronics decision.

Strategies for solution and support-building

LP In the case of Electronics, with market uncertainties rating highly, we see a high judgement score. More important is the observation that judgement is the dominant strategy of the decision strategies (rating even slightly above the computation strategy), with concerns about product quality and company image looming large.

Computations were used to a somewhat below average extent in making the decision to go ahead with this replacement product line; the computations used concerned assessment of the proposed investment upon productivity, and the simple payback method of evaluating returns in preference to other more sophisticated methods such as return on earnings and profitability. These methods perhaps fit the mode of assessing investments in a smaller company where imposed procedures of a remote head office or top management do not impinge to a high degree and where project appraisal can be a more interactive process. The predominance of the simple payback appraisal method in Electronics is supported by the experiment reported in Chapter 4.

Negotiation is high in relation to the overall sample mean. One area of contention concerned the pace at which the decision should proceed with some participants thinking that things were going too slowly. This seemed to indicate the need for urgency over the decision rather than the clock time of the decision since the duration was only 0.77 years, the shortest time of all the decisions studied.

Nevertheless, negotiation was the second most important strategy used; our analysis indicates that the negotiation that took place was able to cope with the relatively low degree of politicality. It was not so much a negotiation concerned with building alliances as mutual-adjustment amongst decision-makers trying to solve problems. Inspiration was used to a moderate degree but it was not a dominant part of the process. Most important was the part played by top management in influencing and inspiring this decision.

MP Whereas the Electronics decision tended to be judgementally built, the Medical decision was driven by inspiration and judgement together. The problem was that in Medical the uncertainties were relatively high. Computations were used to a moderate degree but more in a token manner to satisfy imposed procedures needed to justify the investment to headquarters, an aspect not needed in Electronics. Some key costings were calculated incorrectly.

Influence

Electronics exhibited a pattern of influence that involved a large number of internal interests, especially in view of the relatively small size of the organization. As already mentioned, there were no external interests involved.

In addition to this pluralism, the *LP* decision was driven to a large extent by the interest of the chief executive. This illustrates the interaction between the influence and definition variables.

In Medical Supplier, decision *MP* exhibited a lower level of internal interest. What was different in comparison to Electronics was the high degree of influence exerted by two functions, engineering and marketing, in the decision but a low degree of involvement by top management. There was also a fairly high external interest involved in Medical; this occurred because of the involvement of the French subsidiary in the decision and of the supplier.

Authority was used in the case of Electronics in the sense that the influence by top management (chief executive and chairman) was felt throughout the decision process and, overall, was the highest, but that other people and functions were actively involved.

Conversely, in the case of Medical, authority became a rubber-stamping matter, particularly by the US Headquarters; top management tended to take a 'hands-off' attitude, in this case with marketing and engineering becoming the dominant interests. This goes a long way to explain how the company got into the situation of approving an investment which resulted in an over-capacity of manufacturing facility that, during the effecting of the decision, was appreciated as unnecessary in the sense that the productive capacity became excessive.

The 'hands-off' approach to investment decision-making had been noted by the chief executive officer (CEO) in a post-audit evaluation; for example, there was only one signature on the PAR (the internal project approval review form), that of research and development, instead of a full representation of signatures from all major functions.

Timing

Apart from some dissatisfactions with the pace of the process, the Electronics decision proceeded with little time needed for build-up, few delays, and lasted forty months from inception to implementation. In general the timing was considered to be right for the market and there were few disagreements over the pace at which the decision should proceed.

Medical was quite a long decision and took time to build up. Most significantly for this decision was the realization that the new plant, though technically advanced and working well, was not, after all, needed to fulfil current production targets. However, the chief executive made the point that perspectives on this decision could change if it should be found that the market materializes in the future.

MP, therefore, demonstrates that perceptions of effectiveness can vary over time, even concerning a decision that is considered finished.

Summary

These two decisions provide a contrast in that the Electronics decision illustrates a highly-effective, strategic business decision, reaching agreement quickly, building upon a full appreciation of the organizations situation, while Medical illustrates a business decision that is clumsy, long winded, emphasizing the rituals of financial justifications to satisfy headquarters, derogation of responsibility by top management, while leaving lower level functional interests to control the course of events. At no time during this process could we say that there was a common view developed amongst the participants.

For decision *LP* in Electronics what we see is a decision that is driven by a simple market logic, given impetus by an alert management, where individual inspiration exists but is under control due to management interest. In Medical this interest by top management was missing.

The learning in Electronics was described in terms of learning about a new product market mix. It was also seen as enabling the company to improve its methods of evaluating investment decisions. The tradition in this company was to use relatively simple methods, such as payback, but the management appreciated the need to develop more sophisticated methods.

Learning in Medical Supplier was rated very low by all the actors interviewed. However, this and a number of unsuccessful projects gave the impetus to wide-reaching changes within the organization. The second Medical Supplier decision below elaborates on this.

A HIGH LEARNING/LOW OBJECTIVES DECISION AND A LOW LEARNING/HIGH OBJECTIVES DECISION: MEDICAL SUPPLIER REVISITED (MK) AND THE ELECTRIC COMPANY (ES)

The comparison made above has, in terms of decision effectiveness, compared the best and worst cases. Figure 7.1 shows us two other decisions that can be viewed as diametrically opposed. One decision, to invest in knitting technology in Medical (*MK*) has already been described in depth, rates highly in terms of learning but low in terms of achieving objectives. The other decision (*ES*), to buy the ICL Maestro computer system in Electric Company, rates high in terms of achieving objectives but low in learning.

The significant aspect of this second Medical Supplier decision is that it is an involved story in which many things went wrong but from which the company managed to learn by their experiences. The decision is only recounted to the extent that our analysis compares the processes to those involved in the Electric Company decision.

Settings and definitions

MK The organizational setting for Medical has already been described. Additional aspects relevant to this decision concern the shift to consumer products and away from 'ethicals' in an attempt to increase margins and to cope with a static market, a trend that was later to be reversed. There was, therefore, a vacillation in the strategy of the company that changed the assessment norms for investments.

Interest, both internal and external, was very high for this decision, and so was career implications, due mainly to the involvement of Clive Briggs as described.

Complexity was high due to uncertainties about costs and likely return on investment and due to rarity. The main actors involved were not familiar with knitting technology although, as became apparent, they did not have to look very far to find out.

Politicality also became high due, in particular, to conflicts about objectives and personality clashes. Consequentiality, in particular due to the concern for the competitive aspect of the decision, was high.

What really distinguishes this decision is the lack of agreement about what the uncertainties and disagreements were about and why the decision was considered consequential. This supports the survey results which finds a negative relationship between disparities and the objectives-attainment dimension of effectiveness. Conversely, we should recall the survey finding that disparity can increase the learning achieved from a decision.

Overall, then, the Medical Knitting decision presents an appreciation of an issue that is high in interest, uncertainty, politicality and consequentiality, and in disparities about these variables.

ES The Electric Company decision (*ES*) provides a contrast in term of its simplicity. Electric is a British distribution company which, at the time of the decision, was still in public ownership but anticipating privatization. The main task of Electricity is to purchase electricity, mainly from the Central Electricity Generating Board (CEGB) which has a virtual monopoly of supply within the UK (although the charter of Electric allows it to buy from other sources), for distribution within its own area. This task was enshrined in an Act of Parliament. A number of performance norms are also laid down covering such things as reliability of supply but, on the whole, this is an organization that has a clear idea of what its task is and how to achieve that task.

When we look at the question of how the decision to purchase Maestro was recognized in Electric, we see a decision that had high interest due to the career implications for the managers involved. There was fairly high external interest due to the involvement of the supplier of the system. Consequentiality was quite high due to the need to fit the new system to overall strategy. Consequences of failure was seen as low although the performance of the computer was seen as critical to the organization.

Strategies for solution and support-building

MK   The notable feature about the strategies used during the Medical decision is the high level of negotiation with a lot of alliance building, and the high level of inspiration. This is in contrast to the Electricity decision, which has a low level of negotiation but high judgement.

As we saw in the detailed description of the Medical Knitting decision, quite a high level of computation was carried out but mistakes were made in these. Conversely, Electricity had a fairly high level of computation but negotiation was low and inspiration very low, probably reflecting the low level of uncertainties and disagreements.

ES   The Electricity decision was quite solvable given sufficient information. The norms and general parameters of the decision were quite clear; the only information that participants would have liked that was lacking was to be able to talk to another similar organization that had used such a system before but such a possibility did not present itself.

Influence

The Electricity decision (*ES*) involved only a narrow band of internal interests (4 units, mean 6.7) and was fairly narrowly directed (3 units interests, mean 3.9), but there was high top management support.

In the Medical Supplier decision (*MK*), there was very wide involvement (9 units, mean 6.7) and direction (5 units, mean 3.9). What was missing in this decision was strong top management support or parameters within which decision-makers could operate. The high inspiration in this decision came from quite low down in the hierarchy and never managed to gather support for the decision from the various interests.

Timing

In *ES* there were hardly any disagreements over objectives and so the decision proceeded quite smoothly, with some delays, but with a clear idea of to where they were trying to get.

MK   was a decision fraught with disagreements, driven very strongly by the inspiration of one fairly junior participant in the organization, taking a long time to come to fruition. During the overall process, lasting six years, the strategy of the company changed twice, first strongly shifting towards a consumer policy in which marketing was dominant, then, to some extent shifting back to a more balanced policy between the consumer and medical sides of the business. As a solution to a problem the knitting machine lost support during the decision. It was a decision in which authority could have played a greater role to have prevented the low achievements of objectives by infusing a stronger appreciation of the organization's environment and in preventing domination by research and development, and marketing interests.

Summary

The Electric Company decision (*ES*) to purchase a computer system quite closely followed the rational decision-making path, achieving the initial objectives but with participants not apparently learning much. What this meant for the organization was that the purchase of the computer had little impact other than in achieving the initial objectives. This does not mean, of course, that the organization will not learn from the use of the technology.

The important question concerning the Medical Knitting decision was how this achieved very high learning while apparently not achieving objectives. Disagreements inherent in political decisions can lead to a deeper appreciation of the organization and the issues that it faces.

The in-depth case study of Medical shows how, especially following the appointment of a new chief executive, the organization came to appreciate the need to rethink its structure and general approach to investment decision-making. The chief executive saw clearly that it was the prime responsibility of top management to set the decision rules in such a way to make it clear to lower levels what performance norms were important.

CAPITAL GOODS MANUFACTURER: INSTALLATION OF A NEW MANUFACTURING CENTRE AT THE TURBINE DIVISION (CM)

Another investment decision that tends towards the high objective-attainment but low learning position in Figure 7.1 took place in the subsidiary of a large multinational engineering company, Capital Goods Manufacturer (decision *CM*).

Setting

Capital Goods Manufacturer (*C*) is a very large multinational company operating in many markets but concentrating upon heavy electrical engineering components. The organization has evolved as the result of the bringing together of a number of previously independent companies, many of which helped form the bulwark of the heyday of British engineering.

The decision involves the purchase of a machining centre to replace a number of more conventional machines in the corporation's turbine division. The turbine division operates as a profit centre within the corporation. About twenty existing machines could be replaced by three new ones.

In terms of our two dimensions of decision effectiveness, this decision was rated quite highly on achievement of objectives but quite low on learning (Figure 7.1).

Definition of the issue

The feeling had been growing within the division that the facilities were outdated, costs too high and lead-times too long. A review of the manufacturing facilities had been started three years or so earlier. This specific proposal originated in the manufacturing technical department and was looking ahead as part of a five-year rolling plan. In the end about £4m was committed.

Participants did not see career implications as generally important in working on this project; it was generally seen that, unless proposals were submitted within the budgeting deadlines, the opportunity to invest would be lost. Although a profit centre, headquarters maintained a strict regime over its divisions as regards the procedures and parameters to be used in assessing capital projects.

It was seen as quite a consequential decision, particularly as regards the possible impact of failure and in terms of competitive performance in the market-place. Uncertainties were above the sample mean but disagreements below the mean. There was fairly high agreement as to what the objectives of the decision were. Major uncertainties were seen in the terms of determining the costs and whether finance could be arranged.

Strategies for solutions and support-building

This was a decision in which the computational and judgemental strategies were dominant, and with a fair degree of negotiation evident. A manufacturing technology outline design was produced along with an artist's impression. A considerable amount of talking to machine-tool manufacturers was carried out.

Capital Goods has a formalized system of capital appraisal. Formal approval begins with the submission of a brochure to Head Office. There is then a sequence of steps whereby the proposal moves through different stages of evaluation and enventually ends up with the group finance director and then to the managing director. The primary quantifiable methods of evaluation used were the effect of the investment on profit and sales targets and payback period; this latter was considered to be a highly-favoured method of the chairman of the corporation. A new computer-based technique of financial appraisal called BORIS was used by the company in assessing the investment proposal and this was considered to be a major innovation in terms of the methods of evaluation used.

The decision reached a fairly low degree of negotiation; the negotiations that occurred concerned methods of evaluation of the project rather than the objectives to be achieved. Individual inspiration was low, reinforcing the collective nature of the realization.

The process was seen as long by most of the participants, the decision processes taking about nine months from the working up of the initial proposal to approval but with another eighteen months for implementation.

Influence

A large number (nine) of different units were involved and exerted influence. There was some external influence and direction was also fairly widely dispersed (five units).

Effectiveness

Although a large investment this decision exemplifies a fairly routine investment project in the division of a large multinational capital intensive industry. The objectives of replacing an ageing outdated production facility were efficiently achieved and the new plant was successful in its operation.

CONCLUSION

The core of this chapter consists of four investment decisions presented as two sets of paired comparisons. Each comparison shows what happens when we make a shift from two different starting points along the axes of Figure 7.1.

If we start from the position of decision *MP*, the low objectives-attainment/low learning decision in Medical Supplier, we can acquire an understanding of what is required to achieve higher objectives-attainment by making a comparison with decision *EC*, the computer decision in Electric. The key seems to concern the need to define objectives with clarity beforehand, to keep involvement by unnecessary interests at bay and to build solutions and support by means of the computational strategy of decision-making.

Starting from the same position of decision *MP* we can also get clues as to what is involved in improving learning. Here, lack of clarity in definition of the decision, combined with wide involvement, inspiration and lack of top management guidance, might be argued to increase learning. But all these factors also apply to *MP*. So why did decision *MK* and not decision *MP* achieve high learning?

A critical factor from these cases appears to be that decision *MP* took place before *MK* within the same organization and before the new chief executive arrived. The organization had not yet built up the pressure to change its investment practices. Structures tend to change when sufficient evidence as to the inadequacy of existing practices has accumulated.

In order to explore these questions further we examine more cases and the interrelationships between variables achieved by a more extensive comparison of cases.

8   A new kitchen at Cloth-Dyer

Cloth-Dyer is a wholly-owned subsidiary of the Textiles Division of Associated Industries, a large multinational corporation with chemical and many other interests. Cloth-Dyer prints colour designs on to fabrics on a commission basis, the customer usually supplying the cloth, and agreeing colours and designs with Cloth-Dyer. The white(ish) linen is kept on huge rolls like newspaper print, the process typically involving bleaching, successive stages of printing and drying, again as a continuous process with raw material going in at one end of the factory and the finished product out at the other end. The rate of production is determined by the length of run of one particular design and especially by the drying capacity once the fabric has been dyed/printed. It is essential to production that the colours chosen for printing are consistent throughout a whole run and for future runs.

The colourshop (or kitchen) is therefore at the very heart of finished product quality and the decision to replace this is the capital investment chosen for study. There is only one colourshop but seven printing machines. The colourshop takes basic dye colours and mixes them to the required colour, servicing all seven printing machines, and has two essential functions: (1) to establish a sample and retain the constituent proportions in a data bank (the 'recipe') and (2) to reproduce that sample consistently and repeatedly for batch production. Computers can be used in either or both functions, separately or combined in one system or two. If needed, the existing colourshop has the facility to produce manually.

The colourshop is located in the printing works at Wigan. Turnover is about £3m and the number of employees about 100. Cloth-Dyer has other activities, mainly in associated furniture and textile businesses in two other plants. An approximate organization chart is given in Figure 8.1 showing the main actors involved in this decision.

The Cloth-Dyer temporary managing director, Mike Van, sees the

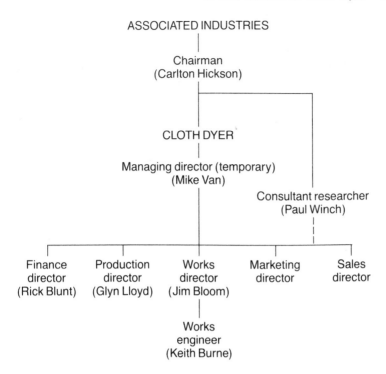

Figure 8.1   Cloth-Dyer's organization

company's business as 'an ability to put colour on cloth in a particular way'. The company's main product area is to print designs for curtain material and soft furnishings. They are increasingly introducing co-ordinated designs and gradually moving to a wider 120-inch-width cloth. Expansion in the UK and then in export markets is fundamental to the strategy. There are three major competitors at the top end of the market all of whom are, to a greater or lesser extent, inferior to Cloth-Dyer according to the general view at the company. As Mike Van said, 'the company is driven by closeness to the customer and the need to respond. Cost reduction is an operational not a strategic tool'.

ISSUE DEFINITION

The original kitchen was built in 1974 for £110,000, representing then the most advanced technology in its field. The anticipated life was ten years but, by the mid-1980s, there was general awareness of the need for replacement. A search was started in 1984 for a new colourshop when the old one started to 'creak' as it was becoming slow and computer components were no longer readily available. Increasing demand and complexity of business required new equipment to produce a quality product and provide consistency of product manufacture.

Textile furnishings in the domestic market have an in-built barrier to entry in that the printing done by Cloth-Dyer is for a unique type of market, domestic and 'colonial', that is, the USA, Canada, Australia, New Zealand and Hong Kong; domestic market share is 50–60 per cent. The products are frequently multicoloured floral patterns, not in demand in the rest of Europe or the rest of the world. Cloth-Dyer therefore operates in an oligopolistic market based upon a notion of a cost quality combination but not lowest price.

According to the managing director, this decision was aimed to emphasize the cost reduction element and the choice of machine was seen as strategically important. Moving away from the core business of furniture fabric and curtains was never considered, although consideration was being given to the addition of a third, as yet unkown, line. Central to the operating philosophy was the need to change colour and design frequently in response to the requirements of the large powerful retailers who are increasingly calling the tune and making it obvious they are willing to buy from Europe.

Investments of up to £100,000 are authorized by the managing director of Cloth-Dyer. In discussing how the colourshop decision would be assessed the managing director said that 'I'm not an accountant; they tend to use words like payback and internal rate of return'. He said, at the start of the colourshop investment, 'people didn't have a clear view of what they wanted at the beginning . . . they were very slow in coming together . . . it was a leadership problem I suppose'. There was a general feeling of caution concerning new technology expressed by the participants in the decision.

APPOINTMENT OF WORKS DIRECTOR

In November 1984 Jim Bloom was appointed works director at Cloth-Dyer from a sister plant where he had experience of installing a colourshop. He noted that the Cloth-Dyer colourshop was becoming slow, and definitely behind on the computer side. At the same time there was also a directive from Group to reduce costs by 2 per cent per year. Paul Winch, a Group consultant researcher, joined the decision team and initially acted as chairman. Jim Bloom was of the opinion that, 'you've got to be certain in your own mind that it's a team decision that's being made and it's not influenced by one particular person and that it is right for the business as a whole'. The main investment criterion was that they should have a system which would take the company forward into the future whilst providing an acceptable, but largely unknown, rate of return. The investment was required primarily to fulfil the needs of business in terms of colour performance, continuity of colour application and labour reduction.

EVALUATION COMMITTEE FORMED

In 1984 Paul Winch and Glyn Lloyd (production director), saw a brochure originating from a representative of a French colourshop manufacturer, CF. It was decided to form an evaluation committee to investigate the possibility of a replacement for the colourshop. Paul Winch and Glyn Lloyd looked to alternative suppliers to see what they had to offer. Cloth-Dyer had not generally been used to initiating investment decisions, this being left to their parent group. At this juncture both Paul Winch and Glyn Lloyd were working together as a team and without complications. Glyn Lloyd at that time was colourshop manager while Paul Winch led the evaluation team. Paul Winch had put in the last colourshop and also helped Jim Bloom put one in at a sister company of Cloth-Dyer. Mike Van also had many years in the business. The finance director, Rick Blunt, was new.

The first alternative to CF considered was a British company, Techcal. An important aspect of the operation of the original colourshop was to eliminate 'standards', a diluted dye in a 'standard' concentration. Dilution was originally necessary because the accuracy of scales and dispensation were not available prior to that. Accuracy of the dye strength was essential and concentrated dye could therefore not be controlled sufficiently so that it was mixed with inert white paste. The first colourshop got rid of the standard completely and handled dyes in a highly-concentrated form. Jim Blunt and Paul Winch went to a machinery manufacturer's fair in Rotterdam. They also did a considerable amount of reading of journals and similar literature.

One problem of colourshop operation is that there are about forty dyes which are dirty and messy to dispense. CF solved this by an elegant method. In making colour for pastes, strong dye is diluted into standards – the early colourshop did away with standards and could deal with concentrated dyes. In the view of Paul Winch 'Techcal were still using standards and had a bad reputation'.

CF, the French firm, offered dye dispensation in concentrated form while Techcal offered only standards. Cloth-Dyer, following on from the principle established in the old colourshop, was trying to retain dispensation in concentrated form. Paul Winch and Glyn Lloyd subsequently visited CF in the spring of 1985.

INSTALLATION OF NEW CENTRAL COMPUTER

An Associated Industries-wide decision was made to install a central computer, the Systemic. As the colourshop decision involved purchasing a computer the Systemic decision laid down important constraints and requirements of compatibility for Cloth-Dyer in the colourshop decision.

The Systemic was installed in Worcester about October 1985. Numerous talks about ways of holding information, what should be held on the machine and where the recipes should be held, took place. Rick Blunt, the finance director, noted, 'there was never anything written down because the users could never specify what they wanted, they just wanted a colourshop that was going to work, and there was not a specification on the information technology side'. Reviewing the feasibility of using Associated's central computing resources was generally estimated to have taken about six months. The Cloth-Dyer evaluators and Paul Winch had an engineering background and was the only company with any information technology or computer-aided manufacturing knowledge.

After reviewing CF, Paul Winch and Glyn Lloyd went to see Victor Woll in Germany, a well-known established company in the field. Victor Woll's system incorporated sampling and batch production so that samples could be taken without disturbing production. Consistent reproduction of colour batches from samples is very important in the colourshop. Unfortunately the Victor Woll valve was not very accurate, but the idea was good and subsequently incorporated into the system specification.

ANALYSIS OF OPTIONS

In autumn 1985, the need for a new colourshop was formally accepted into the capital investment budget. This now established the Cloth-Dyer replacement on the agenda of forthcoming capital expenditures within the Group. About this there was no dispute: the issue was which machine.

Early 1986 saw ST, another German company, come on to the

scene. ST make textile-printing machines and were well known to people in Cloth-Dyer. ST wished to diversify their operations and commenced production of colourshops. Paul Winch considered the ST machine to be unsatisfactory for a number of reasons which he enumerated in detail: (1) fundamentally poor engineering design, (2) it went against the Cloth-Dyer principle of using concentrated dye rather than standards, (3) the software was incompatible with existing systems, (4) it was twice the price of competitors and (5) the perceived arrogance of the company's personnel in refusing to accept customers' requests.

Paul Winch thought the ST sales staff overbearing and favoured either CF, or the British supplier, Techcal, despite its poor reputation, because it was the most software compatible and recipes could then be stored in the group mainframe computer. A lot of investment had already gone into the Systemic mainframe and other divisions were committed to it. Systemic was not IBM-compatible whereas the ST software was. The colourshop would have had to run independently of the Group with the ST machine. The software created for Cloth-Dyer would also be compatible with the Systemic mainframe.

In spring 1986 Glyn Lloyd, Paul Winch and Jim Bloom visited ST and Victor Woll. This visit confirmed previous impressions and Victor Woll was ruled out on the grounds of poor performance, obsolete design, and lack of confidence in the continuation of the software.

Paul Winch was generally considered to be technically very strong and had more or less made his decision before the ST machine came out. A split now opened up in the evaluation group, which had been working less and less cohesively, as Paul Winch now championed CF whilst Glyn Lloyd and Jim Bloom championed ST, the latter's main objection to CF being lack of communication. Jim Bloom and Glyn Lloyd despaired of the French firm (CF), which was run as a traditional family firm dominated by a father who could not, however, speak English. Objections were also mentioned by Paul Winch about ST involving overbearing attitudes and 'over-lavish entertainment'. Also entering into the fray were suggestions from the Group about the preferability to buy British, namely Techcal, Paul Winch's second choice.

There were now four potential suppliers, CF (France), Techcal (UK), Victor Woll (Germany) and ST (Germany). No supplier exhibited both engineering excellence and acceptable, compatible advanced software. Few evaluation documents were prepared by late autumn 1986 – a specification was drawn up by Jim Bloom regarding the machine but a formal report was never produced.

Victor Woll was rejected in the summer of 1986, on the grounds of performance, obsolete design, and lack of confidence in continuance of the software which was produced by, according to Paul Winch, a very charming but elderly gentleman who ran a mysterious software house. Jim Bloom maintained a requirement that in ten years' time they were going to have somebody available who can service or develop it. His opinion, and a correct one in retrospect, was that Victor Woll could not ensure that. Victor Woll was taken over in 1987.

This was the first time the issue of supplier reliability was raised and is one factor in which the attachment of differing weights subsequently heightened the already increasing contention amongst decision-makers. Supplier service and back-up support is thus one of the two or three axes around which this decision revolved.

Techcal was dismissed due to the poor quality of its engineering and the doubts about the continued survival of the company. It was also felt that they bought in too many parts and had become assemblers rather than manufacturers, so extending the supply chain. Techcal was ultimately taken over. The grapevine informed Cloth-Dyer that communication was the problem with CF, nobody was ever in when they were telephoned and nobody except the son spoke English.

One possible solution was to buy the CF hardware and adjust the software as necessary. The CF machine was better engineered than ST in Paul Winch's view. ST operated with a pump. If this pump failed the whole machine was out of commission. Furthermore, software was incompatible with the Systemic mainframe. Paul Winch further noted that ST had no thought about service back-up, but this view was not supported by Glyn Lloyd. The software question became a considerable bone of contention. Paul Winch noted that, 'when you build automation equipment you concern yourself with what you do when it fails and you don't bother with what you do when it works, that's easy, any fool can see that'.

An additional element in the decision was that some of the existing printing machines were ST models and could easily be integrated with a new ST machine because of common computer controls. This would have been more difficult with the other systems. ST, along with CF, had this. This enabled the shorter production runs for the top end of the market to be printed more quickly, and made it possible to get more out of the printing machines.

Jim Bloom's support for the ST system was also based upon the management experience available. How to manage the whole thing was important. Jim Bloom said:

we'd got a company here with a lot of new, inexperienced people and the last thing we wanted to do was to take on a project where you've got to put in a lot of development time and cost yourself if you've got people who are inexperienced.

One or more members of the evaluation team saw five ST system installations, two in the UK, the rest in Europe, spending one year doing so.

Paul Winch's objections to the ST were so great that his eventual choice was to put CF first and Techcal second. No supplier or solution was optimum but a decision had to be made as the original colourshop was showing its age.

After visiting ST, Glyn Lloyd, Jim Bloom, Paul Winch and Keith Burne (the works engineer) set up a scoring system on all four options. According to Glyn Lloyd, ST came out best but Paul Winch still was not convinced. It was Glyn Lloyd, who regarded himself as championing the project, who noted that 'Paul Winch had influenced one or two others to believe that it wasn't the right move'. The Group, without Paul Winch, then took another look at ST in Germany. Glyn Lloyd thought that Paul Winch and Jim Bloom 'were really going for CF and Techcal'.

The Cloth-Dyer management coalition was by now acting more or less independently of the Group consultant researcher (Paul Winch), forcing him either to support them or extricate himself from the team. Paul Winch effectively left the decision arena at this point noting that he felt that 'he no longer had anything to offer'. Rick Blunt saw this event more in terms of Paul Winch 'walking off the project because he was technically overruled by Jim Bloom'. In effect he was asked to leave by Jim Bloom. Paul Winch wrote to the Group managing director putting his point of view.

Glyn Lloyd saw Paul Winch 'as having "a bee in his bonnet" and worrying too much about what would happen if pipes burst'. In comparing the options Glyn Lloyd and Jim Bloom visited each supplier at least twice. As Glyn Lloyd noted: 'you tend to forget what you see on the previous visit. It's only when you go to four different companies with four different machines you see what they can do!'

Glyn Lloyd maintains that Paul Winch and Jim Bloom had a meeting with the Group managing director without him. The managing director told them to go away and rethink the decision, after which (summer 1986) Jim Bloom then supported Glyn Lloyd on the ST machine. Since the order to purchase was submitted Glyn Lloyd testifies that Paul Winch had said to him that he had made the right choice after all.

Carlton Hickson, managing director of the owning group, Associated Industries, took a broader view and opted for the ST system because he was concerned with the reliability and integrity of the company and being able to communicate with the supplier easily. What was not so immediately apparent was the fact that Carlton Hickson already had good relationships with the very senior people at ST. They didn't have that much to do with the colourshop but at least he knew them and could complain if necessary. ST had put a colourshop into Laura Ashley during 1986, receiving singular lessons in both printing and the art of dealing with the customer, their 'intellectual adjustments' as Paul Winch termed it.

One other point for going with ST was that if the machine failed the suppliers assured Cloth-Dyer that it could be repaired 99 per cent of the time within forty-eight hours. As the old machine had only residual scrap value that could be kept as back up. For somebody in the colourshop for thirty years a consistent picture was not emerging. CF was superior in engineering terms but the time taken for the repair of machine failure was highly variable and therefore uncertain. Engineering excellence was traded for perceived reduced down-time. The ST was actually thought to be a more robust machine and potentially more reliable, but less 'elegant'. Towards the end of 1986 a lengthy report was written by Glyn Lloyd arguing for the ST option. ST came out to be nearer the ideal than the other two.

The report went to Carlton Hickson who, according to Glyn Lloyd 'would pick holes in it' requiring some answers. Three versions of the report were written during these iterations but the key points of comparison raised by the report are summarized in Table 8.1.

Rick Blunt considered the deal with ST to be good. In negotiating over prices the Associated Industries manual on foreign bidding was followed. Rick Blunt said that they asked ST for a quote in both Pounds and Deutschmarks, but ST made the mistake of taking the rate of exchange on the day of the quote. 'We were able to take the most favourable rate, which was in pounds, when it came to our bid!'

THE SHIFT TO QUALITY

Following the appointment in early 1986 of Carlton Hickson as the new Group chairman there was a shift in Group strategy away from risky investments to emphasizing investment in more known and established markets. This investment policy was also seen as consistent with the policy to move 'upmarket' as regards products and

Table 8.1 A chronology of events and subdecisions during the colourshop investment decision at Cloth-Dyer

Date	Event	Subdecision
November 1984	*Paul Winch enters process as consultant-researcher with disparate views*	
	This introduces a degree of bargaining into the decision that did not previously exist	
End 1984	GL and PW review brochure on CF system	
	JB appointed works director	
Spring 1985	*Evaluation committee formed*	SD1
	Colourshop Systems Evaluation committee now comprises Paul Winch, Glyn Lloyd and Jim Bloom. Review of alternatives to purchase completed and decision to purchase a new system confirmed	
	Alternative suppliers sought for evaluation	
	CF system seen in France by PW and GL	
Summer 1985	Paul Winch and Glyn Lloyd visit Victor Woll in Germany	
	Engineering specification improved as a result of the trip. Also visit to Techcal in UK	
	Paul Winch wants Rick Blunt's support	
October 1985	*Installation of new central computer*	
	Need for compatibility strengthened	
Autumn 1985	*Replacement colourshop budgeted for in following financial year*	SD2
	Rick Blunt appointed finance director	
Spring 1986	Glyn Lloyd, Jim Bloom and Paul Winch visit ST and Victor Woll. Victor Woll considered obsolete and deleted from the list	
	Techcal also dismissed from considerations	
Summer 1986	*The shift to quality*	
	Paul Winch submits report with preference for CF. Report not accepted, Paul Winch withdraws	
Autumn 1986	*Authorization of the ST option*	SD3
	First capital expenditure voucher prepared	
	Rewritten six times	
to		
Summer 1987	Voucher finally submitted to Group Level and accepted	
Spring 1988	*Machine installed*	SD4

markets. Hence, we can see that there was a change in company policy towards quality, which tended to favour the ST option.

AUTHORIZATION OF 'ST' OPTION

The decision to purchase the ST option was authorized in late summer 1986 by Mike Van. The capital expenditure voucher was prepared after the decision was made.

COMMENTARY

This decision shows a process starting somewhat reluctantly but gathering momentum over time. Formation of the evaluation committee brought the key participants together to consider options; the availability of suppliers soon gave four possibilities.

There was an assumption on the part of Cloth-Dyer that the business was to continue in its present format and markets. The company did not have a strategic plan but had a three-year rolling operational plan. The 'kitchen' equipment is vital to the company; without it they could not carry on with their basic operations.

Initially the specifications of the machine were not defined. Instead, there was searching to find a machine (that is, search for solutions) which fulfilled, as yet, unspecified requirements. Each participant had a set of preferences not necessarily the same as others. As the requirements were not explicit there was general agreement over the need for replacement but no agreement on the specification of a machine. Hence, the decision displays a fairly high degree of disparity over solutions.

The evaluation team were expressing preferences for either, (1) engineering excellence, or (2) software compatibility for group integration. Disparities started to emerge, coalitions were being sought, positioning within the organization was being established. Mike Van was only a temporary managing director and someone would ultimately be recruited to fulfil that role on a more permanent basis. It is worthwhile to note that ST approached Cloth-Dyer via Mike Van who put them in touch with Glyn Lloyd, and not Paul Winch the evaluation team leader. ST's knowledge that Cloth-Dyer were in the market for a new colourshop was put down to 'the grapevine'; as the case shows there were quite a number of informal contacts between Cloth-Dyer and ST, especially through Mike Van.

It is also noteworthy how little input financial calculations of rates of return on investment played. Instead the decision was fundamentally made on the notion that Cloth-Dyer was dealing with a reputable company with whom relations had been built up. Technical constraints of being able to do the job were there, of course, but even that fell by the wayside to a great extent once it was known that 'the boss' had chosen ST.

In addition to the computation strategy, the process demonstrates strong bargaining and judgement and, in the end, some inspiration, especially as the local management wrested control of the decision away from the head offices' consultant researcher. A potential political impasse was resolved by the dissenter, Paul Winch, withdrawing as an active participant. In this sense, disparities were resolved.

THE CHRONOLOGY OF EVENTS AND SUBDECISIONS

Using a similar chronological analysis for this decision as was used in the previous Medical Supplier decision we can identify the principal subdecision and events as summarized in Table 8.1.

Event: consultant researcher enters decision process

The consultant from headquarters, Paul Winch, entered with a number of different ideas and questioned many of the assumptions held by the local management. The main problem arising from this was the disparity introduced into the process since participants were not sure where he stood on the issue.

However, these disparities visibly increased the search for options as possible compromises were sought. This exemplifies the way in which disparities can increase learning.

Subdecision one: evaluation committee formed

Formation of a committee is often a key decision in decision-making since it is through such arenas that interests are voiced. A committee also serves to register an organization's recognition of an issue.

Membership of committees can be critical in determining the course of a decision. The key functional managers, the managing director, finance director and works director were directly involved. Most significant was the interjection of a consulant-researcher from headquarters.

Event:　installation of new central computer

The need for compatibility was strengthened by the new computer system at headquarters. From the viewpoint of economy and central control compatibility became an increasingly important issue.

Subdecision two:　replacement colourshop budgeted

This subdecision registered the colourshop as a necessary investment in the budget of the corporation. Registration of the need for the colourshop replacement had already taken place within the corporate headquarters. The placing of the investment within the capital budget formalized the issue within the company.

Event:　the shift to quality

There was a change in the strategy of the company to emphasize the importance of quality standards. This reinforced the appreciation of the colourshop decision as vital to the survival of Cloth-Dyer. This event illustrates the importance of achieving a strategic fit between the definition of a single decision issue and the stream of decisions that makes up the strategy of the organization.

Subdecision three:　authorization of the ST option

The board agreed to the purchase of the colourshop ST machine. The withdrawal of the headquarters consultant-researcher left the local management free to come to a conclusion quite rapidly and gain approval.

Subdecision four:　implementation of choice

The machines were purchased and installed and put into operation with little problem.

Learning

This turned out to be a high learning decision. This organization had operated in a stable market for over a decade, protected by the umbrella of a large coporate headquarters and with a relatively fixed technology.

The decision to renew the organization's core technology was seen as highly consequential and rare. Learning obviously took place in the technical sense of gaining knowledge about the changes that were occurring in the industry. Understanding of the core technology had been maintained to some extent by informal means but now management had to commit resources.

The decision involved foreign suppliers and the management came to have considerable contacts with these companies. The management of Cloth-Dyer found that having to make a major deal, satisfactorily in their eyes, with a foreign company represented a major breakthrough in their experience.

Finally, learning also was gained in terms of Coth-Dyer's relationships with their parent group. The intervention of the consultant, experienced as he was, was not altogether a happy event. However, by keeping the option they thought best the local management appeared to gain in self confidence.

9 Water Company: the filtration plant investment decision

This chapter presents another detailed case of an investment decision, this time in a Water Company. The decision was to invest in a major new type of water-treatment plant. It was a decision that scores highly in terms of reaching objectives and quite high for learning and provides a useful comparison to the decisions in Electronics and in Cloth-Dyer in that it illustrates decision-making in a more complex organization that had to respond to a number of different and sometimes conflicting institutional norms. The era is the lead up to privatization in the water industry, although the issue began to show itself long before such ideas had entered the arena of British politics.

SETTING

In the nineteenth century the development of public water, drainage and sewerage works was one form of the first major public works and came to have a major impact upon improving health by virtually eliminating the epidemics of disease that plagued the rapidly-growing early Victorian cities. Each village, town and city raised money to finance its own waterworks which became a source of local pride.

Over time amalgamations took place, but local water boards maintained an autonomy and culture of their own, taking pride in developing expertise in the solution of local problems. In general, however, the task of the water industry as a whole was interpreted in terms of ensuring a reliable supply of clean water. Issues to do with acid rain and pollution arising from the accumulation of agricultural chemicals had not yet arisen and neither had the escalation in costs due to these problems and the general problems of providing for an ever-increasing demand for water.

In 1974 the water industry in Great Britain underwent a major reorganization to coincide with the changes in the organization of local government. The general ideology of this reorganization was co-ordination and rationalization which was to be achieved by creating bigger units. Within England and Wales these new units became the ten regional water authorities. Each authority was given responsibility for water supply, waste and sewage treatment and controlling pollution of the rivers in its area.

In line with the other new authorities, Water Company was formed in 1974 out of the amalgamation of a number of previously separate water boards run by various city and town councils. Internally, seven regional divisions were created, these divisions tending to be formed around the boundaries of the old water boards hence bringing with them their separate traditions, histories, know-hows and loyalties.

The Board itself had twenty-five members, twelve appointed and thirteen elected. The structure is shown in Figure 9.1.

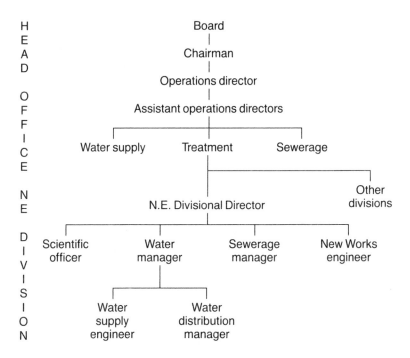

Figure 9.1   Water Company: organization chart of pre-1983 structure

THE WATER QUALITY ISSUE

Following a divisional review sent to the authority's chief executive in the 1970s the north-east divisional water manager, and his colleagues, saw water quality as likely to become a significant problem in the future. The review highlighted the possibility that the division was in danger of not achieving World Health Organization (WHO) and European Community (EC) standards for water quality.

A number of incidents reinforced the importance of the quality issue. Domestic customers were becoming more vociferous; one Monday morning, for instance, the water manager found a contingent of housewives at his office door angrily presenting washing that they claimed had been made dirty by the water. A major industrial user of water, a textile manufacturer, also started complaining about spoilt production. These events were sporadic and no obvious pattern to them could be found.

The case concerns investment in a new water-treatment plant at Brum. The plant was contained within the old north-eastern division which, in a 1980s reorganization, became part of the larger northern division supplying 1.2 million customers of which Brum supplied some 200,000 customers.

The eventual expenditure was £12m spread over a few years. To provide a comparative scale for this project the mid-1980s capital expenditure levels were approximately £120m per year divided approximately into £15m for new demands and growth, £70m for asset replacement and £35m for improvements.

The original Brum works was a simple filtration water-treatment plant dating back to the 1930s comprising eighty-five pressure filters. These are steel tanks holding sand and gravel which filter the water, after a crude straining and chlorination, prior to distribution. The overall capital investment decision process involves the effecting of a number of changes in this existing plant plus the development of a new water-treatment process nearby in order to cope with a number of environmental problems that were adversely affecting water quality.

In the 1970s the water manager called upon the division's chief chemist to look at the possibility of devising a treatment process that could deal with quality problems. Traditionally investment priorities had been defined in terms of ensuring reliability of supply and sewage treatment with little thought being given to investment in quality. At this time there was a big investment programme in building new transmission pipelines and in improving the old ones and moving towards a regional water grid. This was the time of the emergence of the notion of a national water grid, comparisons being made in the minds of the public and politicians with the national electricity grid. The development of a regional grid was accelerated by the drought of 1976. Droughts figure large in the thoughts of water engineers; the water authorities have a statutory duty to ensure a supply and droughts can interfere in this objective.

Other performance factors were beginning to intervene, however. At this time there was increasing political concern to reduce the escalation in costs of local services including water. The issue was increasingly becoming cost reduction.

BRUM MODERNIZATION

Thought was also being given to the modernization of the existing Brum filtration plant. This had become urgent because of increased demands upon the water supply and because the existing filters were having difficulty in coping with an increase in deposits in the water which were causing the sand filters to clog up. There was also an awareness that the plant was expensive to run in terms of labour costs.

Consideration was given to the scrapping of Brum and building a new facility but investment budgets were now being cut. It was decided to invest £1.25m in modernizing the plant with the hope of achieving some manpower reduction through modifications to the filters and the introduction of automated valves. The division supply engineer commented: 'We realized that it was beneficial in reducing manpower but was not doing anything for the quality of the product'.

The general investment philosophy favoured rehabilitation of existing plant rather than replacement. This gave rise to a problem of comparing costs. The general criterion was that internal rate of return had to achieve 5 per cent on new projects. Net returns, the nearest thing to profit in a water authority, were used to pay off loans.

BUILDING OF THE PILOT FLOTATION PLANT

The water manager gave the decision to build a radically new flotation treatment plant at Brum an impetus when he formed a strategy group to examine the overall strategy of treatment in the south-western division. The group comprised: the supply engineer, the chemist, the works engineer, the district manager and the maintenance engineer.

In the late 1970s this strategy group sent a divisional review to the board, and to the then chief executive, highlighting the need for improved water treatment to achieve WHO and EC standards. The water manager gave the divisional chemist the brief to look at a treatment process which would produce satisfactory water throughout the year as defined by WHO and EC standards.

The water manager was generally seen as a forceful character who had strong divisional loyalty and commanded considerable respect from divisional engineers. He retired during the course of this decision process.

There continued a steady deterioration in the raw waters coming from the moors, one unconfirmed theory linking this to acid rain leaching out aluminium and other salts from the peat. The level of complaints about water quality rose commensurately; although easy to recognize it was a rather more difficult problem to solve.

The existing technology

The existing method to treat this problem was to sediment raw waters in reservoirs and then filter at the Brum plant prior to chlorination and supply to consumers through the water mains.

Manganese was getting through to supply because the Brum filters, built in the 1930s, were no longer up to the increasing demands made upon them. The problem of discoloration was exacerbated by the moorland water of the region, particularly in the northern division. This water tends to be 'thin', that is, it contained a small number of particles which takes a long time to settle out as opposed to 'thick' water which is more common in the river basins of the South of England which is more laden with particles.

The filtration plant at Brum was good at removing impurities caused through solid particles but could not remove discoloration which needs changes in the pH value, that is, the acid-alkaline balance, of the water to effect treatment. Moorland water is acidic and has a low pH; Brum could filter at this pH and remove iron and aluminium salts but not manganese. For this the water had to be made alkaline (high pH) through the addition of lime. Hence effective removal of discoloration requires two stages of processing.

Water quality as a problem that needed attention came to be recognized more forcefully in the summer droughts. Market research for the authority showed that customers paid great attention to the aesthetic appeal of water; even though some water looked unappealing it could be perfectly healthy. Further, increasing use of automatic washing machines made coloration more noticeable since clothes could become marked.

Weather also had an effect. As the new works engineer put it: 'in dry years we had problems with virtually all our single stage plants'. This was first noticed at divisional level but was discussed at region. He continued:

> certain scientific elements were regionalized and this was a scientific problem. Moving from a problem towards a solution would have involved an awful lot of people recognizing it was a real problem and that it required additional monies to solve it. But it is not a constant problem as it peaks in certain months, goes away and may not recur for two years.

A favoured, but unproven, theory attributed the increase in these salts to the extra leaching caused by the increase in acid rain due to car exhaust and power-station emissions.

If not removed, manganese tends to settle out in the main pipelines which creates a problem if there is a reversal of the flow when the manganese becomes dislodged and travels through to the consumer. The discoloration increased from an average of 15 hazen (the standard measure of discoloration) in 1976 to 130 in 1985, reaching a peak of 200 in that year. At low levels of hazen a marginal dose of aluminium sulphate coagulent would produce a certain amount of solids which the old Brum filters could cope with but the filters could not cope with such high hazen levels.

There was an increasing awareness that there was a real problem needing attention and that additional monies were required to solve it; it could not be 'operationalized out' of the system with existing funds, as the new works engineer observed, but:

> it took a little time to get this across to the authority that plants which had been operating successfully for fifty years were suddenly no longer OK. Reports were written to highlight the consumer problem. The problem was universally recognized and it needed to be solved. The decision then had to be made on how to solve the problem.

Flotation was being thought about as a solution. 'If it won't settle, make it float; quite simple logic but it takes a little while to come to that sort of decision and to change the direction of thinking', the new works engineer commented. With the help and advice of the water research council it was determined to construct a new pilot treatment process nearby.

As time passed by, consumer complaints increased. According to the supply engineer: 'The investment decision depends on how long the complaints go on and how sustained is the objection to this'.

MORATORIUM ON CAPITAL PROJECTS

A moratorium on capital projects was imposed in the late 1970s due to governmental restrictions on capital expenditure. Nevertheless, a pilot plant was built and operationally assessed. As the degree of the water quality problem varied through the year, the effect of at least a complete year's rainfall cycle had to be assessed and any 'knock-on effects' further down the supply and distribution system considered. The pilot study was crucial in determining the process to use. At this point division and Head Office scientific staff were at odds, the latter believing the flotation process to be too elaborate. The organization was moving from traditional methods of filtration to a chemical engineering process. This was new and innovative.

At this time project proposals tended to arrive at Head Office for approval in a fairly advanced state of design. Head Office held back their support for the flotation method but division was strongly in favour of it. This forward thinking was generally seen to be typical of the water manager and such was his personality that he took other people along with him. As the new works engineer said: 'It is not the Head Office senior management we are talking of here but the scientific community. Consequently, a lot of the decision-making had been around concerning which process to use, polarizing the division and HO'. This comment indicates the enthusiasm with which new technical ideas could get developed within divisions. Divisions could, in a sense, compete with each other to be first in a new method of treatment.

This competitive orientation was exacerbated by the relative independence of divisions. Some went for other types of treatment, the type of treatment used depending heavily upon the beliefs of the scientific officers and the traditions in each division.

During this period the investment priorities emphasized the use of local storage facilities, essentially a way of trying to overcome the investment constraints. But the water quality problem was becoming increasingly acute.

USE OF EXISTING RESERVOIR FOR SEDIMENTATION

By the early 1980s the water quality situation became more desperate, especially since a prominent local textile manufacturer, supplying to Marks and Spencer, was becoming vocal in its complaints following a significant loss of production attributed to manganese deposits. Urgent action was required but the division was under close financial constraints. It was proposed that, as a palliative, an impounding reservoir could be used for 'chemical dosing' so that some of the precipitation took place in Victoria Reservoir, another reservoir downstream in the supply line. Chemical dosing is the adding of chemicals to the water to cause precipitation of unwanted impurities. This could, however, only be a short-term solution until the new plant came into operation since the reservoir would fill up with deposits.

DESIGN OF THE FLOTATION TREATMENT PLANT

During the two-year pilot plant assessment a water treatment strategy for the division was produced by the water manager and his staff. This report made a first attempt at prioritizing the various projects suggested. Priorities were identified relative to:

(a) Public perception of the water they were receiving; complaints were the main measure of whether this was being achieved.
(b) The extent to which the authority was meeting WHO standards or not; reasonably objective tests exist for these standards.
(c) The impact of a new works upon consumers by trying to assess the number of people who would benefit.

It was this strategy and the subsequent specific Brum strategy that was submitted to Head Office in the early 1980s. The scheme was eventually formally sanctioned two years later.

HEAD OFFICE EVALUATION

It took three years for Head Office to sanction the Brum investment and for construction to start. As the chief chemist commented: 'It's a hell of a long time . . . but nobody on the ground had much of an idea what was happening'. He also commented:

These were the days of the corporate management team and trying to involve everybody in the decision-making process so that you moved corporatively forward together. We tried to persuade as many different specialists, including ourselves, that we were doing the right thing. . . . As the project worked its way through there was a lot of side-lobbying, discussion, keeping people informed of what we were doing, presentation, persuasion, even though the formal decision was not being made at that stage, the way was being prepared. Because it was a bottom-up approach there was a divisional alliance to persuade the authority to support our division against other divisions.

In the early stages of thinking about flotation technology it was viewed as a scientific problem. Head Office was aware of it because the scientific personnel had strong divisional affiliation. Traditionally various divisions had tended to experiment fairly independently of one another concerning new treatments. In the opinion of a number of people at division it was the job of the director of operations to co-ordinate such activities but he was seen to be weak. If people needed information or discussions with Head Office they tended to by-pass him and go to the assistant director of operations.

A major problem between the division and Head Office concerned the issue of 'sizing'. In the early 1980s agreement was reached for the process group in the north-eastern division to start designing a flotation plant. Initially this was not a detail design but an outline of the three stages, determining the relative size of units and types of ancillary equipment. This was a departure from the approach used previously when designs were more or less bought in after putting out a tender document giving equipment manufacturers the required performance specifications. This approach had given problems in the past; according to the water manager there were plants commissioned nearly a decade earlier that were still not working to specification.

One option considered during this process was the possibility of scrapping the original Brum plant. However, there were pressures from Head Office to use the existing site because of the investment made in the previous modernization. Hence the 'fresh start' option never got beyond 'back of envelope' calculations. The existing Brum plant was therefore incorporated into the new design as a third stage to a new two-stage treatment plant. The water treatment would now go through two stages in the new plant of adding chemicals and then allowing the impurities to rise to the surface in tanks where a constantly reciprocating wiper would sweep back and forth pushing the coagulent containing the manganese impurities over the lip of the tank to be drained away. The purified water would run out of the bottom of the tanks to go through a preliminary filtration before piping to the original Brum plant half a mile away for final filtration.

One question considered by the study during this time was the question of the size of the plant to be built. It had been thought appropriate to take the total amount of water produced by the collection system and add 25 per cent as a basis for determining size. By the time the overall scheme was presented to the board for approval, it was decided, mainly on the insistence of the assistant operations director, to increase this margin to 33 per cent, overruling division's objections. It was argued that the increase in yield was desirable to permit a greater moving around of water through the water grid which was being developed at the same time. As the supply engineer said: 'From a cost point of view it pushed it up quite a lot'.

Division were also pressing for a three-stage plant, Head Office for a one stage. The supply engineer commented:

> It probably took a couple of years before they were satisfied that three stages were appropriate. Even today there is still some doubt in people's minds regarding the process. There is no doubt in anyone's minds in division. Another division went for a two-stage process but are now quickly rethinking.

BOARD SANCTIONS INVESTMENT

In January 1982 the main board sanctioned the spending of £13m on the construction of a flotation plant at Brum but there followed a difficult process of evaluation with Head Office, especially over the question of sizing.

The corporate planning manager who had recently joined the organization came to review the project proposal, as he put it, 'late in the gestation stage. They (the divisional staff) thought they did not need to involve me'. His concern was to take a corporate view of any investment proposals and in particular to see how they fitted into an overall plan for the authority. The possibility of privatization was now being talked about and the authority was concerned to put itself in a position to cope with such an eventuality.

The corporate planning manager tended to see divisions, the north-eastern division in particular, as been driven by local concerns and, in the case of this project, by strong personalities. The assistant operating director normally vetted investment proposals and this one went round several meetings and discussions involving both Head Office and division staff before being passed to the board. Due to the evaluations the operating director and his team had at Head Office, they considered the capacity of the new plant to be too small. The development of the regional grid meant that no division would in future be able to plan for its own requirements only, and every major proposal would have to take account of the possible need to supply other divisions.

The corporate planning manager saw the process as involving 'healthy and useful discussion of views', a feeling that was generally echoed by others involved, even those at division who had become frustrated by the hold-ups. This investment had a strong effect in bringing about changes to the investment procedures following the 1980s reorganization which merged the divisions to form larger units. A more thorough project appraisal scheme was introduced involving three stages, an initiation stage, an evaluation stage and a sanctioning stage. The idea was to prevent proposals getting too far in the design stage, as this one had, before the alternatives and corporate implications had been fully explored.

Problems in obtaining planning permission for the new building and plant emerged at this time, especially since building the new plant meant using land currently in use by allotment holders, although the land belonged to Water Company. The land had been leased to allotment holders and repossession gave rise to a local enquiry. Residents overlooking the plant claimed loss of amenity. Resolution of these disputes took about one year culminating in a redesign of the lime kiln of the plant.

Detailed design was completed within three years after sanctioning although the operations section and development sections disagreed as to the extent of design detail necessary for the automatic electronic control systems. This probably stems partly from the change to Water Company doing the detailed design rather than external consultants.

Contracts for treatment plant were being placed. Building proper commenced two years later and was completed after a further two years. The final cost was approximately £12m. The original estimated cost was £6 million. Even by this time no decision had been made on what was originally going to be the third stage. Head Office was rethinking the third stage and held this in abeyance. The third stage was not included in the original scheme but mains replacement/refurbishment was, as well as the cost of service reservoirs. The third stage decision process revolved around the replacement of eighty-five smaller filters with ten or so larger filters against refurbishment of existing assets.

COMMENTARY

This was a decision of great consequence in terms of Water Company's public image and relationship with the company's emergent strategy. Although as a public utility and having a virtual monopoly in its area, Water Company could not ignore its relationships with its customers.

The decision did not rate high in terms of concern with failure since the filtration plant, though an important investment and innovation, would not have had a tremendous detrimental effect upon the whole organization if it failed technically or financially. There was great concern with strategic fit, an aspect that grew in importance as the decision proceeded. Initially it was the problem of ensuring that the water quality was improved that dominated the decision, but strategic fit became increasingly appreciated as important in terms of the development of a water grid and then in terms of the need to shift the concern from the more local divisional problem, with the attendant historical loyalties, to a company-wide concern.

We see the decision issue being given an impetus by the combination of a problem (water quality) and the inspiration of the divisional water supply manager who had an interest in the water filtration process. In this impetus we see an interaction between an interest (the manager), the existing organizational setting with its current ideology, strategy and structures, and outside events. In this way an issue is beginning to be appreciated and defined. The long duration of the decision means that we can see how definition of an issue can be an iterative process.

Performance norms emphasized preferences for reliability of supply and treatment, enshrined in the investment priorities of that time, but generally accepted the notion of divisional autonomy. The water supply manager is a key player, helping to define the issue and encouraging the search for solutions within a divisional framework, but in a large diverse organization which, over the duration of the decision, was actively trying to emphasize corporate rather than divisional norms. Hence, interest in the decision remained high amongst a number of key participants.

Uncertainties relating to this issue were fairly high and perhaps most important was the difficulty in achieving agreement as to the objectives of the decision. The question was partly whether the issue was about water quality, cost reduction or finding a use for a technical solution, namely, the flotation process. Management at divisional level became increasingly aware of the quality issue and this happened to match with a developing new technology, the flotation process, for water treatment. But corporate management, as indicated by the advent of a new planning manager, wanted increasingly to take a corporate view, spurred on to some extent by the impending water industry privatization.

Overall, the decision can be seen as an illustration of a garbage can process. The flotation process had been floating around for a long time in the organization. There were participants at divisional level pushing this solution. The water quality issue became a problem to which this solution could be attached. A choice was eventually made after a considerable mixing within the garbage can.

BUILDING SOLUTIONS AND SUPPORT

Overall, the decision rated fairly high on the judgement, computation and negotiation strategies. But it was a decision in which the chronology and the timing of events played a very strong part. It was a long decision, over nine years from the building up of the issue to the completion of the new plant; when the researchers left the site stage three of the overall project was still to be realized.

As a decision where timing plays such an important part it is useful to see the building process as comprising a number of subdecisions which meld over time to produce the appreciation of the issue. A chronological summary is given in Table 9.1

Subdecision 1: the modernization of the Brum plant

The modernization of the Brum plant is an identifiable subdecision which takes as its primary premise the need to ensure reliability of water supply and the need to use existing plant as much as possible. This subdecision came out of the performance figures for the authority and the division and sets premises for future decisions in a commitment to keeping Brum going. Solutions were to be sought within the cost constraints which were increasingly to pervade this decision.

The expenditure of more than £1m to automate valves on the pressure filter shells since manning was at the pre-Second World War level was apparently a manning reduction decision but the main concern at this time was to ensure reliability of water supply and sewage treatment since Water Company has a legal obligation to fulfil these requirements. However, this subdecision set premises for the investment in general since it effectively eliminated the 'fresh start' option.

Subdecision 2: divisional strategy group formed

Although not involving the commitment of funds, the creation of a working group was an important subdecision because, through its membership, it is a significant step towards defining the interests of those who would become involved. It is also a significant commitment of managerial resources. Working group members bring with them their own norms, their own solutions and degree of support.

The creation of a strategy group was a divisional response to an increasing concern to think more strategically, especially as regards the problem of water quality which was coming more to the fore. The

Table 9.1 Chronology of subdecisions during flotation investment decision at Water Company

Date	Event	Subdecision
1974	*Norm change:* Water Company formed	
74	*Modernization of Brum*	
	PG's informal assessment of need to improve water quality	SD1
74/76	Investment priority: reliability of supply	
74	*Strategy group formed*	SD2
	Divisional review to board	
75/78	*Flotation pilot study*	SD3
	Increase in emphasis on water quality due to complaints	
	Problem is sporadic	
76/79	Preliminary design and evaluation. Flotation thought of as possible solution but disagreements between HQ and division	
76	*Norm change:* Moratorium on capital projects	
76/78	Water quality problem in NE division becoming more evident	
	Assessment of pilot	
76/81	Investment priorities emphasize local storage	
77	*Sedimentation as a palliative*	SD4
77/81	Quality situation now desperate	
78	Water treatment strategy produced by NE division	
79/83	*Design of treatment plant using flotation method*	SD5
	NE division strategy report. Proposal to board	
79	Planning objections	
	Norm change: The corporate view develops	
	Investment priority: water quality	
80/81	Size of plant in dispute	
Jan 82	*Board sanctions investment*	SD6
83	Construction starts	
	Norm change: Reorganization and new investment procedures	
84	Detailed plans completed	
83/84	Design of a parallel plant	
87	Awaiting decision re third stage	

setting up of such a group now sets norms as regards who would participate in future decisions and hence signalled the kinds of solutions that might be preferred since the flotation method was already a solution in the minds of some participants. It also set the organization on the road to finding a divisionally-inspired solution to what was to increasingly become an authority-wide problem. Formation of the strategy group had the effect of registering an issue in the organization and by defining the participants, preferences and solutions that would be accepted as appropriate to coping with that issue. Participation was heavily weighted towards the divisional level as was especially focused on the water supply manager who provided the inspirational force.

Subdecision 3: flotation pilot study

A pilot study for the flotation method was carried out and assessed over nearly two years. This helped to reinforce the flotation solution.

Norm change: moratorium on capital programme

This moratorium is an example of a change in the decision performance norms and imposed a pressure towards finding solutions that could be financed out of expenditure. The moratorium was but one way in which government was increasing pressure to control the expenditure of the public utilities such as the water authorities.

This outside influence helped to create the atmosphere in which it was seen as desirable to utilize the existing filtration plant rather than to replace it.

Subdecision 4: use of existing reservoir for sedimentation

This palliative measure was made as a way of coping with the delays imposed by the investment constraints and over disagreements with Head Office concerning the nature of the solution. This was a north-eastern division solution and again further reinforced the conviction for a flotation plant solution since this stop-gap measure clearly could not give a lasting solution.

Subdecision 5: design of flotation treatment plant

The design was allowed to go ahead even though the investment could not be guaranteed authorization in the early stages. Further, the design can be seen as a way of coping with the disagreements with

Head Office concerning the number of stages the plant should contain. At this stage the decision was essentially in a bargaining mode due to the disagreements between Head Office and division over the number of stages to use and the size of the plant. However, the act of designing the flotation plant actually further reinforced this as the solution and, in the end, made the move to the north-eastern division's three-stage solution as inevitable.

Norm change: the corporate view

The appointment of a new Head Office planning manager was indicative of a trend that had been gathering momentum for a number of years. The company's regional grid was an artefact of this trend; now the previously separate divisions were linked together necessitating more co-ordination between divisions. The reorganization of the 1980s, merging the eight divisions into four larger ones cemented this trend. Consequently, the corporate view came to be emphasized in the investment decision procedures and this investment was the first one to go through on such a corporate basis although it was too late for the change to a three-stage formal procedure.

Subdecision 6: board sanctions investment

The main change that eventually brought about the sanctioning of this investment was the change in the investment norms finally recognizing the importance of water quality. Once the overriding necessity to do something had been recognized, the division solution of building a three-stage flotation plant at Brum was accepted. In some respects, implementation had already started during the design stage and before sanctioning of the investment.

We see that the implementation of the decision is by no means the end of the story. Many issues still remain unresolved. The organization as a whole has revamped its structure and procedures for assessing investments, partly as a result of experience gained from this decision. The structure was aimed at reducing the old divisional autonomy and centralizing these kinds of decisions. At headquarters there was a definite feeling of a quantum change in procedures. Nevertheless, the Brum flotation decision set norms for other decisions to come.

Some views on effectiveness

Some general views as to the effectiveness of the decision were expressed by participants. Although the decision was seen to have taken too long, it was thought of as a generally satisfactory decision. The objectives of the decision were achieved in that the plant is working well and water quality objectives are being achieved.

The new flotation process was later used elsewhere in Water Company and so the Brum experiment is providing a useful prototype for evaluating further developments in the technology. The general feeling amongst the divisional managers was that a complete new works would have been the better option but they appreciated that the financial constraints of the late 1980s were too great to allow this. By combining the new flotation plant into the existing filtration plant it was possible to justify the capital expenditure in terms of using existing assets.

A major area of dispute concerned the size of the plant and the procedures used in evaluating the investment which, from the division's viewpoint, had been brought in too late and after a considerable amount of design work had been done, which then needed changing. But in the flotation plant at Brum investment was very instrumental in helping the organization to evaluate and improve the investment-decision process. In particular, post-audit procedures were introduced and a more conscious attempt to plan on a corporate basis.

10 Mainframe replacement in Society: decision SC

The decision to invest in a replacement mainframe computer at a major building society, Society, is a decision that, within our framework for considering decision effectiveness, is rated high in terms of reaching objectives and medium in terms of learning. This decision is presented here in some detail since it provides a contrast to the other in-depth cases already described. As we shall see, it is a relatively simple and straightworward decision, but one in which external influence played an important part.

SETTING

This investment decision eventually involved the commitment of £5.7m to purchase a new computer system for Society. The decision needs to be seen against the background of the merger between the two constituent organizations that came to form Society.

In the mid-1980s the Eastern and Western Building Societies merged to form Society. Eastern already had ICL computer systems and Western had Burroughs hardware (now called Unisys). As far as designing future systems was concerned this was clearly a 'break point' and an opportunity to rationalize, which 'rarely happens in the life of an organization', as Paul Bute, the General Manager of Computer Services, commented. It was seen as preferable for the two parts of what was now one organization to use the same system; while different systems are operating the sunk costs become very high, making rationalization difficult.

The two organizations had quite different cultures. Western was smaller, more local and more traditional in the sense that it espoused more clearly the mutual benefit dimension of building societies. Eastern was larger, more thrusting and liked to think of itself as a smaller version of the Abbey National, the only building society to take the opportunity under the changed financial services regulatory environment of the mid-1980s to leave behind its mutual-benefit status and become a for-profit bank.

A simplified organization chart is given in Figure 10.1 giving the key participants in this decision.

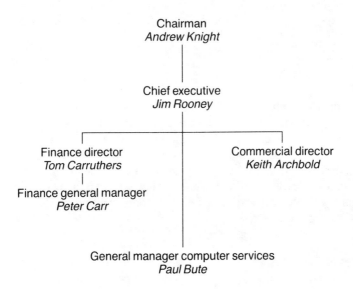

Figure 10.1   Organizational chart for Society

The ex-chief executive of Western, Jim Rooney, became chief executive of the new Society but was forced to retire during the course of this decision process. Officially this was for ill health reasons, but there was a view in Society that his retirement had been forced by the chairman, Andrew Knight. Jim was seen as a traditional 'building society man' who took a long-term view and was interested in developing a team environment: as the Computer Services Manager, Paul Bute, noted, 'I was sorry when he went. His going pushed us into confusion again and the new players haven't yet created their style and culture.'

At the time of the merger consultants were called in to advise on the computer systems. Western had used Burroughs equipment and Eastern had used ICL equipment; the recommendation of the consultants was to use Burroughs equipment throughout Society because they had a strong base within the building society movement. Hence,

Westham, the home of the Western Building Society, was developed as the main computing site with Easthampton, the headquarters of the Eastern Building Society, maintaining a back-up system in their new building.

The merger anticipated the changing face of building society operations due to the new regulatory environment for building societies created by government interest in encouraging competition and diversity in the financial sector. From providers of mortgages to providers of a whole range of other financial services, building societies were increasingly operating in a relatively dynamic environment where their traditional mortgage market had been attacked by the banks but where they could move into the selling of a wider range of general financial services. Management also predicted a greater number of transactions with traditional account holders and hence a greater need for on-site interactive terminals with direct links to the mainframe computer.

The Building Societies Act of 1986 gave building societies the legal right to undertake these wide-ranging activities and to become profit-making enterprises, with public limited liability company status, instead of formally retaining their mutual-benefit association constitutions which was the root of the great building society tradition of the nineteenth century when they acted as a means for thrifty working people to save towards the purchase of their homes. To participate in the expansion due to the foreshadowed opportunities, senior management recognized that the computer would play a key role. It is necessary to have a centralized data processing system so that quick and efficient information can be provided on the state of the hundreds of thousands of accounts. The information system was seen as central to producing new marketing strategies.

According to Paul Bute, there were a number of misconceptions concerning the existing systems in the organization at the time. Although Western had Burroughs hardware, the software had been produced for different purposes. Paul commented: 'the new society majored on ex-Eastern products so a redesign was necessary anyway but it took them six months to go through the cycle to realize that they had made the decision for the wrong reasons'.

As non-profit organizations, building societies are assessed in their task environments by a number of performance indicators. The key from the viewpoint of the members (account holders are technically members rather than customers due to the mutual-benefit constitution) is the interest rate given on deposits and charged on mortgages. As information is easily available to potential borrowers and depositors the extent to which a building society can deviate from prevailing market rates is limited. The tendency has been for building societies to attempt to differentiate themselves by varying the terms and conditions of accounts.

One of the key performance indicators is the expense ratio of a society. These are published annually by the Building Societies Association and are taken as an indication of the efficiency of operation of a society; the idea is that members deposit money for a purpose, entrusting the administration of it to the management, and the expense ratio is supposed to operate as a control on maladministration. The problem, however, within the more dynamic environment, is that of coping with competition and taking opportunities acting more and more as businesses rather than mutual-benefit associations, makes it difficult to keep to the expense ratio as a major criterion of performance. When innovation is required large investments have to be made for future but uncertain returns. In the short term this can increase the expense ratio.

THE CORPORATE PLAN

For a year after the merger senior management worked on a corporate plan. This was not completed until after the investment decision had been made but enough had been done to provide some guidelines for this decision. The lack of up-to-date computer facilities was already clear. Tom Carruthers, finance director, had seen a similar process in operation in a very large society, and another leading society was also doing the same thing:

> There was a sort of management feeling around Society that the merger had not been a success; it hadn't been put together properly and the organization didn't appear to have any particular direction. We realized that we were fundamentally deficient in computer systems; at that time we had a head of computer services who had been around the Eastern for 15 years and his thinking was antiquated. This was imperilling existing business because we were so backward compared to our peers. The existing computer services manager during this period retired and Paul Bute took over and since then we have gone from strength to strength.

Jim Rooney was chief executive of long service with the Western Building Society. Tom Carruthers and Paul Bute both joined Society from large rival societies; Paul had direct experience of using Burroughs computers and joined Society as an Assistant General

Manager with wide experience in the use of computers in building societies and was promoted to General Manager Computer Services upon the retirement of the previous manager:

> They went out into the market to headhunt me. I'm the only person in the country who had exactly the experience they wanted. I had run a complete building society operation for nine years, had installed Burroughs on-line systems and put in Olivetti branch terminals. I deal with Burroughs at all levels. I can quite happily ring up the managing director, although I would only do that if it was a big problem.

The vision of the future that the plan was trying to project, according to Tom Carruthers, was that of a financial services organization which would be 'just like the white goods market, not exactly as a financial supermarket since there would be sales staff and customers would come for a package of services, not just a mortgage but insurance, and so forth'.

DEFINITION OF THE COMPUTER PROBLEM

Soon after the merger the existing computer was increasingly being observed to be a bottle-neck as regards the development of future business plans. This potentially imperilled business planning because the systems were backward relative to the competition. There was, according to Tom Carruthers, 'too much bad feeling between the mainstream society and the computer department'. There were feelings that this situation had come about as a result of outdated thinking on the part of the existing computer manager; this person left the organization and Paul Bute was promoted.

During the corporate planning process, which had been initiated for the first time, the limitations of the computer system were further highlighted 'as woefully deficient' in the words of Tom Carruthers.

Then an event which gave the decision tremendous impetus occurred. The chief executive received a telephone call from the head of Burroughs UK stating that they could offer Society a good deal if it traded in its existing computers for the latest models. This call was followed up a week later by a letter proposing several options including the possibility of rental.

Burroughs had merged with Sperry to produce Unisys and had not been selling enough of its A15 models, the new generation mainframe machines. As Tom Carruthers said:

the deal was attractive in the sense that we were able to give the written down book value of the existing computers even though one of them was only a year old. This is a substantial fall-off so they were making an offer that effectively meant that we were getting one year's use of a mainframe paid for. Society is one of the main Burroughs sites in the UK but the parent US company wanted to see higher sales of the A15 in the UK.

Tom continued: 'the managing director of Burroughs UK telephoned our chief executive to offer a highly advantageous trade-in'. They had also approached six other institutions.

Paul Bute described these events:

It came out of the blue. With the Building Societies Act anything's a bit of a guess as to what capacity we needed. There was a rather garbled phone call from the chief executive of Burroughs to Jim Rooney about wanting to make an opportunity available to us. I said 'forget it' to Jim but they came back later through a letter and other phone calls and explained that they had four of the new A15 machines which initially they had wanted to use internally but were now prevented from doing so by his US headquarters; they now had to hastily find customers. The deal was for us to buy a machine or two and for them to offer a good trade-in price for the existing 7900s. Jim had no feel for how quickly we needed to change and was not conversant with opportunities that people like Burroughs offer. At that time they were very much into the 'sell boxes game'.

SOLUTION AND SUPPORT-BUILDING

Burroughs had indicated the urgency for a decision and asked for a reply in fourteen days. Society's chief executive delegated the job of investigating the proposal to Tom Carruthers and Paul Bute (who had not yet been promoted to General Manager of Computer Services). Although Paul Bute had been involved in the purchase of computer equipment before this was to be his largest deal so far.

In effect, the decision had to be made within ten days. Tom Carruthers spent most of the week upon calculations to determine the bottom-line profit, whether to purchase or lease, and the effect upon annual management expenses. The calculations assumed zero inflation, a five-year life for the machine, a discount rate of 5 per cent and management expenses increasing at 15 per cent per year.

A number of options were considered:

1 Keep the existing machinery and purchase a dual A15 for Westham, moving the existing B7900 to Easthampton for the back-up system. Then in 1991 replace the B7900 in Easthampton.
2 Buy one dual A15, keep one B7900 and at the end of 1987 scrap remaining B7900 moving entirely to A15s.
3 Take the Burroughs option and buy a dual A15 and a single A15 as offered.

Tom Carruthers stated: 'I worked the calculations through not just the A15 generation but also the A17 generation which is going to follow, taking into account trade in values and the need for compatibility'. Another important aspect was the predicted processing needs and Tom asked Paul Bute to reappraise the likely processing needs over the next two years. Urgency was provided by the need to have the machines in place by 31 March for tax reasons. Paul had direct contact with Burroughs, particularly with account manager, Ernest Cain, and between them they did most of the calculations: Ernest Cain did most of the negotiating up and down his organization and Paul Bute did likewise in Society whilst also maintaining close links with Burroughs; he had many years of experience in working with them at all levels.

Paul Bute said:

Although initially against the proposal, I was quickly convinced that it was the right thing to do. We were going to have to increase capacity in 18 months anyway. What we needed is flexibility both in terms of the equipment and its method of purchase. It was a natural progression; there was no possibility that we would change from Burroughs to another supplier. We got a bit off (about £0.25m) but our concern was to get it to a point where the top man in each organization could shake on a deal.

The most important factors taken into account in doing the calculations were impact upon current year's earnings and the effect on the operating cost ratio: As Paul said 'it was a judgement as to whether to hit expense in the current year due to purchasing the computer but to get a future reduction'. Also considered of importance was the fit with strategy reflecting the concern that a computer adapt to future possible changes on the types of service offered.

The question also arose as to whether the computer should be leased or bought. Burroughs were pushing the lease option; Paul Bute supported this since the terms were favourable and it gave flexibility for future changes. The rental plan allowed Society to pay about

25 per cent of the capital cost per year over five years, they paid 125 per cent of the cost but retained to use of the money for that time; it also permitted changing the machine after a certain time if so desired. Purchasing meant negotiating a buy-back price depending upon the market value at the time.

Tom Carruthers strongly opposed rental on the basis:

> that if people have leased mainframes they will tend to turn them over quicker. Buying gives you the discipline of trying to get usable life out of them. You need to buy more capacity than needed at the start of the four-year cycle to give capacity for expansion.

There was little uncertainty concerning the notion that the computer was needed to achieve the plans of the organization. The uncertainties that existed concerned the technical aspect of the extent to which changes were taking place in the computer field and some aspects of the financial calculations as to future costs. In particular, assumptions had to be made about the exchange rate between the pound and the dollar. In the end, as Paul Bute said, 'the real decision was made here in this office. Once I had the conviction that it was right the problem was to ensure the niceties were met.'

AUTHORIZATION BY THE BOARD

Paul Bute presented his paper to the board with a recommendation to purchase from Burroughs at a net price to be negotiated but not exceeding £5.7m. The board agreed. The rental option was put to the board but not accepted mainly, in Paul's eyes, due to financial considerations: 'Peter Carr, finance general manager and an old-time building society man, killed it. The philosphy is that you always buy and not go in for hire purchase. Tom was also sceptical of renting.' The overall time from the inception of this decision as a real live issue (when Burroughs approached Society) was three weeks.

COMMENTARY

The decision was seen as effective as measured by the extent to which the choice of computer met objectives and the final support was high having increased during the process. However, there was less satisfaction with the process due to the imposed time pressure. A fairly high amount of organizational learning occurred.

The chronology of subdecisions and events

Key outside event: the offer by Burroughs

This event, its timing, with the pressure for a quick decision injected by the 'special offer', suggests a considerable appreciation on the part of the computer supplier into the internal decision-making process of Society.

Subdecision 1: the appointment of Bute and Carruthers

A key subdecision is the appointment of Paul Bute and, to a lesser extent, Tom Carruthers to be in charge of the decision. The chief executive is not a computer person and needs to rely upon others to evaluate such a decision. Through the involvement of Paul Bute in this process the acceptance of the Burroughs option, in one form or another, seems almost inevitable. Appointment of people to become involved in a decision is often a key to unlocking particular solutions.

Subdecision 2: authorization of purchase

We see a complex technical decision being made largely upon the advice of the organizational expert in that field. He did not get his way, however, over the method of financing the deal where the financial view prevailed, in particular, the traditional building society ideology that you do not rent, you buy.

Definition of the issue

The change in the regulatory regime of building societies combined with the already-established trend of mergers and general reduction in the number of societies produced a more dynamic and heterogeneous environment. Technology was also changing very fast. Many societies had changed to on-line facilities in their branches and the mastery of modern high-powered computer systems was seen by many societies to be the key to future success.

An important step down the road of a growth and diversification policy was taken when Society was formed out of the East and West Building Societies. Structurally this gave rise to the need for rationalization and for the need to meld the previously separate identities.

The merger of the two constituent societies highlighted the need for a new computer system to integrate the two organizations. Uncertainty was low; the main problems were technical ones concerning the best system. There was never any real doubt as to the necessity of the new computer.

The was little in the way of disagreements over objectives since appreciation of the need for a new computer system had been growing over a couple of years. It was quite a highly-consequential decision, especially in terms of the possible impact upon the survival of the company.

At the beginning of the decision we see the main premises of the decision being formed. In terms of performance norms there is the need to achieve a good expense ratio but at the same time there was also an awareness that the regulatory environment was rapidly changing; the whole field was being opened up to competition and future, but uncertain, possibilities. What had been previously well-tried solutions for dealing with the minor uncertainties that used occasionally to ripple through the building society movement were no longer appropriate for the future. A major norm when considering a computer decision concerned the fact that Burroughs was a long-standing supplier to the organization and that the new chief executive was personally acquainted with the head of Burroughs UK. The appointment of Paul Bute with his Burroughs experience effectively pre-empted questioning of this premise.

STRATEGIES FOR SOLUTION AND SUPPORT-BUILDING

A fair amount of computation was conducted, especially concerning the impact of the new computer upon the critical variable of earnings; the payback method was used to some degree. The concern with quantitative factors reflects the definition of the issue in terms of achieving strategic goals of market growth through increasing the volume and diversity of business rather than with internal operating efficiency.

Judgement also reached an intermediate level in the process, drawing extensively upon the experience and track record of the participants and using qualitative information about product quality; concerns with morale, industrial relations and image figured very low.

Negotiation was low, reflecting the low level of disagreements and the negotiation that occurred centred around the buy/lease issue. Paul Bute was initially against the proposal to change the computer out of suspicion of the motives of Burroughs.

Inspiration played very little part mainly because the impetus for the decision came from the external computer supplier.

The decision was well supported by top management and the level of influential decision-makers within the hierarchy was quite high. The decision went to the board for final approval but this was a largely rubber-stamping operation since they acted upon the advice of the two main participants.

Table 10.1 A chronology of events during the mainframe replacement decision at Society

Date	Event	Subdecision
1/3/83	Merger of Eastern and Western Building Societies to form Society	
1985	Tom Carruthers (finance director), Paul Bute (general manager computer services), Keith Archbold (commercial director) and the chief executive officer were appointed	SD1
	Computer observed to be bottle-neck on expansion plans	
12/85	Burroughs UK need to sell 4 A15s on instructions from US head office	
1986	Building Societies Act	
1986	Working on Corporate Plan for 1988–92. Produced autumn 1986. Deficiencies of computer systems indicated	
4/2/86	Chief executive office received phone call from Burroughs (Unisys) offering special deal for trading in existing ICL machines for Burroughs. Decision required within 14 days	
10/2/86	Letter confirming offer. 14 days to run from date of letter	
11/2/86	Letter to Tom Carruthers and Paul Bute	
12/2/86–24/2/86	Both do computations; Paul Bute in conjunction with Ernest Cain of Burroughs	
18/2/86	Information Technology Committee meeting	
21/2/86	Paul Bute writes to board	
25/2/86	Board presentation and authorization	SD2
31/3/86	Delivery of computer	
4/86	Paul Bute becomes General Manager Computer Services	

The decision was taken in the short time of three weeks hastened by the pressure of the external supplier. No significant delays occurred and the decision proceeded in a straightforward and clear manner. One key outside event and two key subdecisions whose timing was critical during the process can be seen in Table 10.1

11 Appreciating decisions

Our attention now shifts from the detail of decision cases, illustrating the intricacies of organizational decision-making, to the question of whether there are discernible patterns in the processes to enable us to draw some more generalized conclusions about processes that might lead to making decisions more effective.

Table 11.1 summarizes the data that has already been presented in Table 3.3. This is done by concentrating upon those variables that appear to vary significantly across the five groups of decisions already created from the different combinations of the two effectiveness variables. The comparisions are made by means of a simple rating scale using, in the main, low, medium and high designations for variables that originally had numerical designations.

Four decisions (*LP*, *BR*, *WF* and *DK* in group 1) achieve a combination of high learning and high objectives-attainment. Another four decisions (*SC*, *EC*, *JU* and *SS* in group 2) which display a medium degree of learning but still with high objectives-attainment make up group 2. Five decisions (*ES*, *OP*, *CM*, *HO* and *OS*) belong to group 3 which has low learning but high objectives-attainment. Group 4 contains two decisions (*MK* and *BU*) which are high on learning and low on objectives-attainment. Finally, there is one decision (*MP*) which has low learning and objectives-attainment.

PATTERNS FOR EFFECTIVENESS

It can be seen that the number of variables selected for this comparison is considerably less than that presented in the original data set given in Table 3.1. If we initially concentrate upon the strategy variables we can see that group 1 achieves a high level of activity on all across the four strategy variables compared to all the other groups.

Another feature is that in group 1 the computation and judgement

Table 11.1 Summary of the decisions

Variable	Decision group				
	1 (4 decisions)	2 (4 decisions)	3 (5 decisions)	4 (2 decisions)	5 (1 decision)
Effectiveness					
Learning	High	Medium	Low	High	Low
Objectives	High	High	High	Low	Low
Definition					
Disagreements			Low	High	High
Strategies					
Computation	High	High	V. high	Low	Medium
Judgement	High	Medium	Medium	Medium	Medium
Negotiation	Medium	Low	Low	Medium	Low
Inspiration	Low/medium	V. low	V. low	High	Low
Influence					
Authority	Top management	Top management	Parameters	Top management gets involved later	Lack of top management involvement and parameters
	Inspiration linked to strategic objectives			Inspiration not linked to strategic objectives	
Timing					
Pace disagreements	Yes	No	No	Yes	Yes

strategies achieve the highest scores, followed by negotiation and then inspiration. Group 4 (high learning/low objectives-attainment) inspiration is the dominant strategy, exceeding computation. Negotiation is also higher than computation.

We can also note how little effect the definition variables appear to have on the patterns of effectiveness. Disagreements are lower in group 3 (low learning/high objectives-attainment) but high in the single decision that makes up group 5 (low learning/low objectives-attainment).

More significant is the effect of authority. A feature of the decisions in groups 4 and 5 is that top management was not involved either in setting parameters for lower level decision-makers or in terms of taking a direct interest in the decisions during the process. When top management did get involved in *MK* it was after the event and this involvement formed a vital part of the learning process.

We can also note that pace disagreements vary with the groups. In particular, group 1 decisions uniformly exhibited disagreements about pace although the duration of these decisions varied from the speediest decision, *LP* at 0.77 years, to the slowest decision, *WF* at 9 years. A feature of all the decisions in group 1 is that decision-makers had a sense of urgency and sometimes frustration at the pace at which matters proceeded.

Patterns of decision strategies

A prominent aspect of Table 11.1 is that the decision strategy variables show distinctive patterns within each group of decisions. The high effectiveness group, as measured by learning and objectives-attainment, displays high computation and judgement, medium negotiation with some inspiration as shown by the low or medium values on this latter variable.

The single ineffective decision as measured by the objectives-attainment and learning dimensions shows only a medium computation and judgement, accompanied by low negotiation and inspiration. Also noticeable is that the two decisions in group 4 (high learning/low objectives-attainment) display high inspiration but with low computation. Compared with the other decisions this is a 'topsy-turvy' pattern in the sense that these decisions seem to be ruled by inspiration but by comparatively little computation. On the other hand, group 3 (low learning/high objectives-attainment) has very high computation with no inspiration.

Towards some general conclusions

We can now attempt to draw some general conclusions as to the kinds of patterns that might lead to one or other of the two kinds of effectiveness. We present these in the form of propositions which the data, in this summarized form, appear to support:

1 Computation is a necessary but not sufficient condition of effective decision-making on both the learning and objectives-attainment dimension.
2 Inspiration leads to learning.
3 For the highest degree of effectiveness to be attained, both in terms of objectives and learning, a combination of computation, judgement, negotiation and inspiration needs to be used in that order of preference. In particular, computation and/or judgement need to achieve a level of intensity above the level of negotiation, which in turn needs to achieve a level of intensity above that of inspiration.
4 Inspiration is a necessary but not sufficient condition of decision effectiveness.
5 We also have evidence to suggest that top level management involvement increases effectiveness.

LEARNING

Much emphasis has been given to the notion of learning. We now examine in more detail some of the specific ways in which organizations learn from decision-making processes.

Some of the negative features learned by participants within Medical Supplier during and following the knitting decision (*MK*) are revealing. We collected replies to our question: 'What did you learn from this decision?' Following is a sample of the factors stated by a number of participants:

> 'In future we will aske more questions; we discounted too many facts'.
> 'We should have talked more "up-front" with experts'.
> 'We should have got more information'.

All these statements were of a negative nature, emphasizing the things participants did not do, which they had done and resolved to do in the future. In this way the anecdotes of the participants reflect the general finding already reported that dissatisfaction with the decision process and learning are negatively correlated.

Learning about knitting

But learning from decision *MK* also encompassed more positive and concrete actions taken within the organization, particularly by the new incumbent of the position of chief executive. The knitting decision was one of a number of decisions in Medical Supplier which were generally perceived as unsatisfactory in the organization. Another one of these, the new manufacturing plant at Medical Supplier (decision *MP*) has already been described in this study.

The specific actions taken at Medical Supplier to attempt to remedy the problems brought to light by these two decisions centred upon restructuring of the organization along the lines of a more product-oriented configuration. The chief executive was very forthright on the subject:

> The problem has to do with the way the company was organized at that time. I would always put that squarely at the foot of the chief executive. This organization had become leaderless for a period of five or six years; it had been run by a committee of senior politicians.

We must remember that the chief executive had joined the company half way through the process of the *MK* decision:

> Had all the facts been presented to me with all the options open I would never have launched. I was faced with the decision, in a matter of weeks after joining the organization, and the fact that we had already invested £150,000 in knitting and related equipment. The most experienced people we have in textiles were saying that you'll never deliver a product at lower cost using knitting in preference to weaving. We continually brushed them aside because of the power of the Research Director. It's a compromise product and a bad project.

There were some direct effects of this decision upon the capital investment appraisal system:

> A series of bad projects, in which strong individuals drove projects through, have forced us to focus upon our capital investment system. The knitting investment gave one specific example I could get my teeth into.

It is from anecdotes of this type that we gain clues as to the processes behind the general finding noted in Chapter 3, namely, that learning is associated with dissatisfaction with the decision process. But we also see some other aspects of the learning process, in particular the close commitment of the chief executive who, as the 'new boy', had a clear insight into the organizational problems and who was determined to put matters right.

Learning and careers

Learning also impacts upon the careers and aspirations of individuals. Again, the chief executive had some insights:

> People are now going to be nervous about proposing large capital projects because they feel burned.

Clive Briggs achieved 'a modest promotion' and, in the eyes of the chief executive, he could not be punished for his part in the project since he was too junior. However, the effect upon R&D had been considerable since this function was abolished. As the chief executive noted:

> It was amazing how many interesting things we were pursuing but how little they related to the commercial world. . . . The one thing you don't want to do is to turn off the tap for new products, but at the same time you don't want irresponsible investments.

Learning as a systemic process

Most of our responses from participants emphasized the systemic nature of the learning process. This is learning over and above learning which remains at the individual of departmental learning levels. The really significant feature of the knitting decision in Medical Supplier was the way in which lessons have been picked up by a whole range of people in different functions and at different levels. The chief executive had taken up the issues raised by this decision and translated them into organization-wide changes.

A similar, albeit less dramatic, learning process was seen at Water Company. Here there was both a technical and a procedural aspect to the learning achieved. There was learning about a new process but, increasingly important, as the decision proceeded, was the appreciation by the company at higher levels of the need to improve the procedures for capital appraisal.

In Water Company a more centralized system of planning was introduced; the filtration decision just provided one more brick for the higher order building process that was going on in parallel with the filtration plant decision that we studied. This higher-level building involved making other decisions, kinds of meta-decisions, about structures and procedures in the organization.

Significantly, also, was the moving into Head Office of a new planning manager who saw it as part of his mission to introduce more rigorous centralized capital budgeting procedures. We may recall the great emphasis laid upon strategic fit in this decision due to the increasing concern by the top management to tune the organization for a tougher environment in which privatization would be but a starting point. This tougher environment would include the increasing use of market norms to assess the performance of investment projects.

At Cloth-Dyer the learning consisted of an increased feeling of confidence on the part of management who had, in their eyes, successfully brought off a difficult deal involving a number of competing supplying organizations, most of which were foreign. The anecdote of how the company managed to make a shrewd move in terms of the foreign currency market was related with some relish indicating satisfaction with the decision.

But there was also, apparently, sufficient dissatisfaction with the process that acted as a spur to the learning. Initially they were unsure of themselves, they were interfered with by headquarters and they were taking too long over the decision.

HIERARCHY OF DECISIONS

The idea that decisions can have subdecisions, thereby allowing us to conceive of decisions as fitting within a hierarchy of decisions, is not new (Simon 1947). If decisions can have subdecisions, then decisions can also fit into a higher or meta-level of decision-making. The notion of hierarchy provides the basis for the systemic nature of organizational learning.

The argument we put forward is that real learning comes about from the ability to build a decision into a hierarchy. A decision-issue grows out of the subdecisions which are made. In analysing the cases we have identified some of these subdecisions. A key subdecision, in many of the decision cases reported in this book, concerns the creation of some working or task group to consider the issue in question. Who belongs to this group can be very important in determining the subsequent course of events.

The subdecisions inform the decision-issue as depicted in Figure 11.1 with a two-way flow of information between the issue level and the subdecision level. At the same time an issue is located within a network of higher level meta-decisions. In the case studies we have referred to these in terms of events that were taking place during the decision process. These meta-decisions set the premises for the decision-issue; a key meta-decision often concerns the overall strategy of the organization. For example, in *MK* the company made two changes in overall strategy during the decision process, changing in the first place towards an increased consumer orientation and then shifting away from this and developing a product divisonalized structure. Both these changes affected the progress of the decision and created considerable uncertainty for the participants.

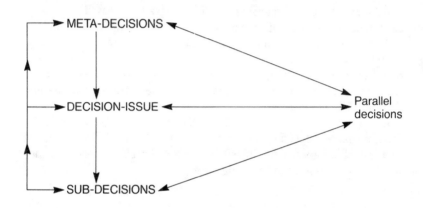

Figure 11.1   The hierarchy of decisions and learning loops

Structural changes, as evidenced by the introduction of more rigorous capital appraisal procedures in the case of Water Company, was another key meta-decision that occurred quite frequently in the decisions we studied.

Meta-decisions inform decision-issues in the sense that premises are determined. But decision issues also inform the meta-premise level as we saw in the Water Company where the new filtration plant decision was instrumental in bringing in new appraisal methods.

Another aspect of the model of learning depicted in Figure 11.1 concerns the parallel decision issues that are going on elsewhere. Often these can be quite separate and not inform a particular issue in any direct way but some parallel issues can be connected as we saw in Medical Supplier. Parallel issues can inform each other and also the meta-level of decision-making.

The system nature of learning can be seen more clearly now from the feedback loops shown in Figure 11.1. The learning generated by a decision issue connects that issue with subdecisions, with meta-decisions and with parallel decisions.

Inspirational decision-making

Inspirational decision-making is perhaps one of the least understood aspects of the decision strategies outlined by Thompson and Tuden and used as a core framework in our model of decision effectiveness. It warrants further examination. Table 3.1 shows that six out of the seventeen decision can be rated as highly inspirational and it is these upon which we concentrate.

It has already been noted that inspiration rates lower than the other three strategies in terms of intensity of use. Further, there is, as Table 3.1 shows, only one decision in which inspiration rates higher than any of the three other processes.

The original idea behind inspirational decision-making as proposed by Thompson and Tuden is that it is a strategy that may be used in cases of extreme ambiguity when both ends and means are unclear. Inspiration is a process whereby individuals, perhaps in a position of formal leadership, but by no means necessarily so, articulate enough imagination or create a new vision or image.

The three most successful of our inspirational decisions show evidence of this articulation. In decision *DK*, Cloth-Dyer's decision to introduce a new 'kitchen', considerable effort was put into developing alternatives and gleaning as much information as possible from suppliers, both quantitative and qualitative. Although there were some participants who had more influence than others, no one person dominated and they were able to achieve a sufficient vision over the new plant to be purchased.

Likewise in Brewer Company, the decision to open restaurants in North America (decision *BR*) was reached through computation and judgemental strategies plus a degree of negotiation in which objectives were questioned and examined in a back and forth process. Power was exerted but there was not domination.

In Electric Company (*LP*), the need to introduce the new electronics product market and technical information was identified. Individuals exerted influence. The problem here was not so much that there was uncertainty about whether there should be a new product but what the design of that product should be and what the cost structure would be.

When we look at those three decisions where inspiration was associated with lower effectiveness, the case of *MP* being the extreme case, we see a lack of conjunction between the four strategies. Inspiration and negotiation overrode computation and judgement. Similarly, in Medical Supplier's new plant decision (*MP*) where the inspiration, centred very much upon one rather junior project manager backed up by an out of control R&D director, drove a project through procedures which had anyway fallen into disrepair. At Brewer a similar state of affairs existed.

When we turn our attention to the kinds of structures needed for inspiration, Thompson and Tuden (1956) also give us some insights. They note that there needs to be interdependence and interaction between people with a need for group decision-making and a set of multiple preferences. More information needs to be introduced during the process of decision-making than can be easily assimilated within the time span and routed through multiple communication channels.

Returning to our relatively effective decisions we can find evidence for this requirement. Electronics Company was very successful in building solutions and support through the processes of information-gathering and dissemination during its decision to introduce a new product (*LP*). This process was assisted by a small organization in which face-to-face communication was relatively easy involving a lot of what Brunsson (1989) calls 'organization talk'.

In the case of Cloth-Dyer's decision to introduce their 'kitchen' (*DK*) we again had a relatively small unit, although the unit was part of a much larger corporation. The hindrance to the process of inspiration that occurred in this instance was due to intervention from headquarters, but the particular person doing the intervening withdrew from the process after having, in the eyes of the local management, caused some disruption.

SUMMARY

This chapter has outlined some aspects of effective decisions. The underlying aspect of effective decision-making is that objectives should be attained and learning be achieved. Learning involves not just finding out more about the technical aspects of the decision in question but also contributing to the meta-level of the organization.

The patterns displayed in the core strategies of decision-making, computation, judgement, negotiation and inspiration are seen to have an impact upon effectiveness. More specifically, computation appears to be a necessary condition for effectiveness, both in terms of objectives-attainment and in learning, but it is not a sufficient condition on its own for decision effectiveness. Additionally processes of judgement, negotiation and inspiration are needed. High inspiration is seen to lead to increased learning but it must not over-whelm the decision-process.

12 Models of capital investment decision effectiveness

In this chapter we examine in more detail the statistical analysis of our interview data in order to develop more explicitly a model of the determinants of effective capital investment decisions. The analysis will be based on the fifty-five individual responses we obtained from our informants. Our sample frame is thus that of individual informants rather than of specific capital investment decisions as in most of the previous discussion. More accurately, then, the analysis of this chapter might be described as reflecting the views of our individual informants as to what factors foster effective capital investment decision-making. This follows from our methodological stance of combining both nomothetic and ideographic methods.

Previous discussion of our capital investment decision-making trade-off experiment, and of particular case studies, has suggested, however, a considerable degree of consensus amongst participants across decisions. This is reflected in this chapter by the fact that our models are, by the usual standards of social science, on the whole relatively successful in explaining effectiveness.

What we may characterize as the 'decision perspective' on our data remains, however, a valid alternative view of it. We exploited this perspective in testing the regression and discriminant analysis results presented here. The way in which this was done, and the detail of our regression and discriminant analysis calculations will be found in Appendix C.

EXPLAINING EFFECTIVENESS

Our approach is essentially one of theory building and testing (Pedhazur 1982) and the principal approaches we shall use to this end are regression and discriminant analysis. As is usually the case in this type of work, many of our variables, and particularly two of our dependent variables, we derived using factor analysis, as already explained in Chapter 3.

The theories have been elaborated in the discussions of the preceding chapters. However, although these theoretical considerations have suggested many variables, many of them may not be important in actual capital investment decision-making. Moreover, in a restricted data-set comprising data from fifty-five informants concerning seventeen individual capital investment decisions, it is unlikely that our data would have found many of the possible explanatory variables to be statistically significant even if they played a part in determining effectiveness; our aim was the modest one of identifying those variables that appear to have the greatest influence. The statistical approaches we shall use to achieve this are stepwise discriminant analysis and stepwise regression.

The effectiveness variables

The two effectiveness variables we shall work with in this chapter are those identified in Chapter 3, namely, objectives-attainment and learning.

Explanatory variables for effectiveness

Explanatory variables fall into four main categories: (1) variables derived from factor analyses; (2) individual variables dropped from the factor analyses; (3) interaction variables; and (4) disparity variables.

Variables derived from factor analyses

As noted in Chapter 3, and as described in detail in Appendix B, a number of potential explanatory variables were derived by factor analysis. These were presented in Chapter 3 in Table 3.2. For convenience, we reproduce Table 3.2 as Table 12.1.

Variables dropped from factor analyses

A number of variables were dropped from the factor analyses of the explanatory variables, as described in Appendix B. These represent potential explanatory variables and were, therefore, incorporated into the analyses.

Table 12.1   The decision-effectiveness model

Phase	Factor (constituent variables)
Dependent variable	
EFFECTIVENESS	*Objectives-attainment*: project success, right choice, (−) unexpected negative outcomes
	Learning: overall learning, (−) satisfactory process
Explanatory variables	
DEFINITION	
Consequentiality	*Failure*: impact of project, failure on corporate financial standing, competitive position, performance of company
	Fit: degree of fit with business strategy, (−) project value
Uncertainty	*Rarity*: novelty of project, supplier uncertainties, production and cost uncertainties
	Performance: market uncertainties, internal and external financial uncertainties
Disagreements	*Personal*: personal objectives disagreements, personality clashes
	Objectives: overall organizational disagreements, disagreements about project objectives
STRATEGIES	
Computation	*Rate of return*: payback, internal rate of return (IRR), productivity
	Reported profit: (−) productivity, earnings, overall computation
Judgement	*Personnel*: impact of project on morale, industrial relations
	Image: impact on image, quality
	Judgement: overall judgement
Negotiation	*Negotiation*: overall negotiation, building of alliances
Inspiration	*Inspiration*: overall inspiration
INFLUENCE	*Internality*: internal involvement and direction
	Externality: external involvement and direction
TIMING	*Deliberation*: duration of decision process, decision building up slowly, delays, pace worries

Note: (−) denotes a negative loading on a variable.

Interaction variables

The logic of our effectiveness model of Chapter 3 is that the effectiveness of a particular capital investment decision depends on the 'appropriate' decision-making strategy being adopted. The appropriateness of a particular decision-making strategy is, from our model, contingent upon the specific values of the individual variables in our four phase categories of definition, strategy, timing and influence.

The implication of our model is that a particular decision strategy should lead to a more effective decision under some circumstances rather than under others. For example, the classic Thompson and Tuden (1956) model would suggest that a negotiation strategy should lead to a more effective decision where ends uncertainty is high rather than when it is low. In statistical terms, this suggests that we need to consider interactions between our decision strategy factors and our other explanatory variable factors. Accordingly, interaction variables are defined as the product of any one of our decision strategy factors with one of the other explanatory variable factors, and are added to the list of explanatory variables. For the computation strategy we used the two derived factors, rate of return and reported profit; for the judgement strategy we used our three derived factor variables of personnel, image and judgement; for the negotiation strategy we used our single negotiation factor; and likewise, in the case of the inspiration strategy (for which no factors could be found), we used the response to a single question, which provided a single, direct measure of the extent to which the decision was perceived as inspirational. The reader is referred to Table 12.1 and Appendix C for further details.

Disparity variables

As noted in Chapter 3, and as suggested by some of the individual case studies, disparity, or lack of consensus between participants in a decision over what was considered important, may have an important impact on the effectiveness of a particular decision. For the purposes of the present chapter we adopted a somewhat more refined definition of disparity than that used in Chapter 3. Instead of the difference between the maximum and minimum responses across all the informants to a case for a particular question (the range), we now use the standard deviation.

Two points might be noted about this procedure: (1) the disparity measures are the same for all informants for a particular decision; (2) decisions for which there was only one informant show zero disparity using the measure applied here. Where there was only one effective decision-maker, whom we interviewed, this is obviously accurate. It is probably also a reasonable approximation to our Japanese investment decision (JU) where we found that our two informants, who count

as one informant because two managers were interviewed simultaneously and came to an agreement as to the replies to give, were
completely baffled by the notion that there could be disagreement
about an investment decision amongst the managers involved. Where,
however, we interviewed only one of several decision-makers our
calculated zero disparity score is likely to overestimate the amount of
agreement in reality.

REGRESSION MODELS OF DECISION EFFECTIVENESS

The various explanatory variables discussed above all stem from
theoretical considerations. However, there were a very large number
of potential explanatory variables. Considerations of model
parsimony as well as the relatively small number of cases, suggested
that stepwise regression be adopted to derive the regression models.
Stepwise regression with a large number of explanatory variables is
well known, however, to be a somewhat unstable process. To deal
with this problem we approached the derivation of the effectiveness
regression models in a systematic way as described in Appendix C.

Two further problems arose from the practical impossibility of
establishing the representativeness of our sample and consequent
threats to its statistical process validity (Cook and Campbell 1979).
The first problem was that certain explanatory variables might have,
fortuitously, shown little variation within our sample. These would
almost certainly be eliminated by a stepwise regression process. These
can be viewed almost as 'non variables' in the sense that they can
remain high, but constant, across the entire sample. The variables of
computation, for example, fall into this category.

The second threat to statistical process validity deriving from the
possible unrepresentativeness of our sample was that certain of the
regression coefficients might be no more than 'data artifacts', that is,
spurious relationships generated by chance features of our sample of
decisions. Here we felt it was possible to do something about the problem. One approach was to use holdout testing methods, that is, we 'held
out' a random sample of informants and derived the regression equation. We repeated this process several times and retained only those
explanatory variables that appeared in all the regression equations thus
derived. In addition, we exploited the fact that our fifty-five informants
had reported on only seventeen decisions. By deriving regressions on
both an individual informant basis and a decision basis, and retaining
only those explanatory variables that appeared in both, we were able to
establish stable regression models, which are reported below.

We confine ourselves to reporting beta coefficients, as a measure of the importance of particular explanatory variables (Berry and Feldman 1985) and R^2 values. Explanatory variables are, where appropriate, named in accordance with Table 12.1. Individual interview schedule variables are given an appropriate name plus a reference to the interview schedule. Interaction variables are given in terms of the variables involved in the interaction. Disparity variables are referred to by tacking disparity on to the name of the interview schedule variable concerned and cross-referencing to the interview schedule. The details of how the effectiveness regressions were carried out can be found in Appendix C.

The objectives-attainment regression model

The regression model for the objectives-attainment measure of effectiveness involved three explanatory variables as shown in Table 12.2.

Table 12.2 Explanations of decision effectiveness: objectives-attainment

Explanatory variable	Beta weight
Inspiration disparity	−0.70
Interaction of personal disagreements and inspiration	+0.18
Negotiation	−0.18

$R^2 = 0.55$

The most important explanatory variable in this equation is inspiration disparity. As explained above, this is the extent to which informants lacked consensus about how far the decision-making strategy might be characterized as 'inspirational'. This is the first instance of the importance of inspiration and associated variables in determining effectiveness. In this case the effect is negative, that is, the greater the disparity amongst informants about whether the decision was made on an inspirational basis, the less effective the decision was in attaining its objectives. The interpretation of this would seem to be that a decision that is tainted with a suspicion of inspiration, that is, where some informants thought that was how the decision was arrived at whilst others did not, is unlikely to be effective in attaining its objective.

The next most important explanatory variable (though only about one quarter as important as the first as measured by beta weights)

was the interaction between the personal disagreements factor and the inspiration decision-making strategy. For the second time, then, inspiration is implicated in the explanation of effectiveness. In this case the beta is positive; the interpretation being that in situations where there is a high level of personal disagreement and inspiration is heavily employed as a decision-making strategy, the decision is more likely to attain its objectives. This makes sense in organizational terms: inspiration, with its charismatic overtones, is indeed a useful way of cutting through personal disagreements.

The third explanatory variable, though with the same numeric beta weight as the second, is negotiation. The implication of its negative sign is that our informants regarded negotiation as detrimental to the attainment of objectives. Case study interviews suggested this was because they tended to see such negotiation as political horse-trading inimical to their organization's interests.

The R^2 for this model at 0.55 is reasonably high by the usual standards of decision-making studies (compare Hickson *et al.* 1986). However, almost the entire explanation is contributed by the inspiration disparity variable; regression on that variable alone having an R^2 of just under 0.5. The reader is reminded that we carried out extensive experiments to ensure the stability of the regression model and, of course, in doing so eliminated many less parsimonious models with considerably higher R^2. For objectives-attainment, however, a very parsimonious model with just inspiration disparity as an explanatory variable would be possible.

The learning regression model

This model involved five explanatory variables all with fairly similar beta weights (in numerical terms), as shown in Table 12.3.

The most important explanatory variable is again a disparity

Table 12.3   Explanations of decision effectiveness: learning

Explanatory variable	Beta weight
Regulation impact disparity	+0.45
Inspiration	+0.40
Interaction of internality and judgement	+0.36
Interaction of externality and judgement	−0.28
Interaction of deliberation and negotiation	+0.23

$R^2 = 0.55$

variable. In this case, it is disparity concerning the extent to which there was uncertainty over the impact of regulations. The implication of this is that decisions where some informants felt that the regulations were unclear whilst others felt that the regulations were clear, were ones that favoured organizational learning. In behavioural terms, this appears plausible. The organizational response to such situations is typically that those who are convinced that they understand the regulations have put a great deal of effort into studying them. They then embark on a process of endeavouring to persuade colleagues as to the correctness of their views. The resulting discussion leads to a close scrutiny of the regulations and their implications. In an era in which organizations can increasingly derive competitive advantage from understanding the implications of the regulations better than their rivals, for example, in financial services, this result is understandable.

The next most important variable was inspiration with a positive beta. Inspiration, then, is seen as conducive to organizational learning. This seems reasonable given the common perception of the association between inspiration and the creative process.

The remaining three explanatory variables are all interactions. The most important of them is the interaction of the internal influence factor (internality) with the judgement decision strategy factor. This has a positive beta whose interpretation is that decisions where an above average number of people within the organization are involved and judgement is an important decision-making strategy are likely to lead to more learning. The connotations of consensual decision-making implicit in this scenario would be expected to foster organizational learning. Alternatively a way to obtain a low value for the interaction term and, hence, a beneficial impact on organizational learning, is to have a below average number of internal staff involved in the decision and make very little use of a judgement strategy. This again seems reasonable in organizational terms. It suggests that a judgement strategy is not effective if there are too few people involved in the decision.

The fourth most important interaction is that between the external influence factor (externality) and judgement. This has a negative beta. Given that one component (judgement) of this interaction and the previous interaction is common, this negative sign compared with the positive one for the previous interaction shows an interesting, though on reflection wholly reasonable, asymmetry between the effects of internal and external influence. The negative beta suggests that decisions characterized by above average external influence where a judgement strategy is adopted are less likely to lead to organizational learning. A plausible explanation for this is that our external influence is likely to be external experts or consultants. What they contribute to judgement is not retained within the organization when the decision is complete. Alternatively a way to get a low value for this interaction term is to have a below average amount of external influence and make little use of a judgement strategy, that is, not using a judgement strategy in situations where advice from outsiders is not available tends to increase organizational learning.

Our final explanatory variable for learning is the interaction of the deliberation timing factor with negotiation. This has a positive beta. It can, therefore, be interpreted as meaning that decisions that are more deliberate than average and where there is a considerable amount of negotiation, are likely to lead to greater organizational learning; or, alternatively, that rapid (in the sense of being below average on deliberation) decisions lead to most organizational learning if there is little negotiation. These results are consistent with the observation that negotiation tends to require time to be effective.

The percentage of the variance explained for the learning model is the same as that for the objectives-attainment model. Moreover, the five explanatory variables contribute more equally to the explanatory power of the learning model so that there is less attraction in paring it down to make it a more parsimonious model.

EXPLAINING THE DETERMINANTS OF EFFECTIVENESS

Having established regression equations for our two effectiveness measures, we now turn to attempting to explain the determinants of effectiveness by regression and discriminant analysis. These equations give rise to further explanatory variables and we then attempt to explain these, in their turn.

Regression equations for the explanatory variables

We attempt to set up regression equations for: (a) the factor (negotiation) appearing directly in the objectives-attainment equation; (b) the other factors that appear in the interaction terms, but do not appear in their own right, that is, personal disagreements, internality, externality, judgement and deliberation; (c) factors appearing as explanatory variables in the regression equations arising from (a) and (b). Note that we did not attempt to produce explanatory models for the interaction terms, since their values are predetermined by the values of the individual factor variables that comprise them.

For the purposes of this exercise, interview schedule variables with the exception of inspiration and disparity variables were considered as given (exogenous variables). No attempt was made to introduce inter-action terms into these regression equations on the grounds of simplicity. However, factors (other than decision strategy factors) were considered as potential explanatory variables in the regression equations for the determinants of effectiveness.

The development of the regression equations for the explanatory variables is discussed in detail in Appendix C. Table 12.4 lists the explanatory variables for which explanatory models were derived along with the type of model derived.

Table 12.4 Explanatory variables for which models were produced

Explanatory variable	Explanatory model type
Deliberation	Regression
Inspiration	Discriminant analysis
Internality	Regression
Judgement	Regression
Negotiation	Regression
Personal disagreements	Regression

The discriminant analysis for inspiration

Since inspiration is a variable measured on a five-point Likert scale, it was felt inappropriate to use it as a dependent variable in a regression equation: discriminant analysis was considered a more appropriate approach.

The development of the discriminant function for the inspiration variable is discussed in detail in Appendix C.

The 'path' models

The results of our further regression analyses and the discriminant analysis can conveniently be summarized by two quasi-path models for objectives-attainment and learning. We refer to them as quasi-path models because of the use of discriminant analysis rather than regression. The form of representation is, however, similar to that of, for example, Van De Geer 1971.

The quasi-path diagrams are shown in Figures 12.1 and 12.2

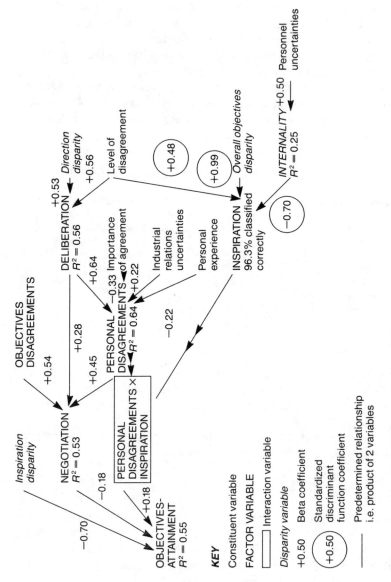

Figure 12.1 Decision objectives-attainment model

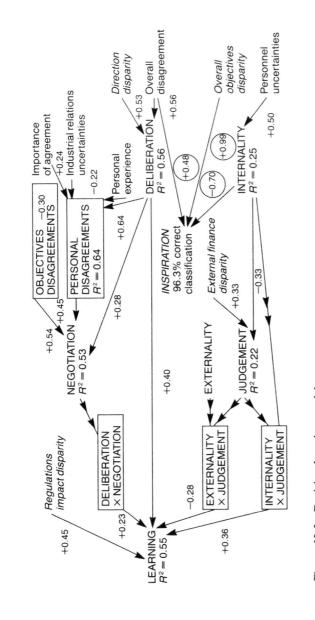

Figure 12.2 Decision learning model

respectively. R^2 values are shown beneath the dependent variable. Beta coefficient values are shown attached to the appropriate link. The predetermined relationships involved in the interactions are shown by double arrows. For our inspiration variable we show, instead of R^2, the percentage of cases correctly specified by the discriminant function and instead of beta values we show the coefficients of the standardized discriminant function. The variables involved are tabulated individually beneath the figures.

Explanatory equations for the common elements of the two path diagrams

We have already discussed the regression equations for the two effectiveness variables, so we now turn to discussing the equations for the explanatory variables that appear as the determinants of the effectiveness variables, that is, we now focus on producing explanatory models for these explanatory variables. The appearance of negotiation and inspiration in both models means that both the quasi-path diagrams have elements in common. We therefore discuss the regression equations and discriminant function associated with those common elements before discussing the additional elements peculiar to the learning diagram Figure 12.2.

Negotiation

The regression equation for this variable has a good, for a social science model, R^2 of 0.55. It involves three variables, all with positive beta weights, objectives disagreements, personal disagreements and deliberation, in descending order of numerical size of beta weights. Disagreement over objectives is essentially the classic Thompson and Tuden (Thompson 1967) ends-disagreement dimension. Negotiation is the recommended decision strategy in situations where such disagreement is high. Personal disagreements, it will be recalled from our discussion in Chapter 3, is another ends-disagreement factor but involving concerns of more personal interest to the decision-maker. Its presence as an explanatory variable is again fully in line with classical theory. Finally, the presence of deliberation in the equation is consistent with the observation that negotiation usually requires a fair amount of time; it is not a feasible decision strategy for decisions that are being forced along.

Objectives disagreements

No regression equation could be found for this variable. It is, therefore, treated as an independent, or exogenous, variable in our quasi path diagrams.

Personal disagreements

The regression equation for this variable has a high R^2 of 0.64. It involved four explanatory variables, deliberation (positive beta), importance of agreement (negative beta), prior personal experience (negative beta), and industrial relations uncertainties (positive beta). The positive beta for deliberation is consistent with the notion that a leisurely decision-making process gives time for managers to reflect on how the decision may effect their own career interests (compare Wilson 1980). The negative beta for importance of agreement again makes good sense; many of our case study informants referred to difficulties in securing agreement when personal objectives obtruded on the decision-making process. Such observations also suggest that the negative beta for prior experience makes good sense.

Finally, the positive industrial relations beta, though fairly small, is not something that seems to us either to be suggested by, or to conflict with, theory. Almost more interesting is the appearance of such a variable. Surveys of decision-making in the UK (Hickson *et al.* 1986), have tended to suggest that managers place very little weight on industrial relations considerations, nor did any of our informants suggest that these played a major role in the decision. None the less, there is a hint in the appearance of this variable, and certain related ones that we shall discuss later, that suggests that such considerations play a larger role than has been thought.

Deliberation

Again, a reasonably high R^2 of 0.56 was achieved for this variable. Only two explanatory variables were involved in this regression equation, overall level of disagreement and direction disparity. That a decision characterized by a high amount of disagreement should proceed at a slower pace seems wholly reasonable.

Direction refers to the presence of a high number of internal interest units that have a high amount of influence (see Chapter 3 and Table 3.3). When there is disparity over direction this means that participants in the discussion differ as to the extent of this direction; there are, in other words, differences as to who is running the decision.

Our finding from this regression equation suggests that direction disparity tends to increase deliberation, that is, to increase the length of time taken to make the decision (duration), that there tend to be more delays, that the decision takes time to build up and that there are associated worries about pace.

Inspiration

As already explained, it was necessary to carry out a discriminant analysis rather than a regression analysis for this variable because it is a discrete rather than a continuous variable. The discriminant function analysis classified 96.4 per cent of the cases correctly.

The variables involved in the standardized discriminant function were, in descending numerical order of discriminant function weight, and with the direction of the effect shown by the sign:

(+) overall objectives disagreement disparity
(−) internality
(+) overall disagreements

Overall objectives disagreement disparity measures a somewhat convoluted concept − the extent to which informants differed in their perceptions as to the amount of disagreement that existed over the objectives to pursue. It would be easy to explain the presence of overall objectives disagreement, itself, in the equation; indeed it is completely in line with the classic Thompson and Tuden theory; the presence of the associated disparity variable poses more problems, though.

However, a little reflection suggests that, if we think about capital investment decision-making as an instance of the negotiation of solutions to non-zero sum games (Aoki 1987), this becomes understandable. If someone within the decision situation perceives the disagreements amongst the remainder of the group as illusory rather than real, the way is open for an inspired solution to the apparent dilemma that allows everyone to feel that the disagreements have been resolved in their favour.

That disagreement in general encourages an inspiration decision strategy is completely in line with the classic Thompson and Tuden theory. That a large number of internal people having an influence on the decision discourages inspiration is, again, wholly consistent with the negative sign implying that such situations are inimical to an inspiration decision strategy.

Internality

The R^2 for this equation, at 0.25, was poor. On the other hand, only one explanatory variable, personnel uncertainties, was involved and this shows a positive beta. This finding appears explicable in that uncertainties about the personnel impacts of the decision would seem likely to cause more different representatives of internal interest groups to be involved. This is a further instance of how human resource management considerations appear to affect capital investment decision-making.

Explanatory equations for variables peculiar to the learning quasi-path diagram

As we have seen, the path diagram for the learning factor of effectiveness is more complex than that for the objectives-attainment factor. We now consider explanatory regression equations for the two remaining variables of Figure 12.2 that are not common with those of Figure 12.1.

Externality

Externality is a measure of the extent to which external interests have an effect on the decision process. No regression equation could be derived for this equation. For the purposes of our model it is, accordingly, regarded as exogenous.

Judgement

A low R^2 of 0.22 was obtained for this factor variable. The regression equation involves two explanatory variables both with numerically equal beta weights: external finance uncertainty disparity (beta = +0.33) and internality (beta = −0.33). Lack of agreement amongst participants about the uncertainties surrounding the provision of external finance would be expected to favour a judgement strategy as implied by the positive beta. The negative beta for internality implies that an above average number of participants involved in the decision is inimical to the exercise of judgement. This seems reasonable: a number of methodologies exist to facilitate the exercise of judgement by groups of decision-makers, for example, Saaty (1980), Lupton and Tanner (1987), Friend (1987); presumably, it would not have been found worthwhile to develop them, if the exercise of judgement by larger groups was an easy matter.

OVERALL ASSESSMENT OF THE PATH DIAGRAMS

The relationships depicted in the path diagrams are on the whole quite strong. Most of the relationships in them turn out to be readily explicable in terms of decision-making theory; those that are less obvious, for example, that for overall objectives disagreement disparity in the discriminant function, seem on closer examination to suggest interesting insights into the capital investment decision-making process. Our process for developing the regression models, as described in Appendix C, suggests that these relationships were fairly robust for our data, at least.

An interesting question is the extent to which our two models explain the two effectiveness measures in terms of the exogenous variables. In a conventional path diagram this could be derived by straightforward computation (compare Pedhazur 1982). In this case, however, the presence of interaction terms and the prediction of the value of the inspiration variable by means of discriminant analysis precludes this approach.

A crude measure of the explanatory power of our quasi path models can be obtained by constructing a regression model for each of the effectiveness measures based solely on the appropriate set of exogenous variables (that is, the exogenous variables involved in the quasi path diagram for the effectiveness measure). This tends, on the one hand, to underestimate R^2 because the interaction variables are, in effect, estimated by regression, whereas in reality they are predetermined, given that they are simply the product of the two variables involved in the interaction. On the other hand, it tends to overestimate the value of R^2 because, (a) direct links are introduced from the exogenous variables to the dependent variable, which, in most cases, do not exist in the quasi path model; (b) the need to adjust R^2 for a fairly large number of explanatory variables relative to the number of cases.

Bearing these reservations in mind, regressions were carried out using only the exogenous variables as explanatory variables. For the model of objectives-attainment using only the exogenous variables of Figure 12.1 as explanatory variables, R^2 was found to be 0.64, that is, markedly higher than the 0.55 for the original regression equation for that measure. Since a single exogenous variable (regulations impact disparity) accounted for nearly 50 per cent of the variance of objectives-attainment, however, we may reasonably conclude that we can explain over 50 per cent of the variance of objectives-attainment from the exogenous variables (in fact, in practical terms, from the exogenous variables overall objectives disparity, direction disparity and regulations impact disparity).

For the model of learning using only the exogenous variables of Figure 12.2 as explanatory variables, R^2 was found to be 0.36, that is, substantially lower than the value of 0.55 obtained from the regression equation for learning itself. However, it does suggest that around a third of the variance of learning can be explained by the exogenous variables alone, which is still a fairly respectable performance for models of this type. In this case, in practical terms, most of the variance explained was accounted for by the variables, overall objectives disparity, external finance uncertainty disparity, overall level of disagreement, regulations impact disparity and externality.

SUMMARY

Regression analyses of our two capital investment decision-making effectiveness factors, objectives-attainment and learning, gave rise to regression equations explaining around 55 per cent of the total variance of each effectiveness factor. By the usual standards of organizational analysis models, this represents fairly high explanatory power.

The regression equation for objectives-attainment was the simpler of the two in that it involved only three explanatory variables. Indeed, the vast bulk of the explanatory power was accounted for by the single inspiration disparity variable. Inspiration was also indirectly involved in one of the other two explanatory variables though, the inspiration × personal disagreements interaction term. The other explanatory variable was that of negotiation. The signs of the regression coefficients of these variables were in line with what might have been expected from theoretical considerations.

The regression model for learning was more complex, involving, as it did, five explanatory variables. These were: relations impact disparity; negotiation; the internality × judgement interaction; the externality × judgement interaction and the deliberation × negotiation interaction.

Interaction and disparity variables therefore played an important role in both these regression equations. The decision strategies of inspiration and negotiation were important either directly, or indirectly through the interactions, in both models. However, their effects were in opposite directions. Our analysis found that inspiration and negotiation are detrimental to objectives-attainment but have a positive effect on organizational learning.

We then turned to deriving equations to explain the explanatory variables in the two effectiveness equations in terms of disparity variables and raw interview schedule variables, which were considered as exogenous variables not requiring explanation. Because inspiration was measured on a five-point Likert scale, discriminant analysis was preferred to regression analysis for explaining this variable. Two 'quasi-path' models were obtained as a result of this exercise, one for objectives-attainment (Figure 12.1) and one for learning (Figure 12.2). Effectively Figure 12.1 is more or less a subset of Figure 12.2, reflecting the greater complexity of the processes surrounding organizational learning. The signs of the coefficients in the two quasi-path diagrams were, in the main, consistent with theory. In one or two cases, where they appeared superficially surprising, it was found possible to derive useful insights from them.

Disparity and disagreement variables appeared to be important in both our quasi-path diagrams. Broadly speaking, the conflict that they imply seems to have a detrimental effect on objectives-attainment and a positive effect on learning.

13 Conclusions

We now try to draw some general conclusions from our results that will be of use to practitioners in making decisions. Throughout our discussions of decision-making processes there is one recurring theme. This theme is located in the tension between computational and inspirational decision-making. The computational approach to making decisions implies careful step-by-step planning and the use of calculations and algorithms to compute an optimal solution before action is taken. The inspirational approach implies acting upon the basis of incomplete information and before the way forward is clear; analysis and reflection will tend to go in parallel or after action has been taken.

The theme for the practitioner that emerges, then, is neatly summed up by Schon's (1983) term 'reflective action'. This implies that managerial decision-making is more of an iterative process in which computation is reflected against inspiration, and inspiration against computation, rather than a linear process whereby decisions are made through the application of step-by-step procedures.

THE MEANING OF DECISION EFFECTIVENESS

The concept of decision effectiveness is, in iteself, problematic and worthy of investigation. We have built upon the idea that effectiveness must go beyond the attainment of initial objectives and include a number of other variables. Our approach has, to some extent, been inductive in that we have asked the participants involved in a number of investment decisions about the variables they considered important in measuring the effectiveness of a decision; from their views we were able to derive two principal factors of effectiveness. These we labelled the objectives-attainment and learning factors.

The objectives-attainment factor accounted for approximately

44 per cent of the variance of all of the effectiveness measures put together and the learning factor for approximately 23 per cent of the variance. These figures indicate the relative weights that decision-makers put upon the two factors of decision effectiveness; from this we can see that attaining objectives is considered to be approximately twice as important as learning. This observation fits well with impressions gained from the case studies and from the more qualitative data gathered from managers during interviews.

The objectives-attainment factor consists of the overall successfulness of the project, the extent to which decision-makers felt that the 'right choice' had been made and the lack of unexpected negative outcomes. The variable of unexpected positive outcomes did not appear in either of the two effectiveness factor variables.

Both our case study findings and the results of our experiment showing the lack of attention paid to the 'best case' rate of return reinforce the idea that managers do not like nasty suprises but appear relatively indifferent to pleasant surprises; at least, they do not base their views of what makes an effective decision upon the hope of finding serendipity, perhaps taking nice surprises as a bonus rather than as an expectation. This finding, to some extent, is in contradiction to Rodrigues's (1980) finding of 'propitiousness' as an aspect of successful decision-making, but supports Mao and Helliwell's (1969) finding that managers are generally averse to taking risks.

The learning factor is negatively weighted upon satisfaction with the decision process, that is to say, when decision-makers see a decision process as unsatisfactory they tend to learn more. This supports the observation made by Cyert and March (1963) that the impetus to a decision can be a perceived performance gap and provides the rationale in much of the strategic planning literature whereby the search is made for areas where performance gaps may appear in the future. In the case of our data we are indicating that performance gaps lead to learning; a notable feature of learning is that it can appear as a result of dissatisfaction with the decision process.

Our regression model for the learning factor is considerably more complex than that for the objectives-attainment factor. The rather simpler regression equation for objectives-attainment, particularly if we base it solely on a single explanatory variable is, perhaps, best explained by the notion that our organizations know how to attain objectives and have well-honed processes for enabling this to happen. The real challenge for them is to develop the reflective organization (Schon 1983), which is much more difficult, as witnessed by the complexity of the learning path model.

INTERACTIONS BETWEEN DECISION STRATEGIES

The advantage of using a combined ideographic-nomothetic method is that we are able to draw general conclusions concerning the processes of effective decision-making and we can also make more refined and specific observations about how these strategic patterns are put into practice.

Interactions leading to objectives-attainment

Inspiration on its own is shown to have no significant effect upon objectives-attainment but inspiration disparity has a strong, but negative, effect upon objectives-attainment. We should recall that disparity in our model of decision-making occurs when the participants do not achieve a high degree of congruence over a particular variable. The use of disparity measures has been an important aspect of our methodology and has demonstrated the usefulness of obtaining the view of multiple informants.

Negotiation, the ability to 'give and take' and build alliances during decision-making, is also seen to have a slight negative effect in attaining objectives.

It seems, therefore, easier to identify factors that decrease rather than the positive factors that increase objectives-attainment. The negotiation strategy, is in part, the outcome of disagreements about objectives and personal disagreements; negotiation can be seen, therefore, as a process that copes with these two forms of disagreements and the model at this point supports the original Thompson and Tuden (1956) conception.

Deliberation (made up by the variables of decision duration, build-up, delays and pace worries) is seen to lead to negotiation. This points to one of the continual dilemmas of decision-making in that time spent coping with disagreements and achieving a greater consensus of views can slow down decision-making. On the other hand, the trade-off between taking time to improve the project design and losing or delaying returns from the capital investment, as discussed in Chapter 2, shows that such delays can be beneficial.

We also find that inspiration interacting with personal disagreements tends to increase objectives-attainment.

Interactions leading to learning

Learning is seen to be strongly influenced by inspiration, an observation already made clear from our discussion of the case studies.

Our analysis shows that inspiration can be put to use in two ways. It can be used in conjunction with personal disagreements to resolve those disagreements, but bearing in mind that it is important for inspiration disparity to be low otherwise objectives-attainment is reduced.

Judgement plays a particularly strong part in learning. Judgement, an overall measure of the extent to which the decision strategy involved an intermingling of quantifiable and intangible factors, interacts positively with internal influence (internality) to form learning. This suggests that the judgemental processes of decision-making works more effectively as a result of a large number of internal participants becoming involved.

Conversely, external influence interacts with judgement in a negative way to reduce learning. It would seem that it is difficult for the more intuitive processes implied in judgement to work effectively with external influence.

The distinction between internal and external influence is at the heart of what an organization is about. Williamson (1975) sees organization as an institutional arrangement whereby the right 'atmosphere' can be generated to assist in the development of special understandings and technical knowledge to enable the process of judgement to work. It follows, then, that learning is a benefit of the internalization of functions that needs to be carefully weighed in current debates about pruning back the core activities of organizations. External interests do not share this internal atmosphere to the same extent as do internal interests.

A decision with a high degree of external influence occurred in Society's decision to purchase new computer software. This decision was given tremendous impetus by the computer manufacturer. In this case Society was buying an 'off-the-shelf' package and so little learning was involved.

The distinction between what we have called the variable of involvement and the variable of direction also needs emphasizing; involvement is a measure of the number of interests that exert at least some influence over an issue, whereas direction is a measure of those interests exerting a great deal of influence. In Cloth-Dyer, the new kitchen decision involved a high number of external units but the externality of influence was low in the sense that these units did not exert stong influence over the way the decision was made. They were involved in providing information but were not a powerful force in making the final choice. If the management of an organization allow themselves to be ruled by external interests they are, in a sense, being usurped by those interests.

Another variable directly increasing learning is deliberation. We see from this relationship that learning needs time, the ability to pause, and allow time for the development of new ideas for an issue, can assist learning. However, the deliberation factor tends to include disagreements over the pace at which a project should proceed, with some participants urging faster action while others want to go slower. The new kitchen decision at Cloth-Dyer is an example of this process. Deliberation, therefore, is not without its cost in terms of anxiety, in addition to the direct cost of managerial time and possible opportunity cost (Sharp 1990).

Computation

At the centre of the decision effectiveness model are the strategies that decision-makers use in resolving issues. These strategies derive from the outline of decision-making strategies given by Thompson and Tuden (1956).

Marsh *et al.* (1988), in their real-time study of UK strategic investment decisions, found that while the companies examined operated systematic and sophisticated capital budgeting procedures, the actual analysis and assumptions were often incorrect or questionable. Some of the conceptual errors identified were significant; managerial bias towards going ahead with the project appeared to affect the analysis conducted, and over-simplified and incomplete financial projections were made to yield a 'good enough' return to justify the project.

However, while the computational approach for the decision was far from perfect, and in part 'ritualistic', Marsh *et al.* found that the use of procedures of this type had many beneficial effects. It forced managers to be more explicit about their assumptions and alternatives; it helped guide decisions and negotiations and revealed new aspects of the decision; it provided deadlines and helped force the pace of the project; and it provided opportunities for face-to-face communication between key players throughout the organization. Knowledge of the procedures and financial requirements enabled the project team to build personal and formal public commitment to the decision's success.

Computation is by far the most heavily-used decision strategy. To make decisions by computation has been part of the scientific management ideology since the early part of this century. Modern management training, through MBA programmes and the like, diffuse the techniques of this ideology and our high score for the computation strategy confirms their success in this regard. The results of our investment experiment reported in Chapter 5, where we asked for managers' views of the kinds of procedures they would use in assessing the synthetic investment projects presented to them, also support the view that modern management is increasingly dominated by computational procedures.

When we come to consider more specifically the role of computations in investment decisions we note the use of payback and internal rate of return calculations as providing the dominant quantitative method of assessing investments. Our observation supports previous research (for example, Pike 1988) in this respect and indicates that computation is a necessary condition for effective decision-making. Those two cases (decisions *MK* and *BU* in Table 3.3) where computations were lower than the other strategies for decision-making were found to be ineffective in terms of objectives-attainment.

Because computation is so universal it is not really acting as a variable in the model but as a constant, although the accuracy and validity of those computations can vary as Marsh *et al.* (1988) point out. The other decision strategy variables of judgement, negotiation and inspiration appear as more variable in our analysis. One overall conclusion is that there is a need for all strategies to be employed in decision-making but that these strategies need to be ordered with computation as the predominant strategy, followed by judgement, then by negotiation and inspiration.

Judgement

Judgement is the second most heavily-weighted strategy for making decisions, but it is not seen to have a role to play in objectives-attainment. It does, however, play an important part in learning through its interaction with the two influence variables of internality and externality.

As with computation, judgement has the characteristic of being a fairly universal aspect of decision-making, although there are some exceptions to this. In particular are two decisions in the low learning/high objectives-attainment group in Household Consumer Goods and Oil Company (decision *HW* and *OP* respectively, Table 3.3). These were both decisions which were highly computational, highly strategic but involving little in the way of disagreements. They were decisions made within quite strict guidelines laid down by headquarters and also display little in the way of negotiation or inspiration.

Negotiation

Negotiation has a negative role to play in the objectives-attainment factor of effectiveness, as already mentioned. This suggests that political factors are seen to be unhelpful in attaining objectives but apparently neutral as far as learning is concerned. However, negotiation, interacting with deliberation, enhances the learning factor. In other words, successful negotiation needs time for the build-up of mutual understandings to be achieved.

At this point we must recall the more general finding derived from the case studies, and mentioned above, that it is the interaction between the four decision strategy variables that is important in determining the effectiveness of the decisions. We were not able to establish this through the use of the regression analysis, partly, we suspect, due to the comparatively non-variable character of computation and partly because the effects appear to involve the application of the decision strategies in a specific order, if they are to be successful, and so we have had to rely upon the case study analysis presented in Chapter 11. We argued that it is the interaction between the four decision strategies that is important in achieving effectiveness of decision-making. Hence, negotiation, when tempered with computation and judgement, becomes an important aspect of effective decision-making.

The knitting decision in Medical Supplier and the UK site acquisition in Brewer were both decisions with high negotiation, especially in terms of alliance building, but were low in computation and judgement. These were decisions that were ineffective in attaining objectives, although they did well in terms of learning.

The negotiation strategy can be seen to be, in part, the outcome of disagreements about the objectives that a decision should try to achieve, and personal disagreements; negotiation is, therefore, a process that copes with these two forms of disagreement. The model at this point bolsters and modifies the original Thompson and Tuden conception since negotiation was seen as a way of coping with disagreements. Here we have drawn a distinction between two types of disagreement.

Lack of agreement

Our regression results suggest that disagreements and disparities seem to foster learning. As can be seen from the path diagram, both types of variable have a positive impact on learning. Given the definition of disparities used, the implication would seem to be that learning emerges from lack of agreement and associated debate and conflict. The role of the negotiation and deliberation constructively interacting can be seen from our individual case studies, with the new kitchen decision in Cloth-Dyer (decision *DK*) providing a good example of this working successfully.

If there is to be disagreement about a capital investment project, participants must have something over which to disagree. In that respect it is interesting to note what disagreement and disparity variables appear in our model. Our disagreement factor variables are essentially two different aspects of the classic Thompson and Tuden ends-disagreement dimension.

It is the disparity variables that provide the most interesting insight as to areas that are the focus of debate. Regulations impact disparity has the single largest impact on learning, yet this apparently technical source of conflict chimes poorly with general perceptions of UK business culture as being, on the whole, uninterested in technical matters. Perhaps such issues provide a suitable focus for constructive rather than destructive debate.

Similarly, the disparities concerning the human resource management-related uncertainties (personnel and industrial relations) seem to provide a focus for a mainly constructive debate. This is a little surprising since various authors (for example, Hickson *et al*. 1986) have found them to be of little apparent concern to managers. One possible explanation is that our findings merely reflect changes in organizational cultures that have occurred in the 1980s. However, in interviews our managers uniformly ascribed a low importance to such considerations. This apparent contradiction may, again, reflect the fact that these areas provide a low risk focus for constructive disagreement.

Inspiration

Inspiration is the least strongly used of the four decision strategies but plays a critical part in decision effectiveness.

Inspiration affects objectives-attainment in two ways. First, inspiration disparity has the strongest effect on objectives-attainment but in a negative direction. Disparity is defined as the lack of agreement amongst participants in a decision over the value of a particular variable. Hence, when participants do not agree upon the degree to which an individual takes over a decision this reduces the extent to which objectives are achieved. Leadership is important, but all must have the same perception as to who the leader is, would be the implication of this finding.

Second, inspiration also interacts with personal disagreements to increase objectives-attainment suggesting that the inspirational decision strategy is particularly suitable for resolving organizational conflicts providing, of course, that the stronger relationship requiring disparity about inspiration to be low is also met.

Inspiration plays an important direct part in learning as already described. Our analysis also shows that personal disagreements lead to inspiration as does disparity about the objectives aimed at by a decision. We also note that internal influence is negatively related to inspiration, indicating that too many fingers in the pie can reduce inspiration.

The notion of inspiration bears a strong affinity to trans-formational leadership which Burns (1978) contrasts to transactional leadership. Transactional leadership occurs where there is a direct exchange of rewards between leader and follower, whereas trans-formational leadership involves a process of building up identification between leader and follower. We suggest that identification amongst participants in a decision with the fundamental goals of that decision will be a necessary part of successful inspiration.

Inspiration can go wrong as we saw in the knitting decision at Medical Supplier (decision *MK*). Here, too much of the inspiration was concentrated upon a relatively junior participant who failed to win this identification and support from key interests in the organization.

TIMING

The question of timing in decision-making is an aspect which is often referred to by practitioners as being critical in producing effective decisions but, surprisingly, this has been little studied. Concern with the pace at which a decision proceeded was a major concern in ten out of the seventeen decisions.

One aspect of timing which we suggest is important is what we called the deliberation variable. Deliberation is a factor consisting of duration, build-up, delays and pace worries. When deliberation is high the picture is of a decision over which decision-makers ponder, put the problem down to pick it up again, tend to take a long time to come to a conclusion and to worry over the time being taken.

Deliberation was not found to directly affect objectives-attainment but to act through other variables, in particular, negotiation and inspiration. Negotiation is partly the outcome of disagreements about objectives, personal disagreements, and deliberation, suggesting that timing is an important aspect of resolving differences.

The role of timing may include a preparedness on the part of management to be bold enough to challenge an existing momentum for a decision to go ahead. Janis and Mann (1977) have used the term 'group-think' to describe a process whereby organizations can apparently cease to question a policy that is in motion. This can happen through management filtering out information that does not fit the existing policy.

In practical terms countering group-think may mean slowing down a decision. For example, Marsh *et al.* (1988) cite the case of a group chief executive referring a project promising strong financial returns back for a complete rethink as a deliberate learning experience for those involved. The result of the rethink was a quite different cheaper alternative offering most of the savings promised by the original proposal.

The knitting decision in Medical Supplier has, perhaps, provided the best example of the combination of poor objectives-attainment and learning, and of a decision that would undoubtedly have bene-fited from management calling for a rethink; the performance of the project was doubtful and, perhaps most importantly, the company had great difficulty in fitting this project into its overall strategy. Although learning in this case led to changes in the procedures for the evaluation of projects, and also to changes in organizational structure, it would have been preferable if management had been more prepared to call for a pause in the decision process.

INFLUENCE

A key question in decision-making is 'who influences?'. From a pre-scriptive viewpoint this means asking 'who *should* influence?'. We have seen how internal, as opposed to external, influence assists the development of inspiration. An aspect of influence investigated by us consisted of the two related constituent variables of involvement and direction.

Involvement is the extent to which interests take part in a decision, including those that do not exert a particularly high degree of influ-ence but who, nevertheless take some part in the decision process. Direction is the extent to which there are interests involved who exert high influence.

Neither involvement nor direction were found to have any direct effect upon either of the two effectiveness variables. Direction disparity, the condition in which there is lack of agreement over who is directing the decision, was found to increase deliberation.

When involvement was divided into internal and external involvement (internality and externality respectively) it was found that internality tended to decrease both inspiration and judgement. However, internality when interacting with judgement tends to increase learning, whereas externality interacting with learning decreases learning. This finding, it has been suggested, reinforces the notion of an organization as an institution to enable the learning process, and that externally-governed relationships are less likely to foster the 'atmosphere' necessary for learning.

That high involvement of interests is antithetic to inspiration is not surprising. The concept of inspiration emphasizes the role of individual volition in decision-making and is contrary to a more collective notion of how decisions should be made.

Herein lies a fundamental dilemma for the successful management of decision-making. To what extent should individuals be given their head to follow their ideas, or to what extent should decision-making seek wide involvement whereby those ideas can be tested and tried but at the risk of stifling initiative and slowing down decision-making?

Our case studies give a pointer as to how this dilemma may be resolved. We found that decision ineffectiveness tended to result from a lack of clear guidance from higher management, that is, from low direction. The strongest example of this was the new plant decision in Medical Supplier (decision *MP*) where we saw that this decision exhibited a high degree of inspiration but where it also lost its way due to lack of firm decision premises to guide it.

Top management guidance can come in one of two forms. Top management can directly intervene, in other words, centralize the decision (Pugh *et al.* 1968), or management can set performance parameters within which decision-makers would need to operate and then delegate the decision to lower levels in the organization.

In Medical Supplier, the lack of guidance came to be appreciated by higher management, especially by the new chief executive in the later stages of the two decisions investigated. The result of these belated insights was to change the organization structure and introduce new procedures for the evaluation of future projects. In general, we found that those decisions exhibiting higher all-round effectiveness were those where top management set overall premises but then gave others in the organization leeway to work out and evaluate options.

DEFINITION OF THE ISSUE

One of the surprising aspects of our data is the low degree of impact of the consequentiality and uncertainty of an issue over the processes that ensued. Disagreements, however, have an affect on objectives-attainment through interacting with inspiration as already described.

The argument is, to a certain extent, circular; we find that disagreements about the objectives of a decision lead to inspiration while inspiration interacts with personal disagreements to improve the objectives-attainment of effectiveness. Again, we need to remind ourselves that it is important that there is congruence (lack of disparity) about the locus of that inspiration in the organization.

What, in more general terms, we seem to have uncovered is the notion that the nature of the issue, while not insignificant, is not as important as Thompson and Tuden (1956) or Hickson *et al*. (1986) would suggest. In a sense, we are discovering the possibility of making a few general statements about the principles of effective organizational decision-making which apply relatively independently of the decision issue.

TOWARDS DECISION-MAKING PRINCIPLES: STRATEGIES FOR REFLECTIVE ACTION

At different points in our discussion we have pointed to the tension between the computational and inspirational decision strategies. The computational strategy is analytical, requiring elaboration of the perfect plan. The inspirational strategy is *ad hoc*, relying upon the energy of one or more individuals and emphasizing action rather than reflection.

This is not a new observation. Over the years a number of terms have been used to describe aspects of this process. For example, Vickers (1965) used the term 'appreciation' to denote a process whereby decision-making adds and builds up understanding about a organization and its situation. This can never be a purely rational process as emphasized by Simon (1960) and March and Simon (1958), since decision-makers do not have access to sufficient information. These arguments have been well covered in Chapter 2.

Schon (1983) has developed this argument by reference to 'reflective-action' which is seen as the kind of decision-making whereby the tension between computation and inspiration may be resolved. Schon presents the reflection-action model (his model II) by contrasting it to what may be seen as a hierarchical model of decision-making (his model I).

Model I can be summarized by noting that decisions would be made in the following way:

- Achieve the task as I (or higher management) define it
- In negotiations try to win and avoid losing
- Avoid negative feelings
- Use rational argument, keep 'cool'
- Act and control the task unilaterally
- Protect yourself
- Protect others even if they do not wish to be.

This model is based upon a certain number of premises about human nature which are also well summarized by McGregor (1960) as Theory X. They are the assumptions of the rational-synoptic decision-maker who believes that it should be possible sufficiently to define the premises to a decision and to make choices according to rational argument. Model I is clearly closely related to the computational strategy as outlined here.

Model II can be summarized thus:

- Give and get observable valid information
- Create the conditions for free and informed choice
- Develop awareness of the values at stake
- Try to gain internal commitment to decisions
- Create conditions in which commitment to action is intrinsically satisfying rather than by external rewards and punishments
- Involve several parties in managing the environment

Model II is an approach to decision-making that does not deny the value of computation but also accepts the importance of judgement, negotiation and inspiration. It becomes more of a total organizational approach, whereby the job of management is to create the surrounding conditions under which these processes can occur.

Through the notion of patterns of decision strategies our findings suggest some specific activities that need to be done in order to achieve effective decisions. If we see inspiration as the action-oriented strategy we can say that, while a necessary part of the decision strategy, it should be built upon computation and other aspects of rational decision-making. From our data we can even give an approximate quantitative assessment of the balance between inspiration and the other strategies. If we assign a score of 100 to be shared amongst the four strategies and taking the means given in Table 3.3 we calculate that the weight to be given to computation should be 41, to judgement 34, to negotiation 17, and 8 to inspiration.

These relative weights are an average across the decisions studied but, they give a perspective on the extent to which inspiration is governed by computation, judgement and negotiation. What Schon calls the 'reflective practitioner' will be someone who knows how to draw upon these four strategies and to give them the kind of relative balance suggested. This observation, drawn from the overall average of all seventeen decisions studied, is reinforced by the case study data; as described above, a notable feature of the decisions which were less effective either in terms of learning or objectives-attainment is that they did not manage to achieve this kind of balance. In general, the less effective decisions were those where computational procedures were lacking.

Another way of making the point is to say that decision-making is 41 per cent computation, 34 per cent judgement, 17 per cent negotiation and 8 per cent inspiration. For managers to 'make it happen' (Harvey-Jones 1990) is less a matter of flashy brilliance and more of hard, steady work. However, the real difference in terms of making effective decisions will come from some degree of inspiration.

To let inspiration run amok will lead to inefficiency (Butler 1991). This condition is created by organizational structures that are too slack or fuzzy for the conditions under which the organization is operating and gives 'decision over-capacity' whereby decision-makers have too much freedom to decide; this situation was clearly seen in the knitting decision at Medical Supplier where there was a great deal of local initiative taken but with insufficient reference to the wider organizational strategy.

On the other hand, to constrain decision processes by forcing a computational perspective will lead to lack of organizational adaptability and lost opportunities. This condition is created by organizational structures that are too crisp (Butler 1991) for the conditions. There will now be a lack of local initiative and an overemphasis upon the pursuit of fixed objectives. The errors here are those of 'decision under-capacity'.

ASSESSMENT

A study of this nature inevitably seems to raise more questions than it answers. Yes, it would have been nice to have had more decisions in the sample but we had to make a compromise in terms of the time that could be spent on survey data in comparison to the time on the case studies. Yes, the concepts of decision effectiveness, strategies and the other concepts in the model need refining. Many of these kinds of issues could, undoubtedly, be improved upon.

However, we do claim to have broken new ground as regards attempting to measure the effectiveness of decision-making and in developing a model with good explanatory power that describes how decision effectiveness can be increased. The idea of managers having to develop a set of decision-making competencies, starting with the four strategies of computation, judgement, negotiation and inspiration, but also having to include competencies concerning timing and influencing, provides a useful case from which to work for practitioner and researcher alike. Furthermore, we have demonstrated that, by taking 'the decision' as a unit of analysis, we can shed light upon the process of management (Butler 1990). The notion of looking at organizational learning as resting upon the extent to which the outcomes from a particular decision affect meta-decisions in an organization allows us to view the processes of organizational change in terms of how actions at the more micro-decision level of analysis interact with wider issues of strategy formulation.

Appendix A – Interview schedule

INTRODUCTION

The interview schedule is designed to collect information about the objectives of an investment decision; the way in which that decision was made; and organizational factors influencing such a decision. Information collected will then help to establish the main non-financial aspects of the decision process. Financial criteria are examined more fully in section 3.

Unless specified otherwise, the following scale will be used throughout:

0 = none
1 = some
2 = reasonable amount
3 = quite a lot
4 = great deal

REFERENCE

Interviewee _____

Organization _____

Department _____

Position _____

Date _____

Place _____

Interviewer _____

1 What is/was the decision about? Is it considered a 'strategic' decision?

2 Approximate value of investment (if known): £_____

3 How and when did it start? When did it finish?

4 Please give a brief description of the main sequence of events with respect to the decision process, from its inception to its completion.

5 In the context of your business, to what extent was this decision unusual?
   Scale: 0 1 2 3 4
   If unusual, why?

6 Did you have prior personal experience of this type of investment?
Scale: 0 1 2 3 4

7 Are there any formal incentive schemes, financial (such as bonuses, etc.) or otherwise, to encourage you to raise capital investment proposals?
If yes, what are they? YES/NO

8 Are there any disincentives to raising such investment proposals?
If so, what are they? YES/NO

To what extent *Extent*

9 was this project successful? 0 1 2 3 4
(0 = total failure; 4 = highly successful)

10 was the way in which the decision was arrived at satisfactory? If unsatisfactory, why? 0 1 2 3 4
(0 = most unsatisfactory, 4 = highly satisfactory)

11 were there any major unexpected outcomes?

11.01 positive	0	1	2	3	4
11.02 negative	0	1	2	3	4

What?

12 in retrospect, was it the right choice? 0 1 2 3 4
(0 = definitely not, 4 = absolutely)
If not, why not?

13 did the decision process used result in useful learning leading to the possibility of future improvements in decision-making? 0 1 2 3 4
If so, how?

14 How important did you regard each of the factors below in reaching your view on the proposal? Please circle appropriate number according to the scale.
0 = none; 1 = some; 2 = reasonable amount; 3 = quite a lot; 4 = great deal

Importance to you

STRATEGIC FACTORS R

14.1	Degree of fit with business strategy	0	1	2	3	4
14.2	Growth rate of markets related to project	0	1	2	3	4
14.3	Competitive position of company/unit (*vis-à-vis* external competition)	0	1	2	3	4
14.4	Performance of company/unit	0	1	2	3	4
14.5	Other (specify)	0	1	2	3	4

QUANTIFIABLE PERFORMANCE FACTORS

14.6	Internal rate of return	0	1	2	3	4
14.7	Impact on current year's earnings	0	1	2	3	4
14.8	Effect on achievement of profit and sales targets	0	1	2	3	4
14.9	Payback period	0	1	2	3	4
14.10	Effect on productivity	0	1	2	3	4
14.11	Other (specify)	0	1	2	3	4

<table>
<tr><td></td><td></td><td colspan="2" align="right">*Importance*
to you</td></tr>
</table>

QUALITATIVE PERFORMANCE FACTORS   R

14.12	Effect on product quality	0 1 2 3 4
14.13	Effect on morale	0 1 2 3 4
14.14	Effect on industrial relations	0 1 2 3 4
14.15	Contribution to corporate image	0 1 2 3 4
14.16	Other (specify)	0 1 2 3 4

RISK FACTORS

14.17	Sensitivity to internal and external economic changes	0 1 2 3 4
14.18	Type of project (e.g. replacement, cost-saving, new technology, etc.)	0 1 2 3 4
14.19	Impact of project failure on corporate financial standing	0 1 2 3 4
14.20	Investment track record of sponsor	0 1 2 3 4
14.21	Impact on personal career/earnings	0 1 2 3 4
14.22	Level of agreement (opposition) from interested parties	0 1 2 3 4
14.23	Any other factors not covered (specify)	0 1 2 3 4

15 What factors are normally required by organizational procedures on the capital request form or other similar documents for a proposal of this type? Please enter a tick under the 'R' column next to the appropriate factor.

16 Consider the four main headings above and comment upon the extent to which the objectives of the decision have been attained in relation thereto on the 0 to 4 scale.
0 = none; 1 = some; 2 = reasonable amount; 3 = quite a lot; 4 = great deal

Extent

Strategic factors	0 1 2 3 4
Quantifiable performance factors	0 1 2 3 4
Qualitative performance factors	0 1 2 3 4
Risk factors (that is, with hindsight, how successful was the decision process in assessing the riskiness of the project?)	0 1 2 3 4

17 Did you assess the riskiness of the project?   YES/NO
If yes, please explain how.

	Informal	Formal
Naïve		
Sophisticated		

18 What risk reduction strategies were undertaken for this project? That is, what steps did you take to reduce the impact of failure or not achieving targets?

19 Consider the following factors and assess on the usual 0 to 4 scale the extent to which they caused difficulty and uncertainty in deciding the best course of action to take.
0 = none; 1 = some; 2 = reasonable amount; 3 = quite a lot; 4 = great deal

There is scope to insert others not thought of.

FACTORS CAUSING UNCERTAINTY OR DIFFICULTY   *Extent of uncertainty*

19.1	Market considerations (e.g., market size, share, growth, competitors actions, government policy, product price changes, etc.)	0	1	2	3	4
19.2	Supplier considerations (e.g., price changes, quality, availability, etc.)	0	1	2	3	4
19.3	Production and cost (e.g., labour, material availability, product quality, etc.)	0	1	2	3	4
19.4	Financial considerations: internal (e.g., meeting required financial return, etc.)	0	1	2	3	4
19.5	Financial considerations: external (e.g., forecasting investment cost, rates of: exchange; interest; inflation; etc.)	0	1	2	3	4
19.6	Technical considerations (e.g., newness, reliability, safety of technology, project life, rate of technical development, etc.)	0	1	2	3	4
19.7	Industrial relations (e.g., strikes and stoppages, wage demands, conditions, etc.)	0	1	2	3	4
19.8	Personnel factors (e.g., impact on morale, absenteeism, turnover, etc.)	0	1	2	3	4
19.9	Regulations (e.g., re: competition, consumer laws, trade policy, employment regulations, tax laws, grants, safety, etc.)	0	1	2	3	4
19.10	Miscellaneous (please specify)	0	1	2	3	4

20 Refer to those factors above which were considered significant (say the 3s and 4s) and, if possible, explain how these caused difficulties in assessing the best course of action to take.

21　This question seeks to establish the type and extent of the information used in arriving at the investment decision. Would you therefore please rate *all* the following statements as to their accuracy in describing the general approach used in making this particular decision on the scale:
0 = none; 1 = some; 2 = reasonable amount; 3 = quite a lot; 4 = great deal

		Description accuracy				
21.1	Decision eventually evolved out of facts and figures perhaps following calculations of varying complexity	0	1	2	3	4
21.2	Facts, figures and calculations referred to but ultimately decision involved weighing up a number of intangible factors not easily quantifiable	0	1	2	3	4
21.3	Decision made by weighing up views of different parties and through bargaining and give and take	0	1	2	3	4
21.4	Nobody seemed able to make up their minds one way or another. Impasse resolved by one person seizing hold of the situation, by some opportune or fortuitous event, by an inspiration	0	1	2	3	4
	If any other description applies better, please specify	0	1	2	3	4

22　To what extent do you think the authorization at the next level up was:

		0	1	2	3	4
22.1	'real'	0	1	2	3	4
22.2	'rubber-stamping'	0	1	2	3	4

(0 = definitely not, 4 = absolutely)
Where do you thing the 'real' decision was made?

23　To what extent do you consider there were delays, interruptions and reconsiderations? (That is, the iterative process.)
Scale:　0　1　2　3　4
In which part of the decision process was it most apparent?

24　To what extent did the decision build up gradually without a clear idea of where things were going?
Scale:　0　1　2　3　4

25　Was there any information you would have liked that you did not have for this project?　　　　　　　　　　　　　　　　　　　YES/NO
If yes, what was it?

26　Was there any information you would have liked earlier?　　　YES/NO
If yes, what was it?

27 Please list below the people that had a major influence on the investment decision and assess their influence on a 0 to 4 scale.

0 = none; 1 = some; 2 = reasonable amount; 3 = quite a lot; 4 = great deal

INTERNAL   [Used to determine variables INEGE1 and INEGE3]

Name/function   *Actual influence*

_____	0 1 2 3 4
_____	0 1 2 3 4
_____	0 1 2 3 4
_____	0 1 2 3 4
_____	0 1 2 3 4
_____	0 1 2 3 4
_____	0 1 2 3 4
_____	0 1 2 3 4
_____	0 1 2 3 4
_____	0 1 2 3 4
_____	0 1 2 3 4
_____	0 1 2 3 4
_____	0 1 2 3 4
_____	0 1 2 3 4
_____	0 1 2 3 4

EXTERNAL   [Used to determine variables INEGE1 and INEGE3]

Name/function   *Actual influence*

_____	0 1 2 3 4
_____	0 1 2 3 4
_____	0 1 2 3 4
_____	0 1 2 3 4

28 What was your attitude to the project when it was first initiated and then after the decision had been made? Please rate on the following scale:

2 = strongly support
1 = support
0 = neutral
−1 = oppose
−2 = strongly oppose

28.1   Initial _____

28.2   Final _____

29 To what extent did people form temporary alliances or subgroups expressly for the purpose of this investment decision?
Scale: 0 1 2 3 4
Please explain a score of 2 or more.

30 To what extent do you think disagreements were in evidence during the decision process?
Scale: 0 1 2 3 4
Concerning which aspects?

		Extent of disagreement
30.1	Objectives of this decision	0 1 2 3 4
30.2	Overall objectives to pursue	0 1 2 3 4
30.3	Procedures to use in evaluating decision	0 1 2 3 4
30.4	Personality clash	0 1 2 3 4
30.5	Personal objectives	0 1 2 3 4
30.6	Pace at which matters should proceed	0 1 2 3 4
30.7	Issue of professional ethics/responsibility	0 1 2 3 4
30.8	Other (specify)	0 1 2 3 4

For those scoring 2 or more, who were the main parties?

31 How strong was the enthusiasm and support for the project:

(a) within the organization generally?   0 1 2 3 4

(b) by particular individuals? (a)   0 1 2 3 4
                               (b)   0 1 2 3 4
                               (c)   0 1 2 3 4

(c) outside the organization?   0 1 2 3 4

By whom and for what reason?

32 Were there any factors you consider important in making the investment decision which have not been covered? Please specify:
Scale: 0 1 2 3 4

Appendix B — Factor analyses and other derived variables

INTRODUCTION

Appendix B gives details of the factor analyses carried out on the questionnaire responses (see Appendix A). The statistical processes by which the various factors were identified are described. However, it must be borne in mind that the factor analyses were driven by the theoretical considerations and previous research discussed particularly in Chapters 2 and 3.

In some cases, certain variables could not be incorporated into factors. Therefore, where appropriate, variables used on their own in certain analyses are also identified.

Factor analysis method used

In all cases factor analyses were carried out using both principal components (PC) and generalized least squares (GLS). In the main there were relatively few differences in the results, so the actual factors used in later analyses were derived using principal components. Scree plots were used to determine the appropriate number of factors in conjunction with the GLS analyses, though in most cases the result was the same as that which would have been obtained using the traditional eigenvalue >1 criterion.

Rotations

In all factor analyses both orthogonal and oblique factor rotations were obtained. In practice, none of the oblique rotations produced results that were much different from the orthogonal rotations. The latter were accordingly preferred on the grounds of simplicity. Only factor loadings of 0.5 or more were considered significant and factors were named as suggested by these loadings.

Dropping variables

The factor analysis was confirmatory in nature. The theoretical considerations of the earlier chapters were used to derive sets of variables on which to carry out factor analysis. Standard statistical tests (principally the Kaiser-Meyer-Olkin statistic, the variable intercorrelations and the Anti-Image Correlation

Matrix: Norusis 1985) were used to eliminate variables from some of these factor analyses where the variables concerned appeared to be relatively unrelated to others in the analysis.

THE PRIMARY DEPENDENT VARIABLES

Defining effectiveness variables

Effectiveness variables were defined by a process of factor analysis. Initial attempts were based on factor analysis of questions 9, 10, 11.01, 11.02, 12, 13, and 28.02. Question 11.02 proved to be poorly correlated with the others so was dropped from the analysis. The final factor analysis produced two factors that explained 67 per cent of the total variance of the effectiveness data. The loadings numerically greater than 0.5 are shown in Table B1 along with various relevant statistics:

Table B1   Effectiveness factors

Question	Objectives-attainment	Learning
12 (right choice)	0.86	
9 (project successful)	0.84	
11.02 (unexpected negative outcomes)	− 0.72	
28.02 (final support)	0.70	
13 (useful learning)		0.83
10 (satisfactory decision process)		− 0.78

Kaiser-Meyer-Olkin (KMO) = 0.66
First factor explained 43.9% of variance
Second factor explained 23.1% of variance
Cumulative % of variance explained: 67.0%

Note: The questions here and the other tables in this Appendix refer back to Appendix A.

The first factor is readily interpreted as an objectives-attainment measure of effectiveness. The second factor can be interpreted as a Learning measure of effectiveness. It is noteworthy that an implication of this latter factor is that organizational learning is negatively associated with satisfaction with the decision-making process; alternatively that out of dissatisfaction with the decision-making process comes organizational learning.

FACTOR ANALYSIS OF POTENTIAL EXPLANATORY VARIABLES

Variables derived from factor analyses

The factor analyses and the resulting number of factors are listed below:

Influence (2 factors)

Based on an analysis of Question 27 the following variables were derived:

Number internal individuals with influence >= 3 (INIGE3)
Number internal individuals with influence >= 1 (INIGE1)
Number external individuals with influence >= 3 (INIGE3)
Number external individuals with influence >= 1 (INIGE1)

Two factors were readily identified from the factor analysis: the first, externality, and the second, internality.

Table B2 Influence factors

Variable	Externality	Internality
INEGE1	0.96	
INEGE3	0.95	
INEGE1		0.92
INEGE3		0.81

KMO = 0.55
First factor explained 54.3% of variance
Second factor explained 32.1% of variance
Cumulative % of variance explained 86.4%

Consequentiality (2 factors)

The initial variables were: 2, 14.01 to 14.04, 14.19. 14.02 proved to correlate poorly with the others. The final factors were therefore based on: 2, 14.01, 14.03, 14.04, 14.19. The first factor proved to load primarily on variables concerned with the impact of failure of the project on the organization, whereas the second factor loaded mainly on variables associated with the fit of the project with corporate objectives. The factors were named accordingly.

Table B3 Consequentiality factors

Question	Failure	Fit
14.19 (impact project failure)	0.81	
14.03 (impact on competitive position)	0.73	
14.04 (impact on Co. performance)	0.73	
2 (value of investment)		−0.84
14.01 (strategic fit)		0.73

KMO = 0.62
First factor explained 37.6% of variance
Second factor explained 24.0% of variance
Cumulative % of variance explained 61.6%

Uncertainties (2 factors)

The initial variables were: 5, 19.01 to 19.09 (uncertainty variables). KMO statistics were poor at just under 0.5. 19.08 was eliminated on the basis of poor intercorrelations with other variables. GLS factor analysis of the remaining variables showed that the factors identified did not load significantly on 19.06, 19.07 and 19.09. These were accordingly eliminated from the analysis and the two factors finally selected using PC analysis were based on variables 5, 19.01 to 19.05 only.

The factor loadings are shown in Table B4:

Table B4   Uncertainty factors

Question	Rarity	Performance
5 (rarity)	0.78	
19.02 (supplier uncertainties)	0.74	
19.03 (production/cost uncertainties)	0.71	
19.01 (market uncertainties)		0.83
19.05 (external financial uncertainties)		0.78
19.04 (internal financial uncertainties)		0.60

KMO = 0.49
First factor explained 34.3% of variance
Second factor explained 28.1% of variance
Cumulative % of variance explained 62.4%

The first factor is one where high values of the factor are generated by a great deal of novelty about the decision and a high degree of uncertainty about suppliers and product cost. It seems fair to interpret this as rarity (a variable that was found important by Hickson *et al.* 1986). The second factor can be interpreted as uncertainties about the financial returns from the project, which we dub performance.

Disagreements (2 factors)

Initial analysis was based on the variables: 30, 30.01 to 30.05, and 30.07. The scree plots were somewhat unsatisfactory. 30 was eliminated from the analysis on the grounds that it was fairly evenly (0.3−0.4) correlated with the other variables. The resulting factor analysis was more satisfactory and led to two factors based on 30.01 to 30.05 and 30.07.

Factor loadings were shown in Table B5:

Table B5   Disagreement factors

Question	Personal disagreements	Objectives
30.04 (personality clash)	0.85	
30.05 (personal objectives disagreements)	0.72	
30.02 (overall objectives disagreements)	0.72	
30.07 (disagreements over professional ethics)	0.55	
30.01 (disagreement over decision objectives)		0.71
30.03 (disagreement over evaluation procedures)		0.52

KMO = 0.67
First factor explained 40.6% of variance
Second factor explained 19.1% of variance
Cumulative % of variance explained 59.7%

The second factor represents disagreement over the objectives of the particular decision studies and the procedures to use in evaluating the decision was called Objectives. The first factor represents disagreements over other aspects of the decision relating more to the individual decision-makers; this we called personal disagreements.

Computation (2 factors)

The variables used were: 14.06 to 14.10, 21.01. The factor loadings are given in Table B6.

Table B.6   Computation factors

Question	Rate of return	Reported profit
14.09 (payback period)	0.85	
14.08 (effect on sales/profit targets)	0.75	
14.06 (internal rate of return)	0.72	
14.10 (effect on productivity)	0.63	− 0.55
14.07 (impact on current earnings)		0.66
21.01 (computation decision strategy)		0.63

KMO = 0.69
First factor explained 39.4% of variance
Second factor explained 21.2% of variance
Cumulative % of variance explained 60.6%

The first factor can reasonably be interpreted as rate of return; the second as a reported profit factor.

Judgement (3 factors)

The initial variables analysed were: 6, 14.12 to 14.15, 14.20, 21.02, 25, 26. 6 did not load strongly in the first analysis whilst 26 was the only variable to load on one of the factors. 14.20 appeared to be only weakly correlated with other variables. 6, 14.20 and 26 were accordingly removed from the analysis to leave as final variables: 14.12 to 14.15, 21.02, 25.

Table B7   Judgement factors

Question	Personnel	Quality	Judgement
14.14 (effect on industrial relations)	0.87		
14.13 (effect on morale)	0.82		
14.12 (effect on product quality)		0.84	
14.15 (effect on corporate image)		0.83	
21.02 (judgement decision strategy)			0.85
25 (needed more information)			0.81

KMO = 0.54
First factor explained 30.7% of variance
Second factor explained 24.0% of variance
Third factor explained 18.2%
Cumulative % of variance explained 72.9%

The factor loadings are given in Table B7. The first factor can clearly be identified with personnel. It seems reasonable to call the second, given the emphasis that organizations have placed, in recent years, on quality in defining their corporate image, quality. The third represents essentially the classic Thompson and Tuden judgement factor which we call simply judgement.

Negotiation (one factor)

The initial variables for this analysis were: 14.22, 21.03, 22.01, 28.01, 29. 14.22 was the sole variable to load on one of the factors while neither 22.01 nor 28.01 loaded significantly on any factor. These three variables were therefore dropped leaving as final variables: 21.03 and 29. The single factor was named negotiation. This is a factor essentially reflecting equally the extent to which the decision was arrived at by bargaining and the extent to which temporary alliances characterized the decision.

Factor loadings were as shown in Table B8:

Table B8   Negotiation factor

Question	Negotiation
21.03 (negotiation decision strategy)	0.84
29 (alliances formed)	0.84

KMO = 0.50
First factor explained 70.1% of variance
Cumulative % of variance explained 70.1%

Timing (one factor)

The variables analysed were: Duration (weeks), 23, 24 and 30.06.
Factor loadings were as given in Table B9:

Table B9   Timing factor

Question	Deliberation
23 (extent delays and interruptions)	0.76
Duration	0.72
30.06 (disagreements over pace)	0.69
24 (gradual build up)	0.66

KMO = 0.62
First factor explained 49.8% of variance
Cumulative % of variance explained 49.8%

A long duration suggests a lack of urgency to the decision. A high score on question 23 indicates a decision characterized by delays and interruptions; a high score on question 24 indicates that the decision was one that built up gradually without any clear direction, a high score on question 30.06 denotes much disagreement about the pace of decision-making. The interpretation of this factor is then: deliberation.

Variables dropped from the factor analyses

A number of variables were dropped from the factor analyses of the explanatory variables, as noted above. These potentially represent dimensions not captured by the factors. Therefore, they represent potential explanatory variables to be incorporated into the regression analyses. However, the poor KMO statistics associated with many of these individual variables suggest that for those variables the problem may be due to rather low variation of the variable within the sample. Practical considerations suggest then that these variables are probably unlikely to contribute much to the regression analyses, while internal validity considerations (Cook and Campbell 1979) also suggest that we are unlikely to be able to detect any significant impacts of these variables in our sample.

The complete list of these variables is:

14.02 (growth rate of markets related to project), 14.20 (investment track record of sponsor), 14.22 (level of agreement/opposition from interested parties), 19.06 (uncertainties due to technical considerations), 19.07 (industrial relations uncertainties), 19.08 (uncertainties about personnel factors), 19.09 (uncertainties concerning regulations), 21.04 (inspiration decision strategy), 22.01 (extent to which authorization was a 'real' decision), 26 (was there any information you would have liked earlier?), 28.01 (initial attitude to project), 30 (overall level of disagreement).

Interaction variables

The Thompson and Tuden (Thompson 1967) framework underlies our study and suggested that, in statistical terms, we need to consider interactions between our decision-making strategy factors (with inspiration, 21.04, being considered a decision-making strategy variable for this purpose) and our other explanatory variable factors. Accordingly, interaction variables defined as the product of one of the decision-making strategy factors with one of our other explanatory variable factors, were added to the list of explanatory variables, which was thus augmented by a set of interaction terms such as: computation × deliberation, personnel × deliberation, and so on.

Disparity variables

Our interviews suggested that agreement or consensus among decision-makers had an important impact on the effectiveness of a particular decision. This idea was further reinforced by our mathematical modelling of the decision-making process which explicitly considered support-building activity (Sharp 1990).

Given that the majority of our case studies were multi-respondent ones it is easy to construct disparity variables as the standard deviation of the response to a particular question from all those associated with a given decision. These variables might more accurately be dubbed disagreement variables since a high standard deviation indicates substantial disagreement amongst respondents. However, to prevent confusion with our disagreement factors we shall refer to them as disparity variables. For these disparity variables: 0 denotes no disparity between respondents and the greater the value of the variable the greater the disparity.

Decisions for which there was only one respondent show complete agreement using the measure applied here. Where there was only one effective decision-maker, whom we interviewed, this is obviously accurate. Where, however, we interviewed only some, rather than all, of the decision-makers our calculated agreement score is likely to overestimate the amount of agreement in reality (though there are plenty of aspects of multi-respondent decisions about which there was complete unanimity). There are then some 'errors in the variables' in our disparity variables which may introduce bias into our regression estimates (Johnston 1972).

The disparity variables were constructed in this way for the following questions: 5, 19.01 to 19.09, 21.01 to 21.04, 23, 24, 30, 30.01 to 30.07.

It should be borne in mind that the disparity variables are decision-level variables, that is, any particular agreement variable takes the same value for each respondent for a given decision. This effectively precludes factor analysing the disparity variables since there we are then reduced to seventeen cases (that is, the seventeen decisions).

Appendix C – Regression and discriminant analyses

GENERAL

Appendix C gives the details of the regression and discriminant analyses carried out on the interview schedule responses. The processes by which these analyses were carried out are described below. All the analyses described were carried out on a stepwise basis with the conventional 5 per cent significance level being used to determine whether or not a variable should be entered.

THE EFFECTIVENESS REGRESSIONS

The dependent variables

The dependent variables for the effectiveness regressions were the objectives-attainment and learning factors discussed in outline in Chapter 3 and in detail in Appendix B. A regression equation was derived for each of these two dependent variables.

Explanatory variables for effectiveness

Explanatory variables for the effectiveness regressions fell into four main categories:

Variables derived from factor analyses
Individual variables dropped from the factor analyses
Interaction variables
Disparity variables

Variables derived from factor analyses

As described in detail in Appendix B, a number of potential explanatory variables were derived by factor analysis. These were, in the terminology of Chapter 3, as shown in Table C1.

Variables dropped from the factor analyses

A number of variables were dropped from the factor analyses of the explanatory variables, as described in Appendix B. These potentially represent

Table C1 The decision-effectiveness model

Phase	Factor (constituent variable)
Dependent variables	
EFFECTIVENESS	*Objectives-attainment*: project success, right choice, (−) unexpected negative outcomes
	Learning: overall learning, (−) satisfactory process
Explanatory variables	
DEFINITION	
Consequentiality	*Failure*: impact of project failure on corporate financial standing, competitive position, performance of company
	Fit: degree of fit with business strategy, (−) project value
Uncertainty	*Rarity*: novelty of project, supplier uncertainties, production and cost uncertainties
	Performance: market uncertainties, internal and external financial uncertainties
Disagreements	*Personal*: personal objectives disagreements, personality clashes
	Objectives: overall organizational disagreements, disagreements about project objectives
STRATEGIES	
Computation	*Rate of return*: payback, internal rate of return (IRR), productivity
	Reported profit: (−) productivity, earnings, overall computation
Judgement	*Personnel*: impact of project on morale, industrial relations
	Image: impact on image, quality
	Judgement: overall judgement
Negotiation	*Negotiation*: overall negotiation, building of alliances
Inspiration	*Inspiration*: overall inspiration
INFLUENCE	*Internality*: internal involvement and direction
	Externality: external involvement and direction
TIMING	*Deliberation*: duration of decision process, decision building up slowly, delays, pace worries

Note: (−) denotes a negative loading on a variable.

dimensions not captured by the factors. Therefore they represented possible explanatory variables to be incorporated into the regression analyses. However, the poor KMO statistics associated with many of these individual variables suggested that for these variables the problem might be due to rather low variation of the variable within the sample. Practical considerations indicated, then, that many of these variables were probably unlikely to contribute much to the regression analyses, while internal validity considerations (Cook and Campbell 1979) also suggested that we were unlikely to be able to detect any significant impacts of such variables in our sample.

The complete list of variables dropped from the factor analyses is, as noted in Appendix B:

14.02, 14.20, 14.22, 19.06 to 19.09, 21.04, 22.01, 26, 28.01, 30

Interaction variables

Interaction variables were introduced for theoretical reasons, as discussed in Chapter 12. They were defined in the usual way (compare Berry and Feldman 1985) as the product of one of our seven strategy factors with one of the nine other explanatory variable factors and added to the list of explanatory variables for regression purposes. The full list of interaction terms thus created using the factor names of Table C1 (which is Table 3.2 repeated), and naming question 21.04 'inspiration', is given in Table C2.

Table C2 Interaction terms for effectiveness regressions

consequentiality factors × decision strategy factors

failure × rate of return	profit × rate of return
failure × reported profit	profit × reported profit
failure × personnel	profit × personnel
failure × image	profit × image
failure × judgement	profit × judgement
failure × negotiation	profit × negotiation
failure × inspiration	profit × inspiration

uncertainty factors × decision strategy factors

rarity × rate of return	performance × rate of return
rarity × reported profit	performance × reported profit
rarity × personnel	performance × personnel
rarity × image	performance × image
rarity × judgement	performance × judgement
rarity × negotiation	performance × negotiation
rarity × inspiration	performance × inspiration

disagreement factors × decision strategy factors

personal disagreements × rate of return	objectives × rate of return
personal disagreements × reported profit	objectives × reported profit
personal disagreements × personnel	objectives × personnel
personal disagreements × image	objectives × image
personal disagreements × judgement	objectives × judgement
personal disagreements × negotiation	objectives × negotiation
personal disagreements × inspiration	objectives × inspiration

influence factors × decision strategy factors

externality × rate of return	internality × rate of return
externality × reported profit	internality × reported profit
externality × personnel	internality × personnel
externality × image	internality × image
externality × judgement	internality × judgement
externality × negotiation	internality × negotiation
externality × inspiration	internality × inspiration

timing factor × decision strategy factors

deliberation × rate of return	deliberation × reported profit
deliberation × personnel	deliberation × image
deliberation × judgement	deliberation × negotiation
deliberation × inspiration	

Disparity variables

The disparity variables were constructed as the standard deviation of the response to a particular question from all respondents associated with a given decision. The disparity variables were derived for the following questions: 5, 19.01 to 19.09, 21.01 to 21.04, 23, 24, 30, 30.01 to 30.07.

Decisions for which there was only one respondent show zero disparity using this measure. Where, however, we interviewed only one of several decision-makers, our calculated zero disparity score is likely to overestimate the amount of agreement in reality (though there are plenty of aspects of multi-respondent decisions about which there was complete unanimity). There are, then, some 'errors in the variables' in our disparity variables which may introduce bias into our regression estimates (Johnston 1972).

It should be borne in mind that the disparity variables are decision-level variables, that is, any particular agreement variable takes the same value for each respondent for a given decision. This effectively-precluded factor analysing the agreement variables since, for these variables, we are then reduced to seventeen cases (that is, the seventeen decisions).

The process of carrying out the effectiveness regressions

The process for the derivation of the stepwise regression models for the two effectiveness factors

Despite the fact that our regression models for effectiveness were to be based on theoretical considerations, as identified in earlier chapters, this still left a very large number of potential explanatory variables.

The major characteristics of the process for the derivation of the stepwise regression models of the effectiveness factors are described below:

(a) *Meansubstitution* As always with a large list of potential explanatory variables, listwise deletion of incomplete cases would have led to a drastic reduction in degrees of freedom. Therefore, it was necessary to use the meansubstitution feature of SPSS[x] Regression to avoid needless reduction in degrees of freedom. There were relatively few missing values and the largest number for any one variable was nine. However, with a full list of explanatory variables this would have reduced the number of cases to about twenty-eight. Of course, this process artificially restricts the range of variation of variables with significant numbers of missing cases, and may, therefore, lead to their elimination by the stepwise regression procedure.

Because we had no effectiveness measures reported for one of our decisions, the effect of meansubstitution was to substitute the mean value of the effectiveness factors (that is, zero, by construction) for the missing responses in two of our cases. This, in effect, induces measurement error in the dependent variable, which, of course, poses no particular problems with the linear regression model.

(b) *Holdout samples* To avoid data artefacts it is useful to examine the robustness of the regression models based on a number of different data-sets. The data-sets were derived by holding out a random sample of five of the fifty-five cases.

(c) *Weighting cases* As a protection against possibly spurious regression relationships arising from a large number of respondents for an idiosyncratic decision (for example, Medical Supplier – *MK*), it was found useful to run regression models: (a) with all respondents equally weighted; (b) with all respondents weighted by the factor (7/number of respondents for the decision). The numerator 7 was the maximum number of respondents for any decision. Weighting (b) effectively weights all *decisions* equally, and creates 119 'notional cases' for analysis, whereas weighting (a) weights all *respondents* equally.

(d) *Stagewise development of the models* This involved the introduction of the different groups of explanatory variables in descending order of complexity. Thus the simplest, most theoretically defensible, variables (factors omitted from the factor analyses) were introduced first, whilst the, in our judgement, most complex explanatory variables (the disparity variables) were introduced last. The aim of this procedure was to identify simpler explanations, wherever possible. The eventual importance of disparity variables in our models is not, therefore, an artefact of our regression approach.

In order to overcome the problems of a very large number of explanatory variables, the regression models were derived by a number of stages. Essentially, these were:

Stage 1

Stepwise regression on the factors and the variables eliminated during factor analysis. The regressions were repeated several times on data-sets derived by holdout methods. Only variables that consistently appeared in all regressions were retained for the next stage. Typically, this led to regression equations with two or three variables.

Stage 2

Stepwise regression was carried out on the variables remaining from Stage 1, together with the interaction variables. In contradistinction to the procedure sometimes adopted in the natural sciences, interaction terms were incorporated even if one or other of the corresponding individual variables had been dropped at Stage 1: this was felt to be more consistent with the contingency theory approach that informs much of our theoretical discussion. This stage was repeated several times on different holdout samples. Again only variables that consistently appeared in the equations were passed to the next stage. At this point, regression equations typically had three or four variables remaining.

Stage 3

Disparity variables were added at this stage and a similar process to that of the previous stages was followed. Both the resulting regression equations for objectives attainment and learning contained five explanatory variables.

Stage 4

All fifty-five cases were used for this stage. The variables remaining from Stage 3 were all entered into the regression equation. Two different sets of regressions were carried out, one weighted on a respondent basis, the other on a decision basis, as described above. For the objectives-attainment model two of the variables proved to have unstable betas, which changed by around 100 per cent, whereas the other betas were all stable (defined as changing by 50 per cent or less). In the case of the learning model, all the betas were stable, so there was no need to proceed to stage 5.

Stage 5

The two variables with unstable betas were eliminated from the objectives-attainment equation, which was then re-estimated using the individual respondent weights. The learning equation from stage 4 derived on an individual respondent basis was judged satisfactory for use. The final regression equations for the two effectiveness dimensions are expressed in terms of beta coefficients. Betas are reported on the basis that they provide a measure of variable importance (Berry and Feldman 1985). The resulting betas and R^2 are tabulated below in the objectives-attainment and learning-sections. Both the betas derived using individual respondent weightings and those derived using decision weightings are reported here, though only those based on individual respondent weightings are reported in Chapter 12.

The regression model for objectives-attainment

The details of this model are tabulated in Table C3 below.

Table C3   Regression model for objectives-attainment

Variable	Beta (respondent weightings) ($R^2 = 0.55$)	Beta (decision weightings) ($R^2 = 0.55$)
Inspiration disparity	-0.70	-0.68
Negotiation	-0.18	-0.28
Personal disagreements × inspiration	$+0.18$	$+0.25$

The regression model for learning

The details of this model are tabulated in Table C4 below.

Table C4   Regression model for learning

Variable	Beta (respondent weightings) ($R^2 = 0.55$)	Beta (decision weightings) ($R^2 = 0.55$)
Regulation impact disparity	$+0.45$	$+0.31$
Inspiration	$+0.40$	$+0.37$
Internality × judgement	$+0.36$	$+0.37$
Externality × judgement	-0.28	-0.28
Deliberation × negotiation	$+0.23$	$+0.30$

Models for the explanatory variables

This section presents models for certain of the explanatory and related variables incorporated into the effectiveness regression models. As explained in Chapter 12, we built quasi path models of the factor variables appearing in our effectiveness regression models either in their own right, for example, negotiation in the objectives-attainment model, or because they comprised part of an interaction term appearing in the regression model, for example, internality in the learning model. We then attempted to model any factor variables appearing in this second set of models and so on back until no factor variables remained to be modelled. For the purposes of this exercise, individual variables omitted from the factor analyses and disparity variables were considered exogenous; therefore, no models were produced for such variables.

All models of this section, save that for inspiration, are regression models. The processes by which they were derived paralleled those used to derive the effectiveness regression models: in particular, both hold-out methods and weighted and unweighted models were used to secure robust models.

As with the two effectiveness models, the results reported in Chapter 12 were derived using individual respondent weights but both sets of betas are given here.

Distriminant analysis of the inspiration variable

The inspiration variable was measured on a five-point scale. Therefore, we attempted to produce a discriminant analysis model for it, rather than a regression model. In order to determine how many categories to use in the discriminant analysis, we produced a frequency analysis of the responses to the inspiration question. This is given in Table C5.

Table C5 Breakdown of responses to inspiration question

	Value	*Frequency*	*Age (%)*
No inspiration	0	34	61.8
	1	10	18.2
	2	2	3.6
	3	6	14.5
High inspiration	4	3	5.5

From Table C5, a two-way split into high and low inspiration seems indicated. After some experiment to determine what to do with the small group of '2' responses, it was decided to assign the values 0, 1 and 2 to a 'low' inspiration category and values 3 and 4 to a high decision category, as this gave a higher proportion of correct classifications.

A stepwise (Wilks) approach was used to determine the discriminant function. As potential classificatory variables we used: (1) all factor variables with the exception of the factors related to the Thompson and Tuden framework, that is, the strategies factors, as defined in Chapter 3; (2) all variables ommitted from the factor analyses; (3) all disparity variables, since there seemed no theoretical grounds for excluding any of these categories.

A discriminant analysis has, of course, no exact counterpart to beta coefficients nor to R^2, so we report instead, in Tables C6 and C7, the coefficients of the standardized discriminant function and the percentage of cases correctly classified for the individual respondent weightings and the decision weightings, respectively. The results reported in Chapter 12 are those given in Table C6.

Table C6   Discriminant analysis of inspiration (individual respondent weightings)

Classificatory variable	Standardized discriminant function coefficient
Overall objectives disparity	+0.99
Internality	−0.70
Overall disagreement	+0.48

Classification results:

Actual group	Predicted group	
	Low inspiration	High inspiration
Low inspiration	45	1
High inspiration	1	8

Overall percentage of cases correctly classified: 96.3%

Table C7   Discriminant analysis of inspiration (decision-based weightings)

Classificatory variable	Standardized discriminant function coefficient
Overall objectives disparity	+0.79
Internality	−0.44
Overall disagreement	+0.69

Classification results:

Actual group	Predicted group	
	Low inspiration	High inspiration
Low inspiration	97	2
High inspiration	11	9

Overall percentage of cases correctly classified: 89.3%

Regression model for negotiation factor variable

As potential explanatory variables for negotiation we used: (1) all factor variables with the exception of the factors related to the Thompson and Tuden framework, that is, the strategies factors; (2) all variables omitted from the factor analyses; (3) all disparity variables, since there seemed no theoretical grounds for excluding any of these categories of variables. Betas corresponding to both individual respondent weightings and to decision weightings are given in Table C8. The betas used in Chapter 12 were, however, those corresponding to individual respondent weightings.

Table C8 Regression model for negotiation

Variable	Beta (respondent weightings) ($R^2 = 0.53$)	Beta (decision weightings) ($R^2 = 0.62$)
Deliberation	+ 0.28	+ 0.21
Objectives	+ 0.54	+ 0.72
Personal disagreements	+ 0.45	+ 0.29

Regression model for personal disagreements

As potential explanatory variables for personal disagreements we used: (1) all factor variables with the exception of: (a) the factors related to the Thompson and Tuden framework, that is, the strategies factors; (b) the objectives factor, which was derived by means of the same factor analysis as personal disagreements; (2) all variables omitted from the factor analyses; (3) all disparity variables, since there seemed no theoretical grounds for excluding any of these categories of variables. Betas corresponding to both individual respondent weightings and to decision weightings are given in Table C9. The betas used in Chapter 12 were, however, those corresponding to individual respondent weightings.

Table C9 Regression model for personal disagreements

Variable	Beta (respondent weightings) ($R^2 = 0.64$)	Beta (decision weightings) ($R^2 = 0.59$)
Deliberation	+ 0.64	+ 0.55
Importance of agreement	− 0.30	− 0.44
Industrial relations ucertainties	+ 0.24	+ 0.22
Prior personal experience	− 0.22	− 0.23

Regression model for objectives

As potential explanatory variables for objectives we used: (1) all factor variables with the exception of: (a) the factors related to the Thompson and Tuden framework, that is, the strategies factors; (b) the personal disagreements factor, which was derived by means of the same factor analysis as objectives; (2) all variables omitted from the factor analyses; (3) all disparity variables, since there seemed no theoretical grounds for excluding any of these categories of variables. No statistically-significant model was found for this factor variable, which was accordingly treated as exogenous in later analyses.

Regression model for externality

As potential explanatory variables for externality we used: (1) all factor variables with the exception of: (a) the factors related to the Thompson and Tuden framework, that is, the strategies factors; (b) the internality factor, which was derived by means of the same factor analysis as externality; (2) all variables omitted from the factor analyses; (3) all disparity variables, since there seemed no theoretical grounds for excluding any of these categories of variables. No statistically-significant model was found for this factor variable, which was accordingly treated as exogenous in later analyses.

Regression model for internality

As potential explanatory variables for internality we used: (1) all factor variables with the exception of: (a) the factors related to the Thompson and Tuden framework, that is, the strategies factors; (b) the externality factor, which was derived by means of the same factor analysis as internality; (2) all variables omitted from the factor analyses; (3) all disparity variables, since there seemed no theoretical grounds for excluding any of these categories of variables. Betas corresponding to both individual respondent weightings and to decision weightings are given to Table C10. The beta used in Chapter 12, was, however, that corresponding to individual respondent weightings.

Table C10   Regression model for internality

Variable	Beta (*respondent weightings*) ($R^2 = 0.25$)	Beta (*decision weightings*) ($R^2 = 0.26$)
Personnel uncertainties	+ 0.50	+ 0.51

Regression model for deliberation

As potential explanatory variables for deliberation we used: (1) all factor variables with the exception of: (a) the factors related to the Thompson and Tuden framework, that is, the strategies factors: (b) the personal disagreements factors, in that the regression analysis (see above) had found deliberation to be an explanatory variable for personal disagreements; (2) all variables omitted from the factor analyses; (3) all disparity variables, since there seemed no theoretical grounds for excluding any of these categories of variables. Betas corresponding to both individual respondent weightings and to decision weightings are given in Table C11. The betas used in Chapter 12 were, however, those corresponding to individual respondent weightings.

Table C11   Regression model for deliberation

Variable	Beta (*respondent weightings*) ($R^2 = 0.56$)	Beta (*decision weightings*) ($R^2 = 0.48$)
Direction disparity	+ 0.53	+ 0.39
Overall disagreement	+ 0.56	− 0.57

Regression model for judgement

As potential explanatory variables for judgement we used: (1) all factor variables with the exception of: (a) the factors related to the Thompson and Tuden framework, that is, the strategies factors; (2) all variables omitted from the factor analyses; (3) all disparity variables, since there seemed no theoretical grounds for excluding any of these categories of variables. Betas corresponding to both individual respondent weightings and to decision weightings are given in Table C12. The beta used in Chapter 12 was, however, that corresponding to individual respondent weightings.

Table C12   Regression model for judgement

Variable	Beta (*respondent weightings*) ($R^2 = 0.22$)	Beta (*decision weightings*) ($R^2 = 0.24$)
External finance disparity	$+0.33$	$+0.37$
Internality	-0.33	-0.32

References

Ackerman, R. W. (1968) 'Organization and the investment process: a comparative study', unpublished doctoral dissertation, Harvard Business School.

Addelman, S. (1961) 'Symmetrical and assymetrical fractional factorial plans', *Technometrics* 4(1), 47–58.

Adelson, R. M. (1970) 'Discounted cash flow – we can discount it?' *Journal of Business Finance* Summer, 50–66.

Aharoni, Y. (1966) *The Foreign Investment Decision Process*, Cambridge, Mass., Harvard Graduate School of Business.

Aoki, M. (1987) *The Co-operative Game Theory of the Firm*, Oxford University Press.

Barnard, C. I. (1938) *The Functions of the Executive*, Cambridge, Mass., Harvard University Press.

Berry, W. D. and Feldman, S. (1985) *Multiple Regression in Practice*, Beverly Hills, Sage Publications.

Bower, J. L. (1971) *Managing the Resource Allocation Process*, Homewood, Ill., Richard D. Irwin.

Brealey, R. and Myers, S. (1991) *Principles of Corporate Finance*, New York, McGraw-Hill.

Bruns, W. J. and Waterhouse, J. H. (1975) 'Budgetary control and organizational structure', *Journal of Accounting Research* Autumn, 177–203.

Brunsson, N. (1989) *The Organization of Hypocrisy: Talk, Decisions and Actions in Organizations*, Chichester, Wiley.

Burns, J. M. (1978) *Leadership*, New York, Harper & Row.

Burrell, G. and Morgan, G. (1979) *Sociological Paradigms and Organizational Analysis: Elements of the Sociology of Corporate Life*, London, Heinemann Educational.

Butler, R. J. (1990) 'Studying deciding: an exchange of views between Mintzberg and Waters, Pettigrew and Butler', *Organization Studies* 11(1), 1–16.

Butler, R. J. (1991) *Designing Organizations: A Decision-Making Perspective*, London, Routledge.

Butler, R. J., Hickson, D. J., Wilson, D. C. and Axelsson, R. (1977) 'Organizational power, politicking and paralysis', *Organization and Administrative Sciences* 8(4, Winter), 54–59.

Butler, R. J., Asiley, G., Hickson, D. J. and Wilson, D. C. (1979) 'Strategic decision-making: concepts of content and process', *International Studies of Management and Organization* 9(4, Winter), 5–36.

Butler, R. J., Davies, L., Pike, R. and Sharp, J. (1987) 'Strategic investment decision-making: complexities, politics and processes', Paper presented at the British Academy of Management Inaugural Conference, University of Warwick, 12–15 September.

Butler, R. J., Davies, L., Pike, R. and Sharp, J. (1991) 'Strategic investment decision-making: complexities, politics and processes', *Journal of Management Studies*, 28(4, July), 395–415.

Butler, R. J., Davies, L., Pike, and Sharp, J. (1992) 'Effective investment decision-making: the concept and its determinants', Paper presented to the British Academy of Management 6th annual conference 'Management into the 21st Century', University of Bradford, 14–16 September.

Butrous, N. F. (1989) 'Effective organizational decision-making: the study of implementation of the Yorkshire Regional Health Authority Strategic Plan using personal interviews with health managers', unpublished PhD thesis, University of Bradford Management Centre.

Carter, E. E. (1971) 'The behavioural theory of the firm and top level corporate decisions', *Administrative Science Quarterly* 16, 413–28.

Carter, E. E. (1977) 'Designing the capital budgeting process', in P. C. Nystom and W. H. Starbuck (eds) *Prescriptive Models of Organizations*, TIMS Studies in the Management Sciences, 5, 25–42.

Christy, G. A. (1966) *Capital Budgeting – Current Practices and their Efficiency*, PhD. thesis, University of Oregon.

Cohen, M. D. (1989) 'Organizational learning of routines: a model of the garbage can type', Paper presented at the conference on the Logic of Organizational Disorder, Venice, Italy, April.

Cohen, M. D. and March, J. G. (1974) *Leadership and the Ambiguity: the American College President*, New York, McGraw-Hill.

Cohen, M. D., March, J. G. and Olsen, P. J. (1972) 'A garbage can model of organizational choice', *Administrative Science Quarterly* 17, 1–25.

Cook, T. D. and Campbell, D. T. (1979) *Quasi-Experimentation: Design and Analysis Issues for Field Settings*, Chicago: Rand McNally.

Cooper, D. J. (1975) 'Rationality and investment appraisal', *Accounting and Business Research* 15(18), 198–202.

Cyert, R. and March, J. G. (1963) *The Behavioral Theory of the Firm*, Englewood Cliffs, N.J., Prentice-Hall.

Dearden, J. (1960) 'Problems in decentralized profit responsibility', *Harvard Business Review* May/June, 79–86.

Dearden, J. (1969) 'The case against ROI control', *Harvard Business Review* May/June, 124–35.

Eisenberg, D. J. (1984) 'How senior managers think', *Harvard Business Review* 62, 80–90.

Friend, J. and Hickling, A. (1984) *Planning Under Pressure: The Strategic Choice Approach*, Pergamon.

Gitman, L. and Forrester, R. (1977) 'A survey of capital budgeting techniques used by major US firms', *Financial Management* 6, 66–71.

Gordon, L. A. and Pinches, G. E. (1984) *Improving Capital Budgeting: A Decision Support System Approach*, Reading, Mass., Addison-Wesley.

Govindarajan, V. and Gupta, A. K. (1985) 'Linking control systems to business unit strategy: impact on performance', *Accounting, Organizations and Society* 51–66.

Haka, S. F., Gordon, L. A. and Pinches, G. E. (1985) 'Sophisticated capital budgeting selection techniques and firm performance', *Accounting Review* 60(48), 651–69.

Harvey-Jones, J. (1990) *Troubleshooter*, London, BBC Books.

Haynes, W. and Solomon, M. (1962) 'A misplaced emphasis in capital budgeting', *Quarterly Review of Economics and Business* 39–46.

Hickson, D. J., Butler, R. J., Cray, D., Mallory, G. R. and Wilson, D. C. (1986) *Top Decisions: Strategic Decision-Making in Organizations*, Oxford, Basil Blackwell, and San Franscico, Jossey-Bass.

Hofstede, C. (1978) 'The poverty of management control philosophy', *Academy of Management Review* July, 450–61.

Hopwood, A. G. (1973) *An Accounting System and Managerial Behaviour*, London, Saxon House.

Issack, T. F. (1978) 'Intuition: an ignored dimension in management', *Academy of Management Review* 3, 917–22.

Janis, I. L. and Mann, L. (1977) *Decision Making: A Psychological Analysis of Conflict, Choice and Commitment*, New York, Free Press.

Johnston, J. (1972) *Econometric Methods* (2nd edn), New York, McGraw-Hill.

Kanter, R. M. (1984) *The Change Masters: Corporate Entrepreneurs at Work*, London, Allen & Unwin.

Kanter, R. M. (1989) *When Giants Learn to Dance: Mastering the Challenge of Strategy, Management and Careers in the 1990s*, London, Simon & Schuster.

Kaplan, R. S. (1984) 'The evolution of management accounting', *The Accounting Review* LIX, July, 390–418.

Kim, S. H. (1982) 'An empirical study of the relationship between capital budgeting practices and earnings performance', *Engineering Economist* Spring, 185–96.

King, P. (1975) 'Is the emphasis of capital budgeting theory misplaced?', *Journal of Business Finance and Accounting* 2(1), 69–82.

Klammer, T. P. (1972) 'Empirical evidence of the adoption of sophisticated capital budgeting techniques', *Journal of Business* 45(3), 337–57.

Klammer, T. P. (1973) 'The association of capital budgeting techniques with firm performance', *Accounting Review* 48(2), 353–64.

Larcker, D. F. (1983) 'Association between performance adoption and capital investment', *Journal of Accounting and Economics* April, 3–30.

Libby, R. and Lewis, B. (1982) 'Human information processing research in accounting: the state of the art in 1982', *Accounting Organizations and Society* 7(3), 231–85.

Lindblom, C. (1959) 'The science of muddling through', *Public Administration Review* 19, 79–88.

Lupton, T. and Tanner, I. (1987) *Achieving Change: A Systematic Approach*, Gower Publishing.

McGregor, D. (1960) *The Human Side of Enterprise*, New York, McGraw-Hill.

McIntyre, A. D. and Coulthurst, N. J. (1986) *Capital Budgeting Practices in*

Medium-Sized Businesses – A Survey, London, Institute of Cost and Management Accountants.

Mao, J. C. T. and Helliwell, J. F. (1969) 'Investment decisions under uncertainty: theory and practice', *Journal of Finance* May, 323–38.

March, J. G. and Simon, H. A. (1956) *Organizations*, New York, Wiley.

Marsh, P., Barwise, P., Thomas, K. and Wensley, R. (1988) 'Managing strategic investment decisions in large diversified companies', in A. M. Pettigrew (ed.) *Competitiveness and the Management Process*, Oxford, Basil Blackwell.

Mintzberg, H. D. (1983) *Structure in Fives: Designing Effective Organizations*, Englewood Cliffs, N.J., Prentice-Hall.

Mintzberg, H. D., Raisinghani, D. and Theoret, A. (1976) 'The structure of "unstructured decision" processes', *Administrative Science Quarterly* 21(2), 246–75.

Mintzberg, H. D. and Waters, J. A. (1985) 'Of strategies, deliberate and emergent', *Strategic Management Journal* 6, 257–72.

Norusis, M. J. (1985) *SPSS-X Advanced Statistics Guide*, New York: McGraw-Hill.

Otley, D. T. (1978) 'Budget use and managerial performance', *Journal of Accounting Research* 16(1), 122–49.

Pedhazur, E. T. (1982) *Multiple Regression in Behavioral Research*, Harcourt Brace Jovanovich.

Perrow, C. (1977) 'The bureaucratic paradox: the efficient organization centralizes in order to decentralize', *Organization Dynamics* Spring 3–14.

Pettigrew, A. (1973) *The Politics of Organizational Decision Making*, London, Tavistock.

Pettigrew, A. (1990) 'Studying deciding: an exchange of views between Mintzberg and Waters, Pettigrew and Butler', *Organization Studies* 11(1), 1–16.

Pfeffer, J. (1981) *Power in Organizations*, Marshfield, Mass., Pitman & Co.

Pike, R. H. (1983) 'A review of recent trends in formal capital budgeting processes', *Accounting and Business Research* 13(50), 201–8.

Pike. R. H. (1984) 'Sophisticated capital budgeting systems and their association with corporate performance', *Managerial and Decision Economics* 5(2), 91–7.

Pike, R. H. (1988) 'An empirical study of the adoption of sophisticated capital budgeting practices and decision-making effectiveness', *Accounting & Business Research* 18(12), 341–51.

Pike, R. H. and Neale, C. W. (1992) 'Capital budgeting', in Drury (ed.) *Management Accounting Handbook*, London, Butterworth.

Pinches, G. (1982) 'Myopic capital budgeting and decision making', *Financial Management* 11(3), 6–19.

Pugh, D. S., Hickson, D. J., Hinings, C. R. and Turner, C. (1968) 'Dimensions of organization structure', *Adminstrative Science Quarterly* 13(1), 65–104.

Rodrigues, S. (1980) *The Processes of Successful Managerial Decision-Making in Organizations: A Comparative Study of Making Successful and Less Successful Decisions in Business and Non-Business Organizations*, Unpublished PhD thesis, University of Bradford Management Centre.

Saaty, T. L. (1980) *The Analytic Hierarchy Process*, New York: McGraw-Hill.

Scapens, R. W. and Sale, J. T. (1981) 'Performance measurement and formal capital expenditure controls in divisionalised companies', *Journal of Business Finance and Accounting* 60(2), 389–419.

Scapens, R. W., Sale, J. T. and Tikkas, P. A. (1982) *Financial Control of Divisional Capital Investment*, London, Institute of Cost and Management Accountants.

Scholl, D., Sundem, G. and Geijsbeek, W. (1978) 'Survey and analysis of capital budgeting methods', *Journal of Finance* 33, 281–7.

Schon, D. A. (1983) *Reflective Practitioner: How Professionals Think in Action*, New York, Basic Books.

Sharp, J. A. (1990) 'Capital investment: an optimal control perspective', *Journal of the Operational Research Society* 41(11), 1053–63.

Simon, H. A. (1947) *Administrative Behavior: A Study of Decision Making Process in Administrative Organizations*, New York, Wiley.

Simon, H. A. (1957) *Models of Man*, New York, Wiley.

Simon, H. A. (1960) *The New Science of Management Decision*, New York, Harper & Row.

Simon, H. A. (1964) 'On the concept of organizational goal', *Administrative Science Quarterly* 9(1), 1–22.

Simon, H. A. (1987) 'Making management decisions: the role of intuition and emotion', *Academy of Management Executive* 1, 57–64.

Simons, R. (1990) 'The role of management control systems in creating competitive advantage: new perspectives', *Accounting, Organizations and Society* 127–43.

Snowball, D. (1986) 'Accounting laboratory experiments on human judgement: some characteristics and influences', *Accounting Organizations and Society* 11(1), 47–69.

Staw, B. M. and Ross, J. (1978) 'Commitment to a policy decision: a multi-theoretical perspective', *Administrative Science Quarterly* 23(1), 40–64.

Thompson, J. D. (1967) *Organizations in Action*, New York, McGraw-Hill.

Thompson, J. D. and Tuden, A. (1956) 'Strategies, structures and processes of organizational decision', in J. D. Thompson, *Comparative Studies in Administration*, University of Pittsburgh Press, 195–216. Also in W. A. Rushing and M. N. Zaid (eds) (1976) *Organizations and Beyond: Selected Essays of James D. Thompson*, Boston, Mass., Lexington Books, D. C. Heath & Co., Ch. 5.

Van de Geer, J. P. (1971) *Introduction to Multivariate Analysis for the Social Sciences*, W. H. Freeman.

Vickers, S. G. (1965) *The Art of Judgement*, London, Chapman & Hall.

Williamson, O. E. (1970) *Corporate Control and Business Behaviour*, Englewood Cliffs, N.J., Prentice-Hall.

Williamson, O. E. (1975) *Markets and Hierarchies: Analysis and Anti-Trust Implication*, New York, Free Press.

Wilson, D. C. (1980) 'Organizational strategy', unpublished PhD thesis, University of Bradford Management Centre.

Zanibbi, L. and Pike, R. H. (1989) 'The capital investment decision-making behaviour of managers and the control of capital investment', Paper presented to International Conference on Research in Management Control Systems, (July), London Business School.

Index